# Paul, in Other Words

# PAUL, IN OTHER WORDS

## A Cultural Reading of His Letters

## Jerome H. Neyrey

Westminster/John Knox Press
Louisville, Kentucky

© 1990 Jerome H. Neyrey

Scripture quotations from the Revised Standard Version of the Bible are copyrighted 1946, 1952, © 1971, 1973 by the Division of Christian Education of the National Council of the Churches of Christ in the U.S.A. and are used by permission.

Chapter 5 is a revised version of "Body Language in 1 Corinthians: The Use of Anthropological Models for Understanding Paul and His Opponents," pp. 129–170 in John H. Eliott, ed., *Social-Scientific Criticism in the New Testament and Its Social World*, *Semeia* 35. It appears with permission of Scholars Press.

Chapter 9, a revised version of "Bewitched in Galatia: Paul and Cultural Anthropology," *Catholic Biblical Quarterly* 50 (1988):72–100, is reprinted with permission of the Catholic Biblical Association.

Chapter 10, a revised version of "Witchcraft Accusations in 2 Cor. 10–13: Paul in Social Science Perspective," *Listening* 21/2 (1986):160–170, appears with permission of the publisher.

First edition

Published by Westminster/John Knox Press
Louisville, Kentucky

PRINTED IN THE UNITED STATES OF AMERICA

9   8   7   6   5   4   3   2   1

**Library of Congress Cataloging-in-Publication Data**

Neyrey, Jerome H., 1940–
    Paul, in other words : a cultural reading of his letters / Jerome H. Neyrey. — 1st ed.
        p.    cm.
    Includes bibliographical references and indexes.
    ISBN 0-664-21925-X

    1. Bible. N.T. Epistles of Paul—Criticism, interpretation, etc.
2. Paul, the Apostle, Saint.   3. Sociology, Biblical.   I. Title.
BS2650.2.N49 1990
227'.067—dc20                                          90-38563
                                                            CIP

# Contents

# Foreword

Interpreting the letters of St. Paul has been a conundrum for Christians from time immemorial. Most Bible readers would agree with the observation in 2 Peter 3:16 that some things in Paul's letters are hard to understand. After all, they are letters, halves of conversations, written to specific groups on specific occasions. Both author and recipients shared a common knowledge of the specific persons, places, and behaviors referred to in the letters, but we often are ignorant of those specifics. Furthermore, each of Paul's letters would call forth in the minds of his first hearers what can really never be explicitly put into a letter, that is, their commonsense, socially shared understanding of reality. It is especially that which cannot be explicitly put into writing by any author that exercises the skill and discipline of the interpreter, scholarly and nonscholarly.

Given the occasional quality and constant extratextual reference of Paul's letters, how does one read between the lines to build up a set of the implicit meanings that run through these documents? One of the most successful ways is the way presented in this book. Jerome Neyrey is a master at applying symbolic anthropology to biblical writings. What he does is sketch out the meanings in Paul's letters as they arise from the characteristics of contextual contours. These contours are shapes deriving from the system of lines drawn around selves, others, nature, time, space, and God(s). For example, if on the smooth surface of a sandbox you proceeded to make three intersecting lines, the shape of a triangle would emerge in the sand. That shape derives its contextual contours from the connecting lines. Erase the lines and the shape disappears. Paul

and his addressees shared a number of such contextual contours. What the reader of this book will learn is how Paul drew
those lines, why they were drawn as they were, and what they
originally meant.

We might say that the type of analysis in this book is based
on the human propensity to draw lines and thus recognize
shapes in their environment. For example, each of us has
learned early on that dirt is matter out of place, because when
we clean, we rearrange matter by placing it where it belongs.
How can we put dirt where it belongs unless there is some
previous set of lines marking off proper and improper places
for matter? But that is not all. We grow up, in fact, being taught
how to recognize amorphous, rather shapeless features of our
environment by learning to impose a set of contextual contours
over segments of that environment, thus defining various items
in our experience. The process is not unlike learning to see cells
under a microscope when what we initially see is smears, or to
see constellations in the sky when what we initially see is ran-
domly situated stars. The cells and constellations that we come
to perceive and appreciate become part of our socially shared
reality.

We are taught to see mother and father, sister and brother,
rooms in a house and the house itself. Along with such perception, we are taught to feel variously about what we are taught to
see. The common perceptions and feelings that are shared by
members of a group constitute the group's culture. People are
enculturated individuals taught to perceive that human beings
estimate what they are *like* essentially in terms of their relationship to other persons and/or in their situation within some
institution; the "I" is the sum of its social roles and statuses, of
social relations and situations.

Richard Jung ("A Quaternion of Metaphors for the Hermeneutics of Life," in John A. Dillon, Jr., ed., *General Systems* 30
[1987]:25–31) has observed that this type of analysis conceptu-
alizes human being in terms of the metaphor of template—a
set of contours resulting from relational contexts. With the
metaphor of template, all phenomena of life can be treated as
having meaning due to a configuration of roles and statuses,
relations and rankings, qualities and capacities deriving from a
system of socially drawn lines. Discrete segments of this system
of lines form niches, and people perceive and evaluate themselves and others in terms of fit in the niches. Thus the template is like the shape formed by a plaster cast. Whatever is put
into the cast or template gets its shape from the surrounding
and supporting walls, here called "the context." Thus the enti-

ties of human experience derive their meaning or form from the characteristic of their relational context. To be a father one must have a son or daughter. To be a pet puppy a beastie must have an "owner."

In this perspective, there is concern about a place for everything as well as that everything stay in its place. To be out of place is to be dirt or deviance. Adequacy is assigned in terms of the fit of the individual within its context. Hence, the main preoccupation urged upon members of society is with appropriate comportment, a sort of harmony that may be discordant at times. The main symbol of this preoccupation is concern for adequacy or fittingness. This is what "kosher" is all about. The preferred philosophical approach, then, is relationalism. As the reader will see, the sets of questions best answered by this approach include those concerning ritual and ceremonial study, symbolic analysis, culture as meaning system, as value system, and the like.

Jerome Neyrey's *Paul, in Other Words* will provide the biblical interpreter, professional and nonprofessional, with a set of tools for analyzing all of the apostle's writings and other biblical documents as well. This analysis will unearth meanings that will surely nurture better understanding of Paul, greater respect for his project, and clearer insight into the flesh-and-blood moorings of his enduring Christian witness.

Bruce J. Malina
*Creighton University*

# 1

# Reading Paul
# in Social Science
# Perspective

Circumcised on the eighth day,
of the people of Israel,
of the tribe of Benjamin,
a Hebrew born of Hebrews;
as to the law a Pharisee.

Philippians 3:5

1.0 What Is This Book?
2.0 Cultural Anthropology
3.0 Symbolic Universe: Cosmology
4.0 Other Assumptions
5.0 The Payoff

## 1.0 What Is This Book?

By his own admission, Paul thought and behaved like a typical, first-century Jew in the Eastern Mediterranean:

> If any other man thinks he has reason for confidence in the flesh,
> I have more: circumcised on the eighth day, of the people of
> Israel, of the tribe of Benjamin, a Hebrew born of Hebrews; as
> to the law a Pharisee, as to zeal a persecutor of the church, as to
> righteousness under the law blameless.
>
> Philippians 3:4b–6

This "confidence" suggests that Paul was clearly socialized into
a Jewish and Pharisaic world. On the micro level, his cosmos
consisted of biblical, temple, and Pharisaic traditions. On the

macro level, Paul shared with other first-century Mediterranean Jews certain cultural perceptions about the cosmos, a
symbolic universe (Berger & Luckmann 1966). These perceptions inform all of his letters, color the way he experienced
reality, and structure the way he behaved. Those who would
understand Paul ought also to share his perceptions, both on
the micro and macro level.

Paul's original readers, who were shaped by similar cultural
perceptions, could be presumed to share them (yet, see 2 Peter
3:15–16). But modern Western readers who study Paul tend to
be twentieth-century Christians, not second-temple Jews, and
so lack an appreciation of how Paul, Jew and Pharisee, thought
and acted. Of more importance, we cannot even begin to imagine the cultural perceptions of the cosmos into which Paul was
socialized. We are postindustrial people, not first-century
peasants. We are Western individualists, not group-oriented
people. We are Europeans and North Americans, not Medi-
terraneans, either Greeks, Arabs, or Semites. A book on Paul,
then, is needed that addresses this cultural chasm between us
and him and that offers some hope of understanding the cultural viewpoint into which he was socialized. What is needed is
a book that talks about Paul *in other words* than those we customarily use to interpret him.

This book is not another theological exposition of Paul's
thought, although it should be part of a conversation on his
understanding of God and Jesus. Nor does it take up specifically historical questions such as Pauline chronology or the
Greco-Roman and Jewish background of Paul, except insofar
as these can illustrate his worldview. Rather, it attempts to
interpret Paul's letters by describing the symbolic universe of
Paul as a first-century Eastern Mediterranean non-elite. This
book examines how Paul and others in his world typically
viewed their cosmos; it aims to discover their perceptions and
values. Its focus, then, is cultural anthropology and social psychology, not history or theology.

## 2.0 Cultural Anthropology

We use cultural anthropology for reasons negative and positive. Krister Stendahl's article "Paul and the Introspective
Conscience of the West" persuasively argued that modern
readers do in fact examine Paul as though he belonged to our
modern culture (Stendahl 1976:78–96). We regularly imagine
that Paul viewed the world as postindustrial, urban, individualistic Westerners do and that he consequently behaved as they

do. But he lived in the first century, in the Eastern Mediterranean, in a group-oriented society. North Americans, for example, have great difficulty understanding the contemporary Middle East, its customs, politics, religion, and so forth; nevertheless, we imagine that we understand Paul, who is a direct ancestor of this geographical region and its distinctive culture. We run the risk of being ethnocentric readers who cast Paul in terms of our culture, rather than in terms of a totally different cultural world. We tend to speak of him in our words, not the *other words* of another cultural world. The considerable cultural differences between Paul and our world have been sketched in Malina & Neyrey (1988:145–151).

Paul, moreover, should not sound like a product of the German Reformation, much less like a Hegelian or an existentialist. We run a further risk of anachronistic reading by having Paul speak the theological language of a millennium and a half later or view the world as a nineteenth-century philosopher or scholar. Yet this anachronistic tendency has always been with us. Surveying various interpretations of Paul, Wayne Meeks described him as the Christian Proteus, a figure who is always changing shape according to the age and place of scholarly investigators (Meeks 1972:435–444). Ethnocentricity and anachronistic reading, then, are the lenses we unreflectingly wear. But they are dangerously inappropriate for an accurate understanding of a figure so far removed in time and culture from us as Paul. Unless we read Paul *in other words* we run the risk of making him into a figure socialized into twentieth-century Europe or North America, not into second-temple Jewish and Mediterranean culture.

There are positive reasons as well for looking at Paul through the lenses of cultural anthropology. In the course of its development as a field of study, anthropology has formally concerned itself with trying to avoid both ethnocentricity and anachronism. It does this by specifying as clearly as possible what presuppositions or lenses are used in one's perception and by finding as appropriate a lens as possible through which to view. A convenient distinction is made between emic and etic interpretations (Harris 1976:329–350). If we asked the natives to describe what is going on, we would get an emic description, that is, a perception by someone in the very culture. Paul is a Jew, and ancient Jews could readily interpret his words and phrases to us. They were the perfect emic readers and hearers; if we would hear Paul accurately, we too must strive to understand Paul in terms of his Jewish and Pharisaic background. As valuable as this might be, it can be supplemented by the analysis and description of professional ethnographers, that is, with an etic description. They ask questions deemed critical for an in-depth understanding of a culture, and they look for patterns of perception and behavior replicated in numerous areas of the culture they investigate. To understand Paul, anthropologists would inquire about his symbolic universe, societal institutions (such as family and politics), economics, cultural values, conflict, and the like. And we would want to know what these look like in a culture clearly other than our own. This data would give us an etic, or professional, look at the pieces of Paul's world and how they overlap and form a consonance in his world. Admittedly, these are not the normal questions of modern readers, but they should be asked if we would begin to understand Paul on his own terms. We must study Paul *in other words*.

We obviously have Paul's letters, and we all claim to be listening to Paul's own voice; therefore, we claim to have emic interpretations of Paul. Yet because of our tendency toward an ethnocentric and anachronistic reading of Paul, we cannot be sure of this emic understanding. We need more formal help in learning to perceive Paul and his world. We need etic, or professional, lenses to help us adjust to a culture totally different from ours and immeasurably removed in time from ours. Just such help can be offered by cultural anthropology.

### 3.0 Symbolic Universe: Cosmology

It would be an encyclopedic undertaking to use all the tools of cultural anthropology to describe the full shape and dynamics of Paul's world (see Meeks 1983a; Malina 1986b). Instead, this book takes up one aspect of that project, the description of Paul's symbolic universe. We start with the painful but necessary observation that Paul was a person from a culture quite different from that of modern Western readers. How shall we understand Paul? We cannot observe him, nor have we any recordings, photographs, or videotapes of him. To say that we have his letters only begs the question. How shall we understand them?

We are not the first to study peoples from other cultures, so we would be wise to employ the models and concepts of those etic observers who do cross-cultural anthropology. We take our inspiration from British anthropologist Mary T. Douglas, as well as from the scholars who have adapted her materials for study of ancient Jewish and Christian culture, be it Qumran (Isenberg 1975), second-temple Judaism (Neusner 1973, 1975,

1978) or Pharisaism (Neyrey 1986a, 1988b). Douglas's two books *Purity and Danger* (1966) and *Natural Symbols* (1982) introduce us to new but crucial ways of analyzing cultures ancient and contemporary.

What is a symbolic universe? How can we know it? All people operate with a set of assumptions about how the world works, assumptions that are usually implicit and unexamined. Is the world orderly? Does it have pattern and purpose? How do people define themselves in relation to this world, whether orderly or chaotic? How do they view or explain the presence of evil and suffering in this world? Is the world just or unjust? Benign or hostile? From birth, people are socialized by family and clan to imagine the world and its workings in certain ways. Whether Jew or Greek, slave or free, male or female, people in Paul's world shared certain general perceptions of the cosmos and how it worked (Isenberg & Owens 1977; Malina 1978a, 1981, 1986a, 1986b).

A "symbolic universe" is a broad general concept that can be specified by examining six specific areas in a given culture. What makes up a cosmos, a symbolic universe?

1. *Purity*: patterns of order and classification
2. *Rites*: either rituals of making and maintaining boundaries or ceremonies confirming values and institutions
3. *Body*: the social perception of the human physical body
4. *Sin*: the social definition of sin and deviance
5. *Cosmology*: who is in the world, and who is doing what?
6. *Evil and Misfortune*: how are they explained?

If we investigate a culture with these questions in mind, we would surely get different answers depending on the particular group about whom we inquire. The Jerusalem priests would surely give a response different from those of villagers and peasants; for the elite of a society tend to represent the "great tradition," whereas the non-elites reflect the "little tradition." Sectarian religious such as those at Qumran would respond differently from the established and ruling segments (Niebuhr 1951). One's symbolic world would necessarily be conditioned by place, time, ethnic group, and social status. The six questions should be asked, but how might we allow for variations based on role and status in that same culture? Scholars working with Qumran, second-temple Judaism, Pharisees, and early Christianity have adapted the six questions enumerated above and have described the following general framework of the symbolic universe of Paul and others in his world. We gladly borrow from those studies and offer their insights as the hypothesis of this book.

**Purity:** Paul and his contemporaries share a strong impulse to perceive order in the cosmos and so to find "a place for everything and everything in its place." Yet people in this world perceive disorder attacking it. Pollution (i.e., what is "out of place") has wormed its way into the system. The rites of purification seem ineffective in eliminating pollution and disorder from what should be an orderly cosmos. Hence, order is perceived and prized, but it is under attack.

**Rites:** Because of the perceived attack on the boundaries of their orderly world, people here concentrate their attention and energy on those boundaries, either making them or maintaining them. They give considerably less attention to ceremonies that confirm the internal order of society, because they perceive even these ceremonies and the internal order they celebrate as attacked. Hence, special attention is given to rituals for expelling the evil that has insinuated itself within the system.

**Body:** The physical body is perceived as a symbol of the social body. The patterns of order and control exercised over the social body are replicated in the way the physical body is ordered and controlled. Given the perception of an orderly and controlled cosmos, the physical body correspondingly will tend to be tightly controlled. Yet, just as the social body is attacked and its boundaries threatened or breached, so the physical body is likewise threatened and attacked. It can hardly be a symbol of life.

**Sin:** On the one hand, in a world so organized and controlled, sin and deviance are associated with the formal violation of the rules and laws of the social group. Yet people also perceive sin as a corruption that insidiously pollutes the whole organism, as does leaven or gangrene. It often happens that internal states of thinking and feeling are considered more important than external behavior.

**Cosmology:** All forces and powers in this cosmos are perceived anthropomorphically. Yet, given the sense of attack and threat, this is a dualistic cosmos of warring forces of Good and Evil. When something happens, the immediate question is, *Who* did this to me? whether the issue is illness, famine, war, or ignorance.

**Evil and Misfortune:** Inasmuch as the world is being attacked by dualistic forces of Good and Evil, it is an unjust place. Evil attacks Good; the wicked prosper. Hence, misfortune is not credited to personal responsibility but to the workings of malevolent forces. Such suffering cannot be eradicated, short of the destruction of the Evil Powers assailing the world.

This, we suggest, represents the general symbolic world of Paul and Jesus and the New Testament. And such is the etic, or professional, perspective from which this book is written. As stated here, it remains quite abstract and devoid of color, shape, and size. This is inevitably so when one asks about the general symbolic world common to most first-century Jews and Christians. In this regard we discover what many people in the Eastern Mediterranean world held in common and how they were alike. Yet these general, abstract perceptions need to be made specific and concrete with reference to particular authors and documents.

When we start examining Paul's letters, we will necessarily begin to employ some emic materials illustrative of these general patterns. For it matters greatly that we strive to see how Paul's socialization as a "Hebrew, of the tribe of Benjamin, trained as a Pharisee" gives specific shape to the general cosmological patterns described above. By focusing on Paul's Jewish background we do not intend to deny or minimize any Greco-Roman influence on Paul (Malherbe 1970, 1987). But in terms of social psychology, Paul was socialized as an observant Jew of Pharisaic stripe, and this gave particular shape to his symbolic universe. A traditional monotheist, Paul believed in the one true God of Israel (1 Thess. 1:9; 1 Cor. 8:4) and his Christ (1 Cor. 8:6); he knew and quoted from Israel's Scriptures (e.g., 1 Cor. 1:19; 3:19–20); he expressed value in terms of Jewish sacrificial language (Rom. 12:1). He understood his life to be structured according to a covenant with God, first that of Moses and then that of Abraham (Gal. 3). He shared Pharisaic concern for purity issues and precise definition. The emic specification of a Jewish symbolic universe is a fitting place to begin to talk about Paul *in other words.*

## 4.0 Other Assumptions

Because it is important in this type of book to be clear about the lenses used to view Paul, we should specify not just the anthropological model and concepts used, but other reading assumptions about Paul.

**Occasional Letters:** For example, in this book we view Paul's letters as "occasional" writings (Beker 1980). That is, they are specific responses to specific questions and crises. The issues at Corinth were not those of Galatia or Philippi; Paul's remarks and arguments are situation specific. Modern scholars give great weight to the particularity of each letter, a thrust followed in this book.

**Inconsistency:** We do not view Paul as a systematic theologian who was working out an elaborately coherent system. If his letters are truly occasional, then their response to issues and questions will likewise tend to be occasional and not consistent.

**Conserver:** Both as Jew and Christian, Paul always maintained basic faith in the one true God and accepted the Scriptures (Rom. 9:4–6). Raised as a strict Pharisee, moreover, he was socialized into an orderly world, a bent he never abandoned. He may substitute Jesus for Torah, but the impulse to order his cosmos on the basis of God's Word persisted long after he left the synagogue. He never advocated lawlessness (*anomia*) despite all the rhetoric about "freedom from the law."

**Reformer:** Yet Paul was not simply a synagogue Jew, a conserver of all things past. He was a follower of Jesus. God revealed that Jesus, whose influence Paul once thought to be pernicious, was truly God's Christ (Gal. 1:14–15). In the light of this new evaluation of Christ (Phil. 3:7–11), Paul began to reform the way Jews should think of Christ, read the Scriptures, and act. Paul was both conserver of ancient traditions and reformer.

**Saint Paul?:** Most people think of Paul as *Saint* Paul and thus ignore or excuse language and behavior that they think inappropriate for a saint. In this book we view him as fully incarnated in his culture and living out the specific expectations of that culture. His world was authoritarian and hierarchical; it was agonistic and ambition ridden. Its view of the roles of males and females would never match what the French and American revolutions have taught us about equality. Yet Paul belongs to that world, not ours. We do not desecrate the icon of *Saint* Paul to note and examine what we consider the more quirky elements of his culture. He was truly a product of his times.

**History:** This book presumes knowledge of Pauline chronology, as well as the rich historical information about specific aspects of Paul's own experience. We are not ignorant of the studies about his working with his hands (Hock 1980), diatribal style (Stowers 1981), catalogs of hardships (Fitzgerald 1988), and the like. An anthropological approach to Paul does not ignore or devalue such pieces of information. But by asking a larger question of Paul's symbolic universe, historical information itself needs an interpretative horizon to be understood correctly.

Furthermore, this book does not conflict with the efforts of contemporary scholars to define the exact historical situation confronting Paul in each document. Accepting the occasional character of his letters, we value the quest for the *Sitz im Leben*, or the situation in history, of the documents. In one sense, this book might be considered a major contribution to that very enterprise, for it aims to describe the very cultural context in which the letters were written, a cultural context shared by Jews, Greeks, and Christians. Consideration of the symbolic universe of Paul is an integral part of the quest for the precise *Sitz im Leben* of his letters.

## 5.0 The Payoff

What will readers know if they read Paul in this way? What will they gain by examining his symbolic universe? What will they know if they know Paul *in other words*? First, this book can begin to provide the adequate scenarios for reading Paul that formally address the problems we all face with ethnocentric and anachronistic reading. It will make Paul strange to us initially—only to clarify the cultural distance between us and him—but will then make him close. If this type of analysis proves congenial to the reader, which is a matter of intellectual aesthetics, then other anthropological perspectives might be used to examine Paul. Second, the models and concepts used here, if they prove accurate and useful for understanding Paul, can be adapted to read other early Christian and Jewish literature. The reading tools of a considerate reader, then, are supplemented by this type of analysis. Using cultural anthropology actually addresses the stated aim of critical biblical scholarship—to study the documents in their proper *Sitz im Leben*, or life situation.

Many readers of Paul's letters read them because they are believers and seek to find in them gospel and kerygma. Students of religion read Paul to learn his theology. In the face of such religious utilitarianism, this book may not at first seem either useful or pastoral. Yet if one's primary aim is to understand Paul on his own terms, then it is useful, and if useful, then informative. For reading Paul *in other words* can begin to provide a reader with the proper and adequate scenarios for taking Paul seriously and critically.

This book takes an anthropological perspective, not just because it is a new fashion, but because it can lead to a fresh and accurate understanding of Paul in his particular cultural context. Although not asking traditional theological questions of Paul, it does ask about his view of God and God's creation, about sin, proper behavior, and evil. It is about his typical cultural concern for order and control, both social and bodily. It is about his intolerance in the face of deviance. It is about his perception of a hostile world and the unjust suffering of the just. The payoff comes in knowing the typical perceptions of Paul and having clarity on characteristic ways he perceives and behaves.

# 2

# Order and Purity
# in Paul's
# Symbolic Universe

God arranged the organs in the body, each one of them, as he chose.

1 Corinthians 12:18

God has not called us for uncleanness, but in holiness.

1 Thessalonians 4:7

## 1.0 Learning to Perceive Like an Anthropologist

Most people prefer a cosmos to chaos and order to disorder. In this chapter we focus on the degree of order people perceive in their world as well as the precise ways they perceive their cosmos to be ordered and structured. For Paul the Pharisee, the world was exactly and precisely ordered; like other Jews socialized to the creation story in Genesis 1, he preferred a cosmos to chaos. He feared anarchy and anomie. The question for us, then, is to discover the redundant forms of order and system in his world.

We begin with an appreciation of general ways in which people typically structure and classify everything in their world: persons, places, things, time, and so forth. We then move on to the more specific ways in which Jews like Paul perceived their world to be ordered. Finally, we can study Paul's letters to learn the precise expressions of his perception of order. We focus, therefore, on perceptions of the world: general ancient Mediterranean perceptions, specific Jewish patterns, and precise Pauline expressions of an orderly and ordered universe. Always we inquire about the way Paul and others tend to organize, classify, and systematize the world around them so as to make sense of what would otherwise be chaos.

*1.1 Order and Disorder/Purity and Pollution* Most social groups are accustomed to perceive and to put order into the chaos of their universe. They value orderly structures and attempt to classify each and every person and thing appropriately. Thus they find "a place for everything and everything in its place." We label this penchant for abstract systems of order and classification "purity," and the concerns for order and classification are called "purity concerns." The term *purity* is a general, abstract word whose utility lies in its abstractness, and so it applies to many different, specific cultural systems. People often label things "pure"/"polluted," "clean"/"unclean," or "holy"/"profane," and in so doing express an abstract sense of right/wrong and good/evil. Curiously, the specific object or action that is pure in one culture might be polluted in another. But the impulse to organize and to label seems to be common and pervasive. This is what we are examining, both the general impulse to label and the specific abstract system that explains the labels. *Purity*, then, is the term used to describe the patterns of order and the system of labeling and classification.

In general, an object or action is pure (or clean, holy) when it conforms to the specific cultural norms that make up the symbolic system of a particular social group. That is, something is pure when it is "in place," when it belongs in a particular, orderly context. This will vary in terms of whether we are examining the cosmos of Japan, Mexico, Iran, Zaire, or Ecuador; each culture has specific ways of perceiving and expressing order. Conversely, things and actions are polluted (or unclean, taboo, an abomination) when they violate the specific cultural system. Pollution refers to what is "out of place," or disorderly.

We can easily enter this discussion by attending to what people generally mean by the terms *pollution* or *dirt* (Douglas 1966, 1969).

> If we can abstract pathogenicity and hygiene from our notion of dirt, we are left with the old definition of dirt as matter out of place. This is a very suggestive approach. It implies two conditions: a set of ordered relations and a contravention of that order. Dirt, then, is never a unique, isolated event. Where there is dirt there is system. Dirt is the by-product of a systematic ordering and classification of matter, in so far as ordering involves rejecting inappropriate elements. This idea of dirt takes us straight into the field of symbolism and promises a link-up with more obviously symbolic systems of purity. . . . To conclude, if uncleanness is matter out of place, we must approach it through order. Uncleanness or dirt is that which must not be included if a pattern is to be maintained. (Douglas 1966:35, 40)

And in another place, she explains:

> The idea of dirt implies a structure of idea. For us dirt is a kind of compendium category for all events which blur, smudge, contradict, or otherwise confuse accepted classifications. The underlying feeling is that a system of values which is habitually expressed in a given arrangement of things has been violated. (Douglas 1975:51)

The labeling of something as "dirty" or "polluted," then, implies that people are socialized to know a group's symbolic universe whereby they appropriately classify, situate, and organize persons, objects, places, and times in their world. *Purity* and *pollution* are but the code names for that abstract system and its contravention.

For example, when consumed at home or at a ball game, a glass of beer is "in place." But it would be "out of place" during a Sunday worship service; it would be out of place at a local chapter of AA. It all depends on the specific system or frame of reference of a given group. Again, when administered in a hospital to a suffering patient, morphine is in place. But it is out of place when used as a recreational drug. Tennis shoes are in place in the gym, but are out of place at a board meeting of bank presidents. Pork is always out of place in Muslim countries. The key element in the labeling process, then, lies in learning the operative cultural context of a group, for that will indicate a system of ordering according to which something will be in place or out of place, and therefore pure or polluted.

One can easily imagine that organizations such as the Vatican, the military, hospitals, and libraries all have systems of order. In each specific context we can learn what is pure, or in place, and what is polluting, or out of place. Purity for the military means authority and discipline; for a hospital it is related to keeping conditions sterile and disease free; for a library, purity refers to its indexing system. But the principle remains clear: pure refers to order and pollution to disorder.

### 1.2 The Bible and Purity Concerns

*1.2 The Bible and Purity Concerns*   We are not the first to employ this way of thinking in regard to the Bible. British anthropologist Mary T. Douglas introduced both the study of order in society and the term *purity* in her study of the roots of Jewish concerns over taboo (1966). She explained why certain persons and things were labeled "unclean," "polluted," or "taboo." Biblical scholars immediately saw the importance of her studies and developed them in regard to Jewish and Christian literature. Jacob Neusner took up Douglas's model and her terminology of "purity" in regard to second-temple Jewish literature in his book *The Idea of Purity in Ancient Judaism* (1973a; see also Baumgarten 1980 and Newton 1985). Isenberg and Owens (1977) and Malina (1978a; 1981:122–152) systematized Douglas's material for interpretation of early Christian literature. The concepts and model have gained acceptance as useful and insightful ways to study the symbolic world of biblical peoples around the turn of the era. So this material comes to us in quite refined form and with much practical application (see Newton 1985:52–114; Neyrey 1986a, 1988c).

We must move now from general considerations of order and purity to more specific expressions of this concept in the world of the New Testament. Anyone familiar with ancient Jewish writings, culture, and archaeology will recognize the frequency and importance of the term *purity* (or *clean*, *spotless*, and so forth) in Jewish culture. Comparably, when we examine the patterns of order and system in Paul's symbolic universe, we investigate how Paul was specifically socialized as an observant Jew, even a zealous Pharisee, to label everything in his world in terms of purity and pollution.

Thus we ask both emic as well as etic questions (Harris 1976).

Emic = how a native perceives and explains = purity
Etic = how an anthropologist or professional
      perceives and explains = order

When we ask an emic question, we want to know how Paul the Pharisee was socialized to perceive and value an orderly and fully classified world and how he would express that in terms of pure/polluted and clean/unclean. For the term *purity* explicitly communicates specific Jewish values, even as it refers to the general principles of order and classification in any society, whether Jewish, Christian, or Muslim. Yet we may ask an etic question about the general tendency of Paul or anyone else to perceive order. Hence *purity* has both emic (specifically Jewish) and etic (general) meaning. It can serve to identify the ordering principles operative in organizations such as the U.S. military, hospitals, the Kremlin, the Vatican, business corporations, and so forth, when these strive to order, classify, and structure their worlds. Purity, then, means order, both general and Jewish.

## 2.0 An Emic Perspective: Purity and the Jewish World

*2.1 Paul, the Jew* People are generally socialized to perceive their world in terms of orderly patterns of classification. Moving from the abstract to the concrete, let us now examine the specific purity system of the Israel of Paul's day. This is the world into which Paul was socialized, and so we must appreciate both the intensity of his socialization into a highly ordered world and the specific details of that particular orderly system.

We must never forget, however, that Paul was socialized to perceive the world as a Jew (Rom. 11:1; 2 Cor. 11:22; Phil.

3:5). He was a Jew's Jew, for as he himself said, "I advanced in Judaism beyond many of my own age among my people" (Gal. 1:14a). Adequately socialized, Paul knew what was expected of him, and he lived accordingly, "as to righteousness under the law blameless" (Phil. 3:6b). What, then, was the system into which Paul was socialized that colored his perceptions of what is pure and polluted?

Although Christian readers all too readily identify Paul as a Christian, he was fundamentally and irrevocably socialized into the purity system of the Judaism of his day: "Circumcised on the eighth day, of the people of Israel, of the tribe of Benjamin, a Hebrew born of Hebrews; as to the law a Pharisee" (Phil. 3:5). It will be important for us to take careful note later on of the ways that being a follower of Jesus changed parts of this system. But for the moment we must take Paul at his word that he was born and bred as an observant Jew, and so his perceptions were shaped in terms of the Jewish system of purity, or order.

**2.2 Jewish Models of Order: Creation and Temple**  How would typical people like Paul be socialized to be good Jews? How would they perceive the world? What patterns would they tend to see operative in the cosmos? How would they tend to classify and identify the people and things in their world? To get at this, let us examine a series of basic "maps" both found in their sacred literature (Genesis 1) and embodied in their major institution (the Temple).

**2.2.1 Creation**  The Jewish God is particularly known in terms of holiness: "You shall be holy; for I the LORD your God am holy" (Lev. 19:2). This phrase "for I am holy" becomes a refrain echoing through the Bible and assuming the status of a major way of understanding God (Lev. 11:44, 45; 19:2; 20:7, 26; 21:8; see 1 Peter 1:16). What does it mean? The Hebrew word for holy (*qdš*) expresses an idea of separation, thus implying a distinctive sense of being "in place." Hence God, who is deathless, is set apart from mortals (1 Cor. 15:50); and God, who is perfect, does not allow what is imperfect into the divine presence (1 Cor. 6:9–10). Thus, for Jews, holiness adequately describes God, particularly as God is set apart.

That is not all it means, however, for God did not remain apart, but created a world. Therein lies a new set of clues about God's holiness. The holy God expressed holiness by creating a holy/orderly cosmos. God acted to bless this creation precisely by the divine ordering and structuring of all relationships.

Writing of the Jewish sense of God's creative blessing, one anthropologist noted:

> In the Old Testament we find blessing as the source of all good things and the withdrawal of blessing as the source of all dangers. The blessing of God makes the land possible for men to live in it. God's work through the blessing is to create order, through which men's affairs prosper. (Douglas 1966:49–50)

Blessing, then, implies order. And the primary act of blessing was creation. We have, then, two meanings of God's holiness: God is holy (1) when set apart from death and sin and (2) when creating order out of chaos. Mortals have never seen the holy God in heaven, but they can know God's holiness in the way God's creation is ordered and structured. We can, then, know God's holiness-as-order as we sort out the various patterns and classifications of creation, especially as these are known from the creation account in Genesis 1.

The creation story in Genesis 1, which is generally known as the "Priestly Account," expresses a rather full sense of the divine order of the world. It encoded various "maps," or patterns of order, that God made for Israel to perceive and follow (Soler 1979). If we would perceive the orderly world as first-century Jews did, Genesis 1 is an excellent window into that world-as-it-was-perceived.

When we read the creation story in Genesis 1, we quickly gain a sense of the mapping of places, persons, times, and things. According to the creation story, God did not make things helter-skelter, but arranged them orderly in a proper cosmos. By constantly "separating" things (Gen. 1:4, 7, 14), God created a series of maps that order, classify, and define the world as Jews came to see it:

**Time:** At creation God separated day and night. When God established "the week," he then separated it into workdays and sabbath rest. God ordained sun, moon, and stars to mark that time precisely. Therefore, the fundamentals of a calendar are thus established. Time was ordered and mapped (see Gen. 8:22).

**Things:** At creation God created animals, birds, and fish in their pure form (no hybrids, no unclean creatures). Each class, moreover, was separated from the others in terms of its proper place, diet, and means of locomotion. Things as well as places were ordered and mapped.

**Place:** At creation God separated the waters above from those below; then the land was created, separating wet from dry. With the creation of animals, birds, and fish, God further separated each creature into its proper place: animals roam the earth, birds fly in the air, and fish swim in the sea. Thus place was mapped, first as wet and dry space, and then as the proper abode for specific classes of things.

**Diet:** At creation God assigned each creature its proper diet. Animals eat grass, birds eat seeds, and fish feed on sea creatures. No animal ate carrion, much less birds; nor did birds feed in the sea. Dietary restrictions existed from the beginning of creation.

**Role/Status:** At creation God established a pattern of authority and hierarchy among creatures. The heavens "rule" over the night and the sun "rules" the day; among the creatures on the dry land, God gave Adam dominion over them all (Gen. 1:26, 28). Thus persons were mapped.

Chaos was conquered, and in its place an orderly cosmos was arranged. Thus Genesis 1 contains many specific instances of separation, order, and classification, which we may conveniently call "maps." Furthermore, creation, which is the holy God's premier act of ordering and classification in the world, conveys to Israelites both the principle that there are maps and specific examples of them.

To think like a Jew, one must read Genesis 1 like a Jew, for it expresses the symbolic world into which Jews, if they would be holy, must be socialized. In summary, the maps of creation define what it means to be holy; when the maps are not followed, pollution occurs. When followed, then persons, times, places, and things are in place and therefore pure. For example, the Sabbath is a day of rest. Hence, working on the Sabbath violates the map of times; it is out of place on that day and therefore unclean. Birds were created to fly in the sky and to eat seeds (proper place, locomotion, and diet); but birds such as cormorants and vultures violate the ideal map by not adhering to proper place or proper diet, and so are classified as unclean.

The holy God expressed holiness precisely through these patterns of classification and order. If Israelites wished to be "holy as God is holy," they must imitate God's holiness as this was expressed in God's orderly creation. For God expressed divine holiness in the precise series of maps of place, things, times, and persons that serve to classify and locate each item in its proper place. Israelites must know the maps and keep them. Therefore, subsequent holiness among God's creatures involves maintaining these distinct categories of creation (Soler 1979:24–30).

### 2.2.2 The Temple

Yet Paul and other observant Jews find the holiness of God not only abstractly expressed in the creation story, but concretely embodied in the temple system in Jerusalem. Observant Jews who went to the Temple for annual pilgrimage and for prayer or sacrifice (Luke 2:41; Acts 21:26) were socialized to patterns that became part of their worldview. What maps would one learn there?

**Map of Things:** Not all animals may be offered on the altar, but only "holy" animals, that is, those that are in accord with the definition of a clean animal and that are physically perfect (unblemished). Specific offerings, moreover, were appropriate for specific feasts or occasions: a lamb for Passover, a red heifer for Yom Kippur, a holocaust for sins, but grain for thanksgiving.

**Map of Persons:** Not just any person could offer the sacrifice, but only a "holy" priest who has the right bloodlines, enjoys an unblemished physical condition, and is in a state of ritual purity. Who may participate in the sacrifice? Only Israelites and only those with whole bodies (see Lev. 21:17–20). Reconstructions of the Second Temple clearly indicate the careful gradations of space on the temple mount, indicating where Gentiles might stand, where women were allowed, where Jewish men could go. Priests entered the general sanctuary area, but only the High Priest entered the Holy of Holies. People, then, were mapped.

**Map of Places:** Sacrifices and offerings could not be made anywhere, but only in Jerusalem's Temple, which is a microcosm of creation. Even within the Temple there are specific and appropriate places for priests, Israelites, women, and Gentiles. Gentiles could read in the Temple the following inscription, which mapped out places permitted and forbidden them: "No foreigner is to enter within the balustrade and embankment around the sanctuary. Whoever is caught will have himself to blame for his death which follows" (Josephus, *Antiquities* 15:417; *Jewish War* 5:194).

**Maps of Time:** Specific offerings were made on a daily, weekly, and annual basis. Certain offerings were appropriate only for certain occasions. All of this is specified in the elaborate liturgical calendar developed around the temple system of sacrifice.

The Temple and its maps of time, place, things, and persons became the concrete structural expression of the core value of God's holiness. After all, the creation account in Genesis 1 is ascribed by modern scholars to the Priestly Tradition in the Pentateuch. Such a system was highly visible, formidably impressive, and culturally dominating.

If there is any truth in the claims that Paul was "brought up in this city at the feet of Gamaliel, educated according to the strict manner of the law of our fathers" (Acts 22:3), then he grew up socialized into a highly structured world that had a place for everything and everything had its place. If he was typical of his culture, then Paul had strong purity concerns to order and classify everything in his world. The basic lines of his classification system would be drawn from Scripture and especially from the Temple.

Yet the picture needs to be expanded. The symbolic world of God's holiness in creation and temple was a system that had its critics and reformers. Not everyone in Israel agreed with the precise way its system operated. The residents at Qumran strongly criticized the temple priests because of their bloodlines and calendar; consequently, they developed their own "reformed" version of Israel's purity system (Yadin 1985:147–191). Jesus, the Jew, is reported to have criticized the temple system as such (Acts 6:14; Mark 11:15–19; 12:29–30), thus implying further reform of the system. The point is, although there was a clear and dominant system evident to all, not all in Israel agreed with it in every detail. The key term is *reform* (Theissen 1978). There were many reformers in Israel in the time of Jesus, and so we learn not only of the typical Jewish system but of attacks on the system. Again it is a matter of perception, but Jesus and others would describe their actions as reform, whereas people such as the temple priests would consider them as subversive of the whole system (see Acts 6:11, 13–14; 17:6; 21:28).

As we turn to examine Paul, let us keep two things in mind: (1) In general, observant Jews in the time of Paul typically valued a highly ordered world, a cosmos. And the pattern of organization was based on God's action in creation and on the worship of God in the Temple. (2) But the exact shape of that system was a matter of ongoing debate and reform. Many reformers, Jesus and Paul for example, challenged certain of the maps and values on which the maps were drawn. Hence we must be sensitive to "order" as well as "disorder" in Paul's letters.

## 3.0 Paul's Orderly Cosmos: 1 Corinthians

As a Jew, Paul was strongly socialized to perceive the world as an orderly cosmos. And as a Jew he shared the same specific cultural definitions of order as this was developed in the Bible and the Temple (Newton 1985). Like other Jews, he frequently used the particular language of clean/unclean and pure/polluted to express his acute sense of order. But at this point we are not trying to affirm Paul's Jewishness, a fact easily done and not to be denied. Like most other Jews in his cultural milieu, Paul strongly believed in an orderly universe, even if he tinkered with the existing arrangement of it and urged reform of it. Clear patterns of order and classification may be found in all of Paul's letters, but we will concentrate here on 1 Corinthians as an apt illustration of this tendency in his symbolic perception of the universe. It happens that 1 Corinthians may not contain illustrations of all the various maps that make up the world. And so, when necessary, we will indicate these in other letters.

*3.1 Paul and the Language of Purity*  From Paul's acknowledgments of his Jewish background, we may confidently assume that he shared the same strong passion for an orderly universe that characterized Israel's politics and piety. What does this look like? One direct way of uncovering this phenomenon in Paul's letters is to note Paul's frequent use of the Jewish terms for order and disorder, i.e., *purity* and *pollution*. Figure 1 (pages 54–55) lists not only the specific terms *purity* and *pollution* but the semantic word field, giving us a rich sense of the synonyms and cognates that convey the sense of order and disorder, clean and unclean. Every thing, person, place, and time could be classified in terms of its purity. Although we do not find all of the various terms listed in Figure 1 in the Pauline letters, that list does show that Paul and his world employed a variety of terms to express a common, pervasive perception. Also, the frequency of the terms used by Paul indicates that this type of perceiving and labeling is a special concern of his, something we would expect of a devout Jew.

Yet we will not stop and examine Paul's specific use of this or that term. Rather, it is enough to note here that Paul shared

with other Jews a strong sense of an orderly cosmos and expressed that sense of order in terms of purity. He was deeply
socialized to appreciate a world extensively classified and systematized, namely, an orderly cosmos. Moreover, Paul the Jew
explicitly used the actual words denoting clean and unclean in
much the same sense that his Jewish countrymen did in regard
to Genesis 1 and the Temple. Here it will be helpful to speak
more in detail about the criteria whereby some thing or person
is labeled "clean" or "unclean."

For a Jew of Paul's period, *clean* might refer to a variety of
persons, places, or things. People are pure when they fully exemplify the cultural definition of what it means to be a person.
Jews are pure who are of the proper bloodlines, who are circumcised, keep the Torah, and are not bodily mutilated. Foods
are pure that conform to the definition of a clean animal given
in Leviticus; if an animal fails fully to satisfy that definition in
any way, it is unclean and may not be sacrificed to God or
eaten at table. Sabbath is a holy day on which one rests and
does not work. Working at this time is unclean.

The human body was especially perceived in terms of purity
in regards to its wholeness. Mutilated or deformed persons
could not offer sacrifice in the Temple (see Lev. 21:16–20).
Bodily excretions were perceived as dangerous sources of pollution; hence bodies are clean that have no flows of blood,
menses, semen, or pus. Bodily surfaces likewise replicate purity; hence skin diseases of any sort (popularly called "leprosy") were unclean (Pilch 1981). Excretions and flaking skin
indicate material that is "out of place." These were no minor
matters for the Jews of Paul's world, for full membership and
complete participation in the group's activities depended on
being pure according to the specific popular understandings of
that concept. For uncleanness there was no sympathy or toleration. This would be especially true for Pharisees, who strove to
act in their daily lives with the same ritual purity usually required only of temple priests. For a fuller discussion of the
meaning of these technical Jewish words, a reader might consult Douglas 1966; Neusner 1973a; Malina 1981:122–137; and
Neyrey 1986a:93–105; 1988b:65–78.

*3.2 Maps of People*   A second way of appreciating Paul's sense
of an orderly cosmos is to attend to the series of implicit maps
in his letters that encode his sense of order and classification.
These reveal just how structured was his perception of the
world as a highly ordered universe. His maps, moreover, are
comparable to the maps implicit in Genesis 1 and the Temple,

which we studied above, and they cover the basic elements of his world: persons, things, places, and time. These maps clearly indicate that for Paul there was a place for everything and everything had its place.

We begin our survey of Paul's maps of order with in investigation of his *maps of people*. Without prejudicing our findings, we will observe how frequently Paul actually speaks of some sort of structured relationship or hierarchy among all peoples, both those in heaven and on earth. To Paul, these maps belong to the natural order of the universe; they are "the given" of creation. Yet Paul's interest in them is not an abstract passion for neatness, but functions directly in regard to the pervasive and ever-present conflicts in the Pauline churches over authority, rank, and status. To settle disputed issues of authority and relationships, Paul appeals to maps of persons to which he was socialized as a Jew.

### 3.2.1 God and Maps of Heavenly Figures

There are four passages in 1 Corinthians that suggest an attempt by Paul to describe the relationship of God first to Christ, but also to Christ and Spirit (1 Cor. 3:21–23; 11:3; 12:3–5; 15:27–28). In examining these passages, the language at times seems strange and forced, but let us examine them and then ask about the function of such *maps of heavenly figures*.

1. *Cosmic Hierarchy*:

> I want you to understand that the head of every man is Christ, the head of a woman is her husband, and *the head of Christ is God*.
>
> 1 Corinthians 11:3

So much modern attention is given to the issue of hierarchical relationship between man and woman/husband and wife that we pay scant attention to the assertion that Christ stands in a hierarchical relationship to God, who is his "head": "the head of Christ is God." In heaven, even the risen Jesus, who must surely enjoy maximum freedom in his resurrection (2 Cor. 3:17), nevertheless remains in a structured relationship with God. In short, there exists authority and differentiation of role and status even in heaven, even between God and Christ.

2. *Heavenly Hierarchy*:

> "For God has put all things in subjection under his feet" [Ps. 8:6]. But when it says, "All things are put in subjection under him," it is plain that *he* [God] is excepted who put all things

under him. When all things are subjected to *him* [Christ], then the Son himself will be subjected to *him* [God] who put all things under him, that God may be everything to every one.

1 Corinthians 15:27–28

In essence, this passage describes the same structured relationship between God and Christ as 11:3. Inasmuch as it comes at the end of the argument in 15:21–28, let us examine the whole of that statement to clarify just what is being said.

As everyone knows, some members of the Corinthian church claimed to share already in the power of Jesus' resurrection. By implication, they were no longer subject to the ordinary laws and maps that structure earthly, fleshly existence. Modern scholars label this erroneous perception of time as "realized eschatology" (Meeks 1983a:121–122). In response, Paul maps out a scenario of "the resurrection," which precludes the social disorder that would follow if group members legitimately thought of themselves as independent of group norms because of their present sharing in Christ's resurrection. According to Paul's map, Christ is indeed the first fruits of the resurrection (15:20); and his resurrection is understood in such a way as to indicate that others too will be raised (15:21–22). But only Christ is *already* raised, no one else yet.

Concerning the resurrection, Paul speaks of a grand map, both of times and of persons.

Each in his own order [*tagmati*]: Christ the first fruits, then at his coming those who belong to Christ. Then comes the end, when he delivers the kingdom to God the Father after destroying every rule and every authority and power. For he must reign until he has put all his enemies under his feet. The last enemy to be destroyed is death.

1 Corinthians 15:23–26

Paul's *map of times* is clear: first Christ (already), then those who belong to Christ at his coming, then "the end" (remote future). The resurrection will be complete when at last "death" is finally destroyed. The precise phraseology here functions as Paul's argument against any claim in the Corinthian church about another map of time. No one but Christ has been raised, for "death" still reigns. No one else will be raised until Christ's coming at "the end."

In this passage we read also of a map of persons in which Christ's surpassing role and status are affirmed. Christ ranks higher than all other maverick or competing figures in a world full of heavenly figures. He will destroy Rule, Authority, and Power, that is, heavenly figures. Moreover, "all enemies" will be put under his feet; finally, *the* enemy, Death, will be subject to him. The description of Christ's superior status indicates that he stands at the top of some map of celestial figures, whether they be heavenly or demonic.

The map that locates Jesus above all other competing figures is not complete until another figure is accounted for, namely, God. A most important part of the map of heavenly figures is described in 15:27–28, a map of precedence among the most prominent figures in heaven, Christ and God. Paul first cites Psalm 8:6, apropos of Christ's superiority over all enemies, Death included: "For God has put all things in subjection under his [Christ's] feet." But as the argument continues, Paul makes a point of clarifying the relative ranking of God and Christ. Taking up Psalm 8:6, Paul carefully interprets each word of the psalm. First, when the psalm states that *all* things are in subjection under Christ's feet, "all" does not mean what it states, for someone is excepted from the literal meaning of *all,* namely, God. "When it says, '*All things* are put in subjection under him,' it is plain that he [i.e., God] is excepted who put all things under him [i.e., Christ]" (15:27a). Put simply, God is not under the feet of Christ! God does not rank lower than Christ!

Having stated the issue negatively in 15:27, Paul immediately states it positively in 15:28: "When all things are subjected to him [Christ], then the Son himself will be subjected to him [God] who put all things under him [Christ]." Indeed, Christ is subject to God, even in heaven, even in the resurrection, even when the perfect order is finally achieved. The principle is immediately clear: "that God may be everything to every one" (15:28b), including Christ.

In a passage where maps of time and persons serve to present a correct perception of a fully ordered universe, Paul affirms a map of heavenly relationships. As we saw in 11:3, Paul insists in 15:27–28 on the legitimacy of social precedence and so of authority and honor ranking even in the heavenly world. If Christ, who enjoys maximum honor and status, is nevertheless "under" God in terms of rank and authority, then the pattern of the heavenly world (macrocosm) legitimatizes similar patterns on earth (microcosm). But the principle is clear: persons, even heavenly figures, are mapped. The same pattern can be observed in 3:21–23.

### 3. *Expanded Heavenly Hierarchy*:

There are varieties of gifts, but *the same Spirit*; and there are varieties of service, but *the same Lord*; and there are varieties of

working, but it is *the same God* who inspires them all in every one.
1 Corinthians 12:4–6

If we are correct in noting Paul's penchant to present a map of heavenly figures, this perception will surely affect the way we interpret 12:4–6. Readers of 1 Corinthians are familiar with the various problems and crises of that church, among which was conflict and competition over spiritual gifts by the persons who exercised them. Paul writes about this problem in 12:1–14:39 ("*Concerning spiritual persons . . .* "). His first remarks distinguish false from true "speaking by the Spirit": only a false spirit could inspire someone to say "Cursed be Jesus!" but the sign of the true Spirit is to confess that "Jesus is Lord" (12:3). "Spirit" denotes for many freedom and the abolition of authority (2 Cor. 3:17); Paul promptly qualifies such a perception by asserting that authentic "spirit" leads one to acknowledge authority. Hence, genuine spiritual speech should acclaim the authority of Jesus: "Jesus is Lord!" Does this imply any pattern of ranking for Jesus and Spirit?

In 12:4–6 Paul no doubt affirms unity amid the diversity of gifts in the group. Unity is expressed in the repetition of "the same" (*to auto, autos*) in regard to Spirit, Christ, and God. It is implied as well in the apparently harmonious relationship among the three heavenly figures mentioned—Spirit, Christ, and God. Clearly there is no rivalry or competition in heaven, in spite of what occurs in the group at Corinth. Yet, are the heavenly figures equal in rank and authority? Does Paul imply some differentiation among them? Are they listed here in a way that suggests a structured relationship? Let us examine the map of persons here.

God, of course, remains sovereign and enjoys the highest place on the map, just as God did in 11:3 and 15:27–28 (see also 8:5–6). Furthermore, in 12:3 Paul implies that authentic "spirit" acknowledges Jesus' exalted position ("Jesus is Lord!"); hence, after God, Jesus enjoys maximum status. This means that "spirit" is mapped in third place, as servant of the Lord Jesus. Therefore, it seems that in 12:4–6 the paramount figure in the triad listed must be God, and that Paul lists the figures in ascending order, affirming differentiation in role and status among Spirit, Lord, and God. Paul, then, does not allow Spirit to disrupt God's orderly world (see 1 Cor. 14:32–33), and so Spirit is perceived in relationship to other figures and is even subordinate to them (Neyrey 1988d:180–196). Paul, then, lists the figures in 12:4–6 in such a way as to convey a *map of heavenly persons* who are not equal in role or status.

*or in function*

At first, the language seems forced and the concepts odd. Why such a structured list? Why clarify by means of a map of heavenly figures the relationship of "Spirit" and Lord and God? The answer lies once more in the domestic conflicts in the Corinthian church. Certain pneumatic elite appear to Paul to be exalting "spirit" and pneumatic gifts in ways that threaten Paul's perception of an orderly group (14:33, 40). Paul senses that pneumatic celebration of freedom means denial of authority and divinely affirmed patterns of roles and statuses, not only on earth but also in heaven. Hence, "spirit," when first mentioned, is described in relationship to other heavenly figures, first to Jesus who is Lord and then to Lord and God. By speaking of spirit in relationship to other heavenly figures, Paul suggests a pattern of orderly relationships, a map of heavenly figures. If patterns of different roles and statuses exist in heaven, then comparable patterns are expected on earth in the church. The macrocosm serves as the model for the microcosm, the church.

**3.2.2 Maps of People Within the Church** After examining maps of people in the heavenly realm, we turn now to the earthly world and its maps. We look first at Paul's maps of people within the church (12:28; 15:5–11; 12:14–25), then at his way of mapping members and nonmembers, then at his maps of creation (15:38–41).

1. *Ranking of Resurrection Manifestations*:

> [Jesus] appeared to Cephas, then to the twelve. Then he appeared to more than five hundred brethren at one time, most of whom are still alive, though some have fallen asleep. Then he appeared to James, then to all the apostles. Last of all . . . he appeared also to me. For I am the least of the apostles, unfit to be called an apostle, because I persecuted the church of God. But by the grace of God I am what I am, and his grace toward me was not in vain. On the contrary, I worked harder than any of them, though it was not I, but the grace of God which is with me.
>
> 1 Corinthians 15:5–10

This list of those to whom Jesus manifested himself has enormous importance for Paul, because those to whom Jesus appeared were thereby ascribed a specific role in the church ("Am I not an apostle? Have I not seen Jesus our Lord?" [9:1]), with specific rights and duties. The list bespeaks the legitimate ascribed authority of those listed. To be listed at all is of great significance.

Cephas is listed first, probably because Christ appeared to

him first in time (Luke 24:34) and/or because Christ affirmed his leadership among his brethren (Luke 22:31–32; John 21:15–19). Paul stands last, not simply because he might well have been the last in time to receive Jesus' manifestation, but because he is "the least of the apostles, unfit to be called an apostle" because he persecuted the church. A map of persons is replicated then by a map of time.

The primary function of the list lies precisely in getting Paul on it in the first place, for it is a list of duly authorized persons with ascribed legitimate authority. It is not news to readers of Paul's Corinthian correspondence that his authority, role, and status at Corinth were constantly challenged (Dahl 1977:47–55). Among more gifted people, Paul seemed "un-wise," "non-eloquent," "non-pneumatic," and "un-strong." Why should anyone listen to him, respect him, or pay heed to his teaching? But Paul is not content merely to include himself on the list of authorized persons in 1 Corinthians 15:6–8. Nor is he satisfied to remain "last" and "least." He describes himself as gifted by God ("by the grace/*charis* of God I am what I am"), which should serve to include him among the other elite and gifted people at Corinth. In regard to Cephas and the others, Paul boasts that "I worked harder than any of them." On the list Paul may be "last" in time and perhaps "least" because he persecuted the church, but he is hardly content with that position. Therefore, the very list in 15:5–11 serves as a map of persons to whom the Lord Jesus gave legitimate authority. Paul's very presence on the map bespeaks his ascribed authority in the church.

### 2. *Ranking of Prominent Persons*:

> God has appointed in the church *first* apostles, *second* prophets, *third* teachers; *then* workers of miracles, *then* healers, helpers, administrators, speakers in various kinds of tongues. Are all apostles? Are all prophets? Are all teachers? Do all work miracles? Do all possess gifts of healing? Do all speak with tongues? Do all interpret?
>
> 1 Corinthians 12:28–30

This list occurs in the midst of a discussion of spiritual persons and their gifts (12:1–14:40). We know from Paul's letter that certain gifts were prized over others, and in the eyes of some indicated higher status. Spiritual gifts, then, functioned to map people, wise over unwise, those "in the know" over those *not* "in the know," the free over the nonfree. The paramount gift was the gift of tongues. In the face of the local list of celebrated gifts, Paul puts forth his list, which appears to function as a corrective to certain elitist tendencies in Corinth.

The list in 12:28–30 is carefully structured. A map of time seems to be indicated: "first . . . second . . . third . . . then." In a world where the dominant temporal pattern was "earlier is better, later is weaker," the claim to be first in time implies a claim to higher role and status (see 3:6, 10). Although we probably should not look too carefully at the total arrangement of this list, the beginning and ending are important for the way they map out certain gifts and persons. At the beginning are the most important persons and their gifts (apostle, prophet, teacher), but at the end Paul lists the gift that seems to be causing the most division (speaking in tongues). By mentioning them first on the list, Paul ranks "apostle, prophet, and teacher" as superior to those noted last and at the bottom. The list, moreover, enumerates the sequence of gifts twice, first with a temporal twist (12:28), and then with an argument that not everybody has all of the gifts. Finally, after affirming the need for all the gifts, Paul exhorts the group to aspire for the "higher gifts" (12:29–31). The gifts are not simply equal, on a par. There are higher gifts. The gifts, then, are mapped in a hierarchical pattern. The list of them has a clear shape to it, and its rhetorical structure constitutes its argument, both polemical and apologetic.

From other places in 1 Corinthians we know that Paul greatly prized his own role as apostle (9:1; 15:8–10). Comparably, he tended to list speaking in tongues in the last and lowest position, first of all in the list of manifestations of the Spirit in 12:8–10 and then throughout chapter 14, where prophecy is always ranked higher and better than speaking in tongues. The list in 12:28–30, then, functions as a map of persons, indicating rank and status in the group.

### 3. *Ranking of Church Members*:

> If the *foot* should say, "Because I am not a *hand*, I do not belong to the body," that would not make it any less a part of the body. And if the *ear* should say, "Because I am not an *eye*, I do not belong to the body," that would not make it any less a part of the body. . . . The *eye* cannot say to the *hand*, "I have no need of you," nor again the *head* to the *feet*, "I have no need of you." On the contrary, the parts of the body which seem to be weaker are indispensable, and those parts of the body which we think less honorable we invest with the greater honor, and our unpresentable parts are treated with greater modesty, which our more presentable parts do not require.
>
> 1 Corinthians 12:15–16, 21–24a

Paul remarked concerning the "body of Christ": "one body—
Jews or Greeks, slaves or free" (12:13). Paul said this in support of the oneness of the body of Christ: "Just as the body is
one and has many members, and all the members of the body,
though many, are one body, so it is with Christ" (12:12). Such
remarks must be seen in conjunction with Paul's distress at the
division of the church into competing factions (1:11–12; 3:3–4;
11:18–19). But he did not at all mean that the one body had no
appropriate *map of persons/parts.* Oneness does not preclude
diversity or differentiation.

In defense of the unity of the body, Paul phrases his remarks
in 12:14–25 to speak about a perceived division of the body
between the "weak" (12:14–19) and the "strong" (12:20–25).
First he paraphrases what might be the complaints of the non-
elite: "If a foot should say, 'Because I am not a hand, I do not
belong to the body.' . . . If an ear should say, 'Because I am
not an eye, I do not belong in the body'" (12:15–16). Paul
does not say that all the body parts are the same or equal.
Rather, he argues that the foot and the ear indeed "belong to
the body," although they do not have the same rank or place in
the body as the hand or the eye. The argument supports unity
but does not deny differentiation. Furthermore, arguing from a
sense of God's order in creation, Paul states: "God arranged
the organs in the body, each one of them, as he chose" (12:18).
The *map of bodily members* is based on the original and
programmatic map of persons that Paul perceives as given
in creation.

After defending the status of the lesser members, Paul then
speaks more aggressively in correction of the way the elite
might express their superior role and status. "The eye cannot
say to the hand, 'I have no need of you,' nor again the head to
the feet, 'I have no need of you'" (12:21). Again, Paul does not
argue that the body should not be mapped in terms of head/
feet, eye/hand, and so forth, but that the order of creation was
not intended to support rivalry and division but to establish
order. Whatever else Paul says about the way the body members should relate to one another, the argument in 12:14–25
functions on the unchallenged premise that there is a map of
parts/persons that is established by God in the primal act of
creation.

Only three examples are listed above the map of persons. But
there are many others that, when examined, convey the same
message, namely, that within the church there are diverse roles
and statuses indicative of differing degrees of legitimate authority (e.g., 1 Cor. 16:10–16). These *maps of people in the*

*earthly world* should be seen vis-à-vis the maps of heavenly figures. For the principle seems to be the same: In an orderly cosmos there is a clear and structured hierarchy of roles and statuses, in both the macrocosm and the microcosm. One might ask further about the social utility of such maps, who articulates them, and who benefits from them. From what we know of the Corinthian church, for example, when Paul's role and authority were challenged and when rivalry and competition set members of the church at odds, then Paul tended to spend extra time articulating these maps to locate himself and his challengers and rivals more accurately on the map. The maps would also serve as supportive to the weak and corrective to the elite.

### 3.2.3 A Map of the Church: Members and Nonmembers

As everyone knows, when Paul speaks of the members of the church, he operates out of an implicit map of persons that divides the world into two groups: those on the map who belong to the body of Christ and those not on the map who do not belong (Meeks 1983a:84–96). In other words, Paul employs dualistic terms in defining membership. Some of the major expressions he used are as follows:

1. *Defining the Church—Us vs. Them:*

| | | |
|---|---|---|
| saints (*hagioi*) | vs. | nonsaints, nonjustified (*adikoi*: 1 Cor. 6:1, 9) |
| saints | vs. | the world (1 Cor. 1:20–28; 2:12; 3:19; 5:10; 6:2; 7:31, 33ff.; 11:32; Gal. 4:3; 6:14; Eph. 2:2; Col. 2:8, 20) |
| insiders (*hoi esō*) | vs. | outsiders (*hoi exō*: 1 Cor. 5:12–13; 1 Thess. 4:12; Col. 4:5) |
| believers | vs. | unbelievers (1 Cor. 6:6; 7:12–15; 10:27; 14:23; 2 Cor. 4:4; 6:14) |

The dualistic patterns, of course, are rooted in the ancient description of Israel as a "chosen people, a people set apart." In fact, the Hebrew Scriptures constantly use this expression for mapping persons and places in Israel. Not only is Israel God's chosen people (Deut. 7:6–7; 14:2; 1 Kings 3:8; Ps. 33:12), but from among the chosen people there were groups specifically chosen, such as Levites (Deut. 10:8), or individual figures such as Aaron (1 Chron. 23:13) and David (2 Sam.

6:21). Places were chosen as well, either the specific place
where God will put his name (Deut. 12:11, 14; 14:23–25) or
the royal city (1 Kings 11:13, 32). But the basic perception
seems to have been the description of Israel alone being on the
*map of covenant people*, whereas all others are not on the map.

This dualistic perception is likewise reflected in the way Paul
subsequently described the members of the church. The key to
the map is the awareness that God has done something unique
to certain people, either chosen them, sanctified them, loved
them, or known them.

### 2. *Dualistic Terms Illustrative of a "Chosen People"*:

| | | |
|---|---|---|
| sanctified (1 Cor. 1:2) | vs. | unsanctified |
| called (1 Cor. 1:2, 24; | vs. | not called |
| Rom. 1:6–7; 8:28) | | |
| loved "Jacob I loved" | vs. | not loved "Esau I hated" |
| | | (Rom. 9:13) |
| "my beloved" | vs. | "not beloved" (Rom. 9:25) |
| known by God (1 Cor. 8:3; | vs. | not known by God; and |
| Gal. 4:9) | | do not know God (Gal. 4:8; |
| | | 1 Thess. 4:5; 2 Thess. 1:8) |
| "my people" | vs. | "not my people" |
| | | (Rom. 9:26) |
| heirs, sons (Gal. 4:6–7) | vs. | not heirs, not sons |
| of Abraham, by | vs. | of Abraham, by other sons |
| one son (Gal. 3:16) | | (Gal. 4:22–23) |
| enlightened | vs. | not enlightened (Rom. 10:2) |
| Israel of God | vs. | old, false Israel (Gal. 6:16) |
| justified | vs. | still sinners |
| | | (Rom. 1:18–3:20) |
| (pre) destined | vs. | not destined |
| (Rom. 8:29) | | |
| children of light | vs. | children of darkness |
| (2 Cor. 6:14ff.; | | |
| 1 Thess. 5:4–11; | | |
| Eph. 5:7–14) | | |

### 3. *Distinctions Within the Church*:

Along these same lines, we find dualistic expressions used
constantly in Paul's letters to distinguish members of the
church in terms of status and prowess. At this point it does not
matter whether Paul himself contributed to such expressions or
merely repeated what he heard others saying in the churches.
Of importance is the phenomenon of mapping even the chosen
people in terms of some sort of ranking and honor system.

| | | |
|---|---|---|
| in the know | vs. | not in the know |
| *pneumatikoi* | vs. | non-*pneumatikoi* |
| strong | vs. | weak |
| wise | vs. | foolish |
| honorable | vs. | nonhonorable |
| presentable | vs. | unpresentable |
| superior | vs. | inferior |
| adults | vs. | babes |

Such maps may strike the heirs of the French Revolution as quite at variance with the ideals of egalitarianism and brotherhood we have come to treasure. But they are clearly found in the Pauline letters, and it behooves us to note them and see what function they play. Clearly, according to Paul's sense of an orderly world, if the heavenly world (macrocosm) admits of ranking and hierarchy even among God, Christ, and Spirit, such patterns are appropriate in the earthly world (microcosm). In studying this material, modern readers can clearly see the great cultural gulf between Paul and themselves, for he is neither embarrassed nor defensive about such maps of people. They served the distinctive social function of making clear the unique identity of Christians by distinguishing them from all others, Jews included.

### 3.2.4 Maps of Persons in Creation
Paul's penchant to map everything in his ken extends not only to persons in heaven and earth, but to animals and birds on earth, and to stars, sun, and moon in the heavens.

### 1. *Earthly and Heavenly Bodies*:

> But God gives it a body as he has chosen, and to each kind of seed its own body. For not all flesh is alike, but there is one kind for men, another for animals, another for birds, and another for fish. There are celestial bodies and there are terrestrial bodies; but the glory of the celestial is one, and the glory of the terrestrial is another. There is one glory of the sun, and another glory of the moon, and another glory of the stars; for star differs from star in glory.
>
> 1 Corinthians 15:38–41

In their context, these remarks answer the specific question "How are the dead raised? With what kind of body do they [the dead] come?" (15:35). From the rest of the argument in 15:42–49 and 50–54, Paul basically stresses the change that will occur in those who are resurrected. The perishable is raised imperishable; the physical body is raised a spiritual body (15:42, 44): "We shall be changed" (15:52). But let us look more closely at the passage precisely for the maps it encodes.

Given the elaborate map in 15:38–41, might one not ask whether all those who are raised will have the same glory in God's kingdom? In short, will there be a map of persons in heaven, even as there is on earth? Such maps seem to function in Revelation, where spatial proximity to God's throne serves as the criterion of differentiation (Rev. 4:2–11; 7:9–12). From 15:38–41 one might draw a comparable conclusion. First Paul draws on the fundamental map of Genesis 1, in which Adam was given dominion over all creation (Gen. 1:26, 28). Arguing that "not all flesh is alike," Paul lists "terrestrial bodies": "men . . . animals . . . birds . . . fish" (15:39). The list ranks man as the highest of God's creatures, affirming his unique role and status; below him are mentioned earth animals, sky birds, and sea fish. Parallel to the microcosm of earth, the heavenly macrocosm also enjoys a *map of glory*: "There is the glory of the sun, and another glory of the moon, and another glory of the stars" (15:41a). A considerate reader must remember to take off Copernican glasses and put on Ptolemaic ones. And even among stars there is a map: "Star differs from star in glory" (15:41b). On earth and in heaven there are maps that locate and classify. In fact, all creation must be ordered according to some series of maps.

We spoke above of a *map of body parts* in 1 Corinthians 12:14–26, which serves also as a map of persons in the church. That map of body parts lists foot and hand, ear and eye, weaker and stronger parts, and honorable and less honorable parts. To repeat, Paul does not consider them equal in role, rank, or status. He never obliterates the ordering of the body parts; for, as he himself states, "God arranged the organs in the body, each one of them, as he chose" (12:18). What 1 Corinthians 12:14–26 presents us with, then, is another highly articulated map based on God's ordering actions in creation.

**3.3 Maps of Things** It is characteristic of Paul and others in his world to try to put all things within their ken in some form of order. We can observe this especially in the way he lists related items and arranges them in some sequence. For example, when speaking of the materials that one might use to construct a building on a foundation, Paul enumerates the items on the list in a hierarchical manner: "Now if any one builds on the foundation with gold, silver, precious stones, wood, hay, straw . . . " (1 Cor. 3:12). The sequence proceeds systematically from the most precious materials to the least valued. This example, then, cautions us to pay attention to Paul's lists to discover the pattern of arrangement and the values embodied in the sequencing of things.

### 3.3.1 Gifts Differing, but Nevertheless Ranked

On the relative importance of spiritual gifts in the church at Corinth, Paul labors again and again to classify them as more or less valuable and to list them in ways that suggest this classification. We discussed earlier (see 3.2.2) the listing of gifts in 12:8–10 and 28–31 insofar as these lists imply a corresponding map of persons. But the lists are first and foremost a ranking of spiritual gifts precisely with a view to promoting some to prominence and demoting others. In both lists, "speaking in tongues" is put last to signal its diminished importance in Paul's perspective. The same phenomenon might be noted in regard to the ranking of prophecy over tongues in 1 Corinthians 14. Comparing and contrasting these two gifts, Paul states that those who prophesy are greater than those who speak in tongues (14:5). In a third example of this phenomenon, the whole of 1 Corinthians 13 contains Paul's attempt to compare and contrast gifts in such a way that one gift, love, achieves paramount status. The discussion began with the exhortation "Earnestly desire the *higher gifts*" (12:31) and ends with "So faith, hope, love abide, these three; but the *greatest* of these is love" (1 Cor. 13:13).

*[margin note: Only in relation to edification the church, not an individual]*

### 3.3.2 Better and Best: A Form of Ranking

The impulse to list and to order need not always issue in a catalog of things. It may be present in the effort to rank two things. For example, in 1 Corinthians 7 among Paul's remarks about marriage and sexuality, his impulse to rank items clearly emerges. It is "better" (*kalon*) for a man not to touch a woman (7:1), but marriage is permitted because in principle "it is better to marry than to be aflame with passion" (7:9). Later in the discussion he ranks the unmarried state as better than marriage (7:25–35) on the principle that "Who marries . . . does well . . . who refrains from marriage will do better" (7:38).

Can commandments be ranked? Paul's remarks in Romans 13:8–10 about love sound comparable to the discussion in the gospel tradition about the greatest commandment (Mark 12:28-34). He lists the commandments: "You shall not commit adultery, You shall not kill, You shall not steal, You shall not covet." But there is another commandment that ranks above all these, "Love one another." Paul begins and ends this piece of exhortation with the ranking of the love commandment as paramount: "Love one another; for he who loves his neighbor has fulfilled the law" (13:8); and "Love does no wrong to a neighbor; therefore love is the fulfilling of the law" (13:10). Just as love may be ranked above faith and hope, so the love commandment is perceived as greater than the others.

Once we become sensitive to Paul's tendency to order and classify everything in his world, we begin to recognize more clearly the phenomenon of comparative adjectives and adverbs in his letters. The many references to "better," "older," "stronger," "greater," and "more" serve as further examples of the socialized need of Paul to label each and every thing as accurately as possible.

**3.4 Maps of Times** As well as Paul maps persons and things, he likewise maps time. We are not speaking so much of holy days, such as Sabbath or the first day of the week (1 Cor. 16:2), but of larger classifications of time that serve to legitimate the time of Jesus and the church. Because 1 Corinthians does not contain a full sampler of Paul's various maps of times, we take the liberty of introducing examples from his other letters for the purpose of adequate illustration of the principle.

**3.4.1 Then/Now** Paul is not unique among the writers of the New Testament in his sense of how time can be mapped. As a follower of Jesus, he perceived time primarily mapped in terms of "time before Jesus" and "time after Jesus." Nils Dahl (1976:32–33) speaks of four variations on this basic map of times. In his analysis, Dahl argues that such patterns were commonplace perceptions in the early church; by this he indicates how typical Paul's perspective was.

1. *"Then" vs. "Now"* (Gal. 4:8–9; 3:23–27; Rom. 6:17–22; 7:5f.; 11:30; Eph. 2:11–22; 5:8)
2. *"Once" but "Now"* (Gal. 4:3–7; Rom. 1:18–3:20/3:21–8:39; Col. 1:21–22; Eph. 2:1–10; Titus 3:3–7)
3. *"Mystery hidden" vs. "Mystery now revealed"* (Rom. 16:25–26; 1 Cor. 2:6–10; Col. 1:25–27; Eph. 3:4–7, 8–11)
4. *"Mystery promised" vs. "Mystery now given"* (2 Tim. 1:9–11; Titus 1:2ff.; 1 Peter 1:18–21)

Dahl was specifically identifying formulae in early preaching, and to his list we might add other ways of expressing the same contrast between two periods of time that are not phrased as concisely as the patterns noted above.

Paul especially perceives a map of time that classifies human history into two distinct periods—old creation and new creation (2 Cor. 5:17; Gal. 6:15). Along the same lines, he describes two periods of time, first when God's "wrath was revealed" (Rom. 1:18–3:20) and a later time when "God's righteousness was revealed" (3:21–8:39). A further specification of this occurs in his comparison and contrast of Adam and Jesus in Romans 5:12–21. Comparable to this is Paul's contrast of the period when the "leaven of malice and evil" abounded with the time after "Christ our passover has been sacrificed," when we are "unleavened" and free from sin (1 Cor. 5:6–8). By mapping time in terms of "before/after" and "then/now," Paul situates the followers of Jesus in a context where holiness and sinlessness are the expected way of life.

This map of times, of course, should be seen alongside a map of persons; for the perception of a "before" and "after" implies a sense of "bad" and "good" time that corresponds to a sense of a sinful state of being before discipleship with Christ and a holy state as his follower. The value and importance of being a believer in God and follower of Jesus is once more emphasized by this type of expression. Such maps of time, then, replicate the maps of persons.

### 3.4.2 Childhood/Adulthood

In a similar vein, Paul contrasts childhood with adulthood. This classification goes beyond the before/after distinction mentioned above, for it functions in regard to people who are already members of the church. In fact, it would seem to be an apologetic device used by Paul against charges that his preaching contains only stuff that children should learn, whereas other preachers speak to the group about adult matters. Turning such criticism to his advantage, Paul explains that because of the "jealousy and strife among you," they were *not* adults and so he could not tell them adult things: "I could not address you as spiritual men, but as men of flesh, as babes in Christ. I fed you with milk, not solid food; for you were not ready for it" (1 Cor. 3:1–2).

Variations on this child/adult pattern return in 1 Corinthians. In a general way Paul urges the group to "grow up" in Christ: "Do not be children in your thinking; be babes in evil, but in thinking be mature" (14:20). In a more polemical mode, Paul urges the group to outgrow its fascination with certain charismatic gifts and to behave as adults: "When I was a child, I spoke like a child, I thought like a child, I reasoned like a child; when I became a man, I gave up childish ways" (13:11). The context of this remark has to do with the *map of gifts* created by certain pneumatic people, who prize "prophecy, tongues, knowledge" (13:8). Of these Paul says that they "pass

away" and "cease"; and well they should, for they are "imperfect." Such things fascinate "children" but should not continue
to influence adults. This variation on a map of time, then, replicates the *map of things* that Paul would establish.

### 3.4.3 Fixed Moments: Points on a Map

If maps have any
value, they fix certain points exactly. This was true of the first
pattern; there is an exact point in time when then becomes now
and before becomes after. In articulating the differences between Jews and Christians, and pagans and Christians, Paul
was acutely concerned with such precision in his maps of time.
For him there are certain points in time whose exact moment
can and must be fixed.

For example, it is of considerable importance for Paul in his
description of Abraham's covenant of faith in Romans 4 to
note that Genesis 15:6 ("[Abraham] believed the LORD; and he
reckoned it to him as righteousness") occurred *before* the command in Genesis 17:10, when God ordained circumcision. Justification by faith, then, was prior to works of the law: "Was it
[righteousness] before or after he had been circumcised? It was
not after, but before he was circumcised" (Rom. 4:10). This in
turn rests on an implicit cultural map of time according to
which earlier is better and later is degenerate. In a similar
mode in Galatians, when comparing and contrasting the two
covenants of God (Abraham vs. Moses), Paul notes that God's
first, and therefore more important, covenant was the covenant
of promise with Abraham. He speaks with exactness about
when and why the second covenant was added: "[It] came four
hundred and thirty years afterward" (Gal. 3:17); but the covenant that followed "afterward" does not annul a covenant previously ratified by God. This second covenant, moreover, is
strictly a temporary dispensation, which in turn will have a
definite terminus: "until faith should be revealed" (3:23) and
"till the offspring should come to whom the promise had been
made" (3:19). Paul's map of times, then, legitimates the Christian covenant by linking it with the ancient Abrahamic covenant; what was promised to Abraham is fulfilled in Jesus. And
Paul's map of times functions necessarily to argue for the obsolescence of the covenant with Moses. These are hardly minor
matters. The mapmaker, then, wields considerable power.

### 3.4.4 Jesus' Death: A New Map of Time

Paul's map of times
indicates certain exact moments relevant to the covenant with
Abraham, moments that confirm its superiority to the covenant with Moses. In a second example, he puts great stress on

another exact moment in time, the death of Jesus, which creates a new map of time.

Several maps of time are implicit in Paul's understanding of the death of Jesus. In keeping with the then/now pattern noted above, Paul describes Jesus' death as the end of one age (then) and the beginning of another (now). Sin, which entered the world through Adam's sin, "was reigning" until Christ; the obedience of God's Christ ended that reign and inaugurated a new period of grace (Rom. 5:12–21). Similarly, Christ the Paschal Lamb ended the time of leaven and sin; now we are to celebrate the festival, "not with the old leaven . . . of malice and evil, but with the unleavened bread of sincerity and truth" (1 Cor. 5:7–8). Christ's death, then, constitutes a fixed moment on a map of time, which is replicated in the *map of life time* of each follower.

An important variation on Christ's death as a key moment on a map of time occurs in Paul's constant discussion of the relationship of the covenant of Moses with justification by faith. In Galatians, Paul not only notes the sequences of God's covenants, first with Abraham and then with Moses; he labors to fix with precision just when the second and temporary covenant ended. Christ, of course, was "born under the law" and so during the waning days of the legitimacy of that second covenant (Gal. 4:4). That temporary covenant definitively ended when Christ hung on a cross and so "redeemed us from the curse of the law" (Gal. 3:13–14; Wilcox 1977). Such precision in terms of maps of time serves Paul well in his argument against Judaizers that the old is ended and past! The temporary covenant served its purpose, but now we live in the time of the promise, the period of faith, and the gift of the Spirit.

Paul uses a comparable argument in Romans 7:1–6 to indicate the temporary character of "the law" and its inevitable end. A woman, he remarks, is bound to her husband so long as he lives; but at his death, she is free to marry another (7:1–3). Likewise, Christians once had a relationship with "the law"; but with the death of Jesus "we are discharged from the law, dead to that which held us captive" (7:6). How important it is, then, to know the precise moment of death, namely, Christ's death.

*3.5 Maps of Place* Like their neighbors, ancient Jews had an acutely developed sense of space. First of all, the land of Israel was set apart from all other lands; it was God's promised land, and so it sat in the center of any *map of place* that mattered. Within the land, moreover, space was also mapped, indicating a graded sense of holiness as one moved from the periphery to the center. There are ten degrees of holiness:

1. The *Land of Israel* is holier than any other land . . .
2. The *walled cities* (of the land of Israel) are still more holy . . .
3. *Within the walls* (of Jerusalem) is still more holy . . .
4. The *Temple Mount* is still more holy . . .
5. The *Rampart* is still more holy . . .
6. The *Court of the Women* is still more holy . . .
7. The *Court of the Israelites* is still more holy . . .
8. The *Court of the Priests* is still more holy . . .
9. *Between the Porch and the Altar* is still more holy . . .
10. The *Sanctuary* is still more holy . . . The *Holy of Holies* is still more holy . . . (*m. Kelim* 1:6–9)

The Jerusalem Temple itself was elaborately mapped in terms of internal lines indicating where Gentiles, women, Israelites, and priests might stand. Paul was socialized to the principle of mapped space and to the specific maps relative to the "land," "Jerusalem," and "the Temple."

Yet we note one important difference: Paul's map of places seems to be focused on boundaries, the lines at the edge of the map, not on internal structures. This difference can be explained in terms of a Jewish sense of fixed space (Jerusalem, Temple) vs. Paul's sense of fluid space (see John 4:20–24). Important studies of sacred space include Sack 1986; Cohn 1980; Gordon 1971; and Helgeland 1980.

**3.5.1 Sacred Space: Fluid, Not Fixed**  Like most people in his world, Paul did not regard all places on earth with equal regard. As a Jew, he made pilgrimages to Jerusalem and its Temple (Acts 20:16), which Jews regarded as the most sacred space in the world. As a follower of Jesus, Paul transferred that socialized sense of sacred space from Mount Zion and the temple building to the assembled Christian group. Like other Christians, Paul actually called the assembly of Christians "God's temple," the place where God is praised and where the Spirit operates (1 Cor. 3:16). This is not fixed space in the sense that Jerusalem is a fixed city and the temple site a specific mount. Rather, it is fluid space; whenever and wherever the followers of Jesus gather, they constitute then and there a sacred space, a true temple of God.

Temples, however, had rules about who may enter, where they may stand, and what activities they may perform. We noted above (2.2.2) specific Jewish restrictions on where Gentiles, women, Israelites, and priests may stand in the total temple complex; the Temple would be defiled if such spatial arrangements were violated. Comparably, when Paul likens the church to a temple in 1 Corinthians 3:16, he too indicates that a *map of sacred space* still informs his perceptions, for he prohibits uncleanness in the holy space of God: "If anyone destroys God's temple, God will destroy him" (3:17). Comparably, public behavior at the Christian assembly, which constitutes "a temple," would be seemly. What might be acceptable in the private space of a house (1 Cor. 11:34) could be considered unacceptable in the public space of the assembled "temple" (11:17–22). Because Paul perceives the public space as a map of sacred space, he expects correspondingly sacred behavior. The acute sense of public and private space had direct bearing on the activity of women in the church (Barton 1986).

Paul likewise described the church as a body (1 Cor. 12:12–25; Rom. 12:3–8). This image envisions the church as space that is clearly defined with precise boundaries that are jealously guarded. Each human body perceives itself as an independent entity whose integrity must be maintained at all costs. No body willingly admits to amputations of its members. The external lines, then, that define the body serve as the lines of a map. Bodies, moreover, are themselves internally mapped, with the prominent part, the head, at the top, and the menial parts, the feet, at the bottom. The various bodily organs are classified as honorable and nonhonorable, indicating a cultural perception of differing social roles and statuses. The body, then, conveys a sense of space mapped first to distinguish what belongs from what does not belong, and second to rank the bodily members in some sort of hierarchy. As such, it functions as an excellent map of space. A body would be considered pure if it enjoys integrity (no missing limbs) and when its parts take their proper roles.

### 3.5.2 Who Belongs? In and Out

Not unlike other Jews, Paul perceived the world divided into two spheres—"us" and "them": "saints" vs. "the world"; "insiders" vs. "outsiders" (see 3.2.3 above). Paul locates the saints and insiders in the center of his most basic map of space, whereas all others stand off at the map's edges or simply do not appear at all on it. The dualistic passage in 2 Corinthians 6:14–7:1 clearly expresses not just this basic map, but the corresponding radical behavior that flows from perceiving the world in such terms (compare with 1 Cor. 5:9–13). Whether Pauline or not, it expresses the common Jewish and Christian map of space.

Even Paul's fundamental map has further defining lines, which correspond to his perception that Peter was sent to the circumcised and himself to the uncircumcised (Gal. 2:7–9). Thus, the basic map of space is itself divided into two equal spheres. This of course suggests first and foremost a map of persons, Jews and Gentiles. But that map has spatial implications as well, for Jews will tend to be found in Jewish space, either in Israel or in Jewish sections of cities outside Israel (Esler 1987:76–86, 148–50). Gentiles are those who reside outside of *Eretz Israel*. But what happens when Jewish Christians and Gentile Christians attempt to share the same space—in particular, to share the same food and the same table? Commensality of this sort was and remained a painful situation throughout the period of the early church, as texts such as Acts 11:3; 15:19–21 and Galatians 2:13–14 so clearly indicate (Dunn 1983; Esler 1987:71–109).

### 3.5.3 Fences and Turf

According to Galatians 2:7–9, Paul perceived the world divided into two spheres, one in which Peter worked among the circumcised and another in which Paul worked among the uncircumcised. It is surely bold of Paul to claim half of the universe as his turf. Like a good Jew, Paul valued the principle of fences to protect his territory. Good fences make good neighbors because they clarify what belongs to whom. Fences, then, indicate a map of space. Yet when fences do not work, we expect to hear of a commotion where the fence is breached and unauthorized people trespass where they do not belong.

In 2 Corinthians 10:13–18, Paul expresses anger at certain "superlative apostles" crossing the fence into his territory. He has always made it his boast *not* to cross fences himself and labor where others have labored (Rom. 15:18–21; see 1 Cor. 3:10). We will discuss 2 Corinthians 10:13–18 in greater depth in Chapter 10 on witchcraft accusations, but suffice it to note here the map of space reflected in that passage. Paul states his principle clearly: "We do not boast beyond limit, in other men's labors" (10:15); and again, his aim is to "preach the gospel in lands beyond you, without boasting of work already done in another's field" (10:16). Paul boasts, then, that he respects fences, or maps of space. But he complains that others do not respect such maps.

Trespassing on another's apostolic turf seems to have occurred quite regularly, to judge by Paul's remarks on it. Sometimes Paul can do nothing about it but complain (Phil. 1:15–18). If the trespassers are popular, Paul's remarks are all the more delicate, but nonetheless critical (1 Cor. 3:5–9, 10–15). But at other times, Paul labels the trespassers as malefactors, calling them disguised agents of Satan (2 Cor. 11:3, 13–15) and "bewitchers" (Gal. 3:1). These Pauline remarks confirm, then, his acute map of space, in particular a map of his turf and his acute sensitivity to the fences guarding his turf. When these fences are breached, Paul perceives a world attacked and threatened with uncleanness. Things and persons are "out of place."

## 4.0 Conclusions

From this analysis we should be able to draw some conclusions. We take it as adequately demonstrated that Paul tends to perceive the world as an orderly place in which all persons, places, things, and times can and should be classified. Everything in its place, and a place for everything. He shares this perception with other synagogue and temple Jews. Time does not allow a detailed analysis of the presence and importance of creation language or temple imagery in Paul, but these two areas would surely surface the emic or Jewish character of Paul's obsession with an orderly cosmos.

We did not do a detailed study of the exact use of *pure*, *spotless*, and other terms designating purity. That useful exercise will only confirm the larger interest in noting how Paul prizes order and exact classification. He does indeed have a purity system.

A considerate reader need not agree with Paul's mapping of persons, places, things, and time. That is not the point of this investigation. Advocacy of Paul's point of view is hardly the question here. Rather, we must learn to see the world through his eyes, and his eyes see maps everywhere and perceive order and structure ubiquitously. At stake is our ability as considerate eavesdroppers on another culture to see what Paul saw and to ask how his maps functioned for him.

We focused in this chapter on 1 Corinthians as a rich illustration of Paul's perception of order. If our modeling has been adequate, we trust that readers can take these insights and clues and conduct their own analysis of similar patterns in Romans, 2 Corinthians, 1 Thessalonians, Philippians, and Philemon. Only a full study of all of Paul's letters can confirm the beginning made here, namely, that Paul perceives the world as a cosmos replete with maps of persons, places, things, and times. The specific maps that appear in a given letter must then be studied in terms of the argument of that letter. But the project seems sound.

A fully contextual analysis of passages from 1 Corinthians indicates that Paul's maps serve a specific rhetorical function. Granted, he tends to think this way; certain maps serve him well in his arguments in the local church. But this is an important clue, for Paul is a religious reformer. In the next chapter we will see many examples, not of Pauline maps of order, but of disorder. The point is that Paul may occasionally contest certain societal or group patterns of order with a reforming agenda. In short, we must attend to the way patterns of order and disorder serve the argument of Paul, the Pharisaic reformer.

## Figure 1

### Semantic Word Field on Clean and Unclean

A. *Terms for "Purity"*
1. clean, to cleanse, cleanness (*katharos, katharizō, katharismos*): Luke 2:22; 5:12; 11:41; Acts 10:15; 15:9; Rom. 14:20; 2 Cor. 7:1
2. sweep (*saroō*): Luke 11:25//Matt. 12:44
3. pure, to purify, purity (*hagnos, hagnizō, hagnotēs*): Acts 21:24, 26; 24:18; 2 Cor. 6:6; 7:11; 11:2, 3; Phil. 4:8
4. holy, to make holy, holiness (*hagios, hagiazō, hagiotēs, hagiasmos*):
   *hagiazō*: Rom. 15:16; 1 Cor. 1:2; 6:11; 7:14; 1 Thess. 5:23
   *hagiasmos*: Rom. 6:19, 22; 1 Cor. 1:30; 1 Thess. 4:3, 4, 7
   *hagios*: Rom. 1:7; 7:12; 8:27; 11:26; 12:1, 13; 15:25, 26, 31; 16:2; 1 Cor. 1:2; 3:17; 6:1, 2, 19; 7:14, 34; 14:33; 16:1, 15, 20; 2 Cor. 1:1; 8:4; 9:1, 12; 13:12; Phil. 1:1; 4:21, 22; 1 Thess. 3:13; 5:26, 27; Philem. 5, 7 (references to "Holy" Spirit not included)
5. innocent (*akeraios*): Matt. 10:16; Rom. 16:19; Phil. 2:5
6. spotless (*amiantos*): Heb. 7:26; 13:4; James 1:27; 1 Peter 1:4
7. unstained (*aspilos*): James 1:27; 1 Peter 1:19; 2 Peter 3:14
8. blameless (*amōmos*): Eph. 1:4; 5:27; Phil. 2:15; Col. 1:22; 1 Peter 1:19
9. blameless (*anegklētos*): 1 Cor. 1:8; Col. 1:22; 1 Tim. 3:10; Titus 1:6–7
10. faultless (*anepilēmptos*): 1 Tim. 3:2; 5:7; 6:14

11. innocent (*amemtos*): Phil. 2:15; 3:6; 1 Thess. 2:10; 3:13; 5:23
12. innocent (*athōos*): Matt. 27:4, 24
13. innocent (*akakos*): Rom. 16:18; Heb. 7:26

B. *Terms for "Pollution"*
   1. defilement, to defile (*miasmos, miainō, miasma*): John 18:28; Titus 1:15; 2 Peter 2:10, 20
   2. defilement, to defile (*molysmos, molynō*): 1 Cor. 8:7; 2 Cor. 7:1; Rev. 3:4
   3. unclean (*akathartos, akatharsia*):
      *akatharsia*: Rom. 1:24; 6:19; 2 Cor. 12:21; Gal. 5:19; 1 Thess. 2:3; 4:7
      *akathartos*: 1 Cor. 7:14; 2 Cor. 6:17; Eph. 5:5
   4. spot (*spilos, spiloō*): Eph. 5:27; 2 Peter 2:13; James 3:6; Jude 23
   5. stain (*mōmos*): 2 Peter 2:13
   6. common, profane (*koinos, koinoō*): Acts 10:14–15, 28; 11:8–9; 21:28; Rom. 14:14
   7. defilement (*alisgēma*): Acts 15:20

# 3

# Divine Disorder
# in Paul's Cosmos

I will destroy the wisdom of the wise,
and the cleverness of the clever I will thwart.
1 Corinthians 1:19

## 1.0 Paul and Disorder

In the previous chapter we examined an extensive set of maps implicit in 1 Corinthians. In them we find clear evidence of Paul's tendency to perceive the universe in terms of orderly and systematic classification. But Paul is also a reformer of the system into which he was socialized (Theissen 1978). Like many other people in his world, he does not accept certain patterns and offers his own variations of them.

Although Paul tends to reflect the maps of Jewish culture into which he was socialized, he broke with the Pharisaic circle and abandoned the Temple. A Pharisee's Pharisee, Paul became a follower of Jesus; nevertheless, he remained loyal to the God of Israel and the Scriptures. He preached a reformed vision of God and the Covenant; this reformed vision included new ways of perceiving order in the cosmos.

By his own admission, Paul once persecuted the church (1 Cor. 15:9; Gal. 1:13, 23; Phil. 3:6). That is, as a purity-conscious Pharisee, he evaluated Jesus as a corruption of Judaism. But God revealed his Son to Paul (Gal. 1:16), thus leading him to see Jesus, not as a sinner, but as "Son of God in power according to the Spirit of holiness by his resurrection from the dead" (Rom. 1:4). What he formerly considered unclean, polluting, and deserving of destruction he came to reckon as holy, anointed by God, enthroned at God's right hand, and worthy of evangelization. Conversely, what he formerly considered of value (Torah, Pharisaic purity concerns, circumcision, etc.) he counted as loss and refuse (Phil. 3:7–8). To those in synagogue and Temple, Paul had opted for disorder, not order. But in his own perspective, he came to see that certain maps needed to be redrawn in light of God's revelation of Jesus as the Christ and Holy One of God. God legitimates new maps. Thus Paul should be considered a reformer.

Despite what others would say, Paul would never call his reforms "disorder." He grounds them on his perception of patterns in the way God has always acted in history and Scripture. Yet his new patterns will tend to be perceived by the surrounding world as disorder because they appear to "turn the world upside down" (Acts 17:6). It depends, then, on one's perspective whether something is order or disorder. Like beauty, order and disorder are in the eye of the beholder (Malina & Neyrey 1988:35–38, 42–48). It depends on how one is socialized, and people are socialized to different patterns of order and disorder. Although we might describe Paul's new patterns that upset the old order as "disorder," they form the basis for a new system of classification. Order, then, is ultimately maintained.

Despite the traditional portrait of God as the creative orderer of the universe, Paul likewise perceives God acting in ways that upset traditional patterns of order. So we begin with a consideration of the different ways that Paul understands God's workings in the world, for these form the basis for new modes of ordering and classification, modes that may be at variance with traditional Pharisaic notions. Yet to legitimate his new maps, Paul must appeal to God's will as this is known in history and Scripture. Paul's theology, then, forms the foundation for his reform of traditional patterns of order.

## 2.0 God's Different Maps

Paul and other Jews perceived patterns of order in the world, inasmuch as they were socialized by their sacred literature (e.g., Genesis 1) and by religious practice (e.g., the Temple) to value an orderly cosmos. Had these remained the only values and patterns in his experience, Paul would undoubtedly have remained a Jew who worshiped in the Temple and prayed in the synagogue. But Paul became a follower of Jesus, broke with synagogue and Temple, and ultimately devalued the covenant of law and its elaborate maps (Gal. 1:13–16). In the eyes of other Jews, Paul abandoned his ancestral religion and thus rejected God's clearly expressed will in Bible and Temple. In their eyes, Paul was unclean because he himself was "out of place" and urged others to act likewise.

Yet Paul claimed ever to be a faithful worshiper of God (1 Thess. 1:9; 1 Cor. 8:6; Rom. 11:36) and a loyal adherent of God's Word (Rom. 9:6; 16:25–26). He drew from the Scriptures texts that exemplify patterns, not of God's order but of divine disorder. Paul's understanding of God's approbation of Jesus conflicts with his understanding of God's workings when Paul was a Pharisee. It is hardly accidental, then, that Paul grounded his new, "disorderly" social agenda in God's actions; for God is free to do as God wishes. And God's actions, which are beyond reproach, become programmatic for the covenant people.

Socialized as a follower of Jesus, Paul came to see God acting in ways quite different from those celebrated in synagogue and Temple. These new ways of God legitimate for Paul a new set of maps, not of traditional order but seemingly of disorder.

*2.1 God's New Map of "Chosen People"* The traditional doctrine of the one, true God of Israel (Deut. 6:4) served to distinguish God from all idols, demons, and false gods (Dahl 1977:179–182). Correspondingly, this implied a further distinction between a few holy people who worship this one God and all other peoples in the world who worship idols (see Rom.

9:27; 11:5). This monotheism reflects the traditional Jewish view of God and, at times, the viewpoint of Paul (see 1 Thess. 1:9–10; 1 Cor. 8:4–6). One, true God corresponds to one, authentic people.

**2.1.1 God's Inclusivity**  Yet at other times Paul can take the same confession that "God is one" and use it, not to distinguish believers from Gentiles, but to include Jews and Gentiles alike in the inclusive election of the one, universal God (Dahl 1977:188–191). One of the subtexts in Romans seems to be the affirmation of the full status of Gentiles in the covenant of the God of Israel. Paul frequently speaks of God's actions toward humankind in the phrase "the Jew first and also the Greek." The gospel of God is the power of salvation "to the Jew first and also to the Greek" (Rom. 1:16). God will be just to both and bring tribulation to those who do evil, "the Jew first and also the Greek," but glory and honor to those who do good, "the Jew first and also the Greek" (2:9–10). Although the phrase acknowledges the historical election of the Jews prior to that of the Gentiles ("first" . . . "also"), it does in fact include the Gentiles in God's election. How different such a perception is from the "separating" actions of God in Genesis 1 and the distinguishing patterns of the Temple! Both God's justice and God's mercy, then, are impartial and inclusive (Bassler 1979).

It is precisely in this vein that later in Romans Paul talks of God's "law (*nomos*) of faith," the principle whereby divine righteousness is manifested. Unlike the contrasted covenants in Galatians 3:6–12, Paul does not argue that God has two principles of justification, one for Jews ("the principle of works") and another for Gentiles ("the principle of faith"). He argues in 3:27–28 that God acts according to one principle only, the "principle of faith," which is valid for both Jew and Greek. Paul asks: "Is God the God of Jews only? Is he not the God of Gentiles also? Yes, of Gentiles also, *since God is one*" (3:29). Traditional theology employed the axiom "God is one!" to distinguish Jew from Gentile. But Paul cites it here to argue just the opposite, that God makes no distinction between Jew and Greek and that God justifies all on the basis of the same criterion.

We call this an example of divine "disorder," for as Paul understands and uses this theological confession, God is not preferring one people over another but showing impartiality to all. This, however, clearly contradicts the old *map of persons* fundamental to Jewish self-understanding. Order in the cosmos meant that Israel alone was "chosen." According to his new axiom, Paul reforms that traditional map of persons, which exalted the "chosen people" and excluded all others. Rather, he sees a new map of persons, which looks like radical disorder in the eyes of those socialized to traditional Jewish perceptions. For Paul it constitutes a new order, but to synagogue Jews, a disorder.

*2.1.2 God's Impartiality*  A variation of this new map of persons appears in the profession that God "shows no partiality" and "makes no distinction." In traditional Jewish theology, we regularly hear that God chooses Israel as a special people who are thus "set apart" from and above all others. But in Romans, Paul argues to legitimate the genuine status of Gentile Christians in Rome and to ask their support for Paul's mission to other Gentiles in Spain (Bassler 1984). In this context, he argues that God does *not* choose or favor one people above another, thus *choosing* Israel but *not choosing* the Roman Gentiles. On the contrary, God shows impartiality to all, both in justice and mercy (Rom. 1:18; 3:22–23).

First, Paul affirms God's impartial justice: "There will be tribulation and distress for every human being who does evil, the Jew first and also the Greek" (Rom. 2:9). Balancing that, he asserts impartial divine mercy: "Glory and honor and peace for every one who does good, the Jew first and also the Greek" (2:10; see 3:22). An unexpected and surprising principle emerges: "God shows no partiality" (2:11). In regard to impartial mercy, Paul recalls this divine "disorder" and affirms: "There is no distinction between Jew and Greek; the same Lord is Lord of all and bestows his riches upon all who call upon him" (10:12). Finally, Paul issues his clearest statement of divine impartiality in mercy and justice later in the letter when he states: "God has consigned all . . . to disobedience, that he may have mercy upon all" (11:32).

In Paul's perception, God can act in ways strange and disorderly in our eyes. But then: "O the depth of the riches and wisdom and knowledge of God! How unsearchable are his judgments and how inscrutable his ways! 'For who has known the mind of the Lord, or who has been his counselor?' " (Rom. 11:33–34). Truly, God's ways are not our ways; our perceptions of disorder may be order in God's eyes. By acting with impartiality, God writes *new maps of persons*, which become the maps to which the followers of Jesus must then be socialized.

*2.2 God's "Reversals"*  According to Genesis 1 and the temple system, God would be seen as acting in predictable ways, reflecting a sense of constancy and fairness in the world. When expedient to his argument, Paul argues the same way. But at other times, Paul perceives God reversing patterns of honor and turning upside down the old maps of persons. He sees God reversing patterns of preference and precedence.

The first letter to Corinth contains numerous illustrations of Paul's sense of divine "reversal" concerning traditional maps of persons. He begins the letter with the greatest example of this, the Crucified Christ. According to the *map of honorable persons* shared by both Jew and Greek, Christ Crucified has no place there; he is "a stumbling block to Jews and folly to Gentiles" (1 Cor. 1:23). Yet according to God's new map of persons, Christ Crucified is truly "the power of God and the wisdom of God" (1:24).

Two perceptions clash. How can ordinary people know which perception and which map is correct? In citing Isaiah 29:14, Paul appeals to God's Word to legitimate a principle of divine reversal that establishes a new order: "I will destroy the wisdom of the wise, and the cleverness of the clever I will thwart" (1:19). God, then, may act contrary to patterns of order commonly accepted in the world, even patterns to which observant Jews were socialized.

Paul echoes the same idea later when he argues that the wise among the Corinthians had better become "fools"; for the wisdom of this world is folly with God. How does Paul know this? He cites both Job 5:13 and Psalm 94:11 in regard to God's reversal of human maps: "He catches the wise in their craftiness" (3:19); and again, "The Lord knows that the thoughts of the wise are futile" (3:20). These assertions of divine reversals are not without their polemical and apologetic function within the argument of 1 Corinthians. Indeed, a full appreciation of them would require a reader to see them functioning vis-à-vis their respective contexts. But they illustrate dramatically God's new maps. Customary maps of honorable persons have been reversed. God has other ideas of wisdom and honor.

Immediately after citing the paradigmatic example of Christ Crucified in 1:18–25, Paul applies this new principle of God's action in the world to the social relations in Corinth: "Consider your call, brethren . . . " Affirming that many at Corinth were not ranked high on any map of persons, Paul then describes God's new map of persons in which status is reversed:

> God *chose* what is foolish in the world to shame the wise, God *chose* what is weak in the world to shame the strong, God *chose*

what is low and despised in the world, even things that are not,
to bring to nothing things that are.

1 Corinthians 1:27–28

As in the case of Christ, who appeared weak and foolish to the
world, so in regard to the non-elite at Corinth God reverses
the expected map of persons based on honor. One might apply
the same principle in regard to Paul himself in 2:1–16, where
his honor and status are challenged.

Earlier we studied maps of persons in 1 Corinthians 12, according to which people are ranked in terms of status and
honor. This ranking was based on God's action in creation
(12:18). In terms of affirming the legitimate place of authority
in the church, Paul clearly agrees with this map. Yet the discussion has not ended. Paul concedes that there is a map of
persons that ranks people as "strong" and "weaker," as "honorable" and "less honorable," and as "superior" and "inferior." But he surprisingly states that we ought to "invest with
greater honor" the less honorable parts and "to treat with
greater modesty" our unpresentable members (12:23). In part
this is based on the implicit system of Jewish dress codes in
which nudity is shameful. But Paul makes another principle
explicit in his appeal to God's reversing tendency: "God has so
composed the body, giving the greater honor to the inferior
part" (12:24). In this regard Paul sounds remarkably similar to
the Lukan formulation of God's reversing principle in Mary's
Magnificat (Luke 1:51–53), which is itself based on a pastiche
of citations about God's surprising actions in the Scriptures.
Yet it is clear that for Paul and Luke, God does not act always
in predictable ways to affirm traditional maps of persons. God
also draws new maps that seem to reverse the expectation of
divine favor.

**2.3 God's Sovereign Freedom**   Although known as the creator
God of Genesis 1, the biblical deity was first and foremost the
God who elects and chooses, namely, the God of covenant.
Although the foundation stories of the call and election of
Abraham (Isaac and Jacob) and David tell a story of God's
surprising choice of these persons, Israel's history tended to
focus rather on the abiding social awareness of Israel as a
"people chosen and set apart." The descendants of Abraham
and David had a considerable stake in these special covenants.
For, having made his choice, God's election became a foundational moment in the past that determined subsequent history.
From this came a strong sense of God's "order"; only they

belonged on the *map of covenant persons* who are true descendants of Abraham or David (see Matt. 3:9; John 8:33–42).

But Paul and other early Christians tell a different story about God's election and so draw different maps of covenant persons. In history Paul perceives a different pattern, which has important social consequences for the expanding mission of the early church. For Paul perceives disorder and reversal in the pattern of God's election and choice, namely, that God tended to choose the younger son over his elder sibling. In Galatians, Paul compares and contrasts the two covenants of God, which he finds symbolized in Abraham's two wives and their respective sons (4:21–31).

| Covenant of Law | Covenant of Promise |
| --- | --- |
| Hagar | Sarah |
| Ishmael | Isaac |
| slave son | free son |

Although Ishmael is the elder son, God's abiding favor rests on Isaac, the younger son. Of course, given the allegorical nature of Paul's explanation, we are not surprised that the free son is preferred to the slave son. In this there is no disorder.

But in Romans 9, when Paul enumerates the abiding blessings and benefits given to Israel, he cannot simply repeat the allegory of Galatians 4. As much as he defends God's fidelity to his promises ("it is not as though the word of God has failed," 9:6), Paul also argues for God's freedom to be gracious to a new people, the Gentiles. In this context, he goes beyond emphasizing the distinction among the "true sons of Abraham" (9:6–9) and tells the story of another pair of sons, Jacob and Esau. And in this he finds a pattern of divine reversal. Examining the story of the sons of Isaac, Paul fixes on two phrases from the scriptural report about Jacob and Esau:

"The elder will serve the younger." (Rom. 9:12//Gen. 25:23)
"Jacob I loved, but Esau I hated." (Rom. 9:13//Mal. 1:2–3)

According to the rules of ancient culture, an honor ranking existed among a man's sons, which gave certain sons specific rights and duties. The elder son, by right of primogeniture, traditionally inherited more than his siblings; upon marriage, he tended to bring his wife to live in his father's house, in anticipation of his assumption of the role as head of the clan. Thus his precedence was evident to all inside and outside the family. These typical patterns of social order Paul declares reversed by God's characteristic but surprising action of preferring the younger son to the elder. Although Paul cites but this

one example of Jacob and Esau, the Hebrew Scriptures pre-
serve numerous examples of this reversal of the status of sons:
Abel over Cain, Isaac over Ishmael, Joseph over his brothers,
David over his brothers, and Solomon over his royal siblings
(Clements 1967:47–60).

Paul knows that he is enunciating a new theological principle
when he cites the example of Jacob and Esau, for he says apropos of Isaac's sons: " . . . in order that God's purpose of election might continue, not because of works but because of his
call" (Rom. 9:11). God is free to reverse existing patterns of
order and act in sovereign freedom.

By reversing expected patterns of order, is God therefore
"unjust" (Rom. 9:14)? Is not God free to act as God wishes? In
response, Paul cites two examples that confirm God's freedom
to act in ways that mere mortals with their systems of order
and classification might label as disorder or injustice. First,
Paul cites Exodus 33:19 to the effect that God enjoys sovereign
freedom to élect and to choose: "I will be gracious to whom I
will be gracious, and will show mercy on whom I will show
mercy." Inasmuch as this axiom is treasured by those on whom
God showed mercy and compassion, it was seen as legitimating
a certain order, not upsetting it. Furthermore, in Romans
9:19–24 Paul echoes the Scriptures as he describes God as a
potter who makes vessels of glory and vessels of wrath (Isa.
29:16; 45:9; 64:8; Jer. 18:6). In their original context, these
images and scriptural passages illustrated the sovereign freedom of God to choose the Jews.

Yet Paul uses these traditional descriptions of God's freedom to legitimate God's new actions, the election of Gentiles.
At stake is the right of the potter, human and divine, to exercise freedom to make whatever vessels he wills. God, then,
does not act unjustly when he acts in freedom to choose and to
bless, not just Jews but also Gentiles. This new action may
strike those Jews socialized to see themselves as the chosen
vessels of God as capricious, and it certainly disturbed expected patterns of order. But Paul argues the principle firmly:
God enjoys freedom to choose whom he will.

It is important to contextualize this type of argument. Inasmuch as Paul addresses a Gentile church in Romans and asks
for their assistance in his projected journey to other Gentiles in
Spain, the principle of divine freedom and "disorder" functions in light of the particular audience and situation. It serves
as the basis for Paul's further remarks about God's election of
outsiders (even Gentiles). He quotes Hosea 2:23 and 1:10 to
illustrate how a group of outsiders became insiders by virtue of

God's "call": "Those who were not my people I will *call* 'my people,' and her who was not beloved I will *call* 'my beloved' " (Rom. 9:25). God's freedom, therefore, to call, choose and elect can create new maps of persons. This freedom creates disorder in existing social perceptions according to those whose privilege is thus restricted. Once more, then, Paul finds in Israel's Scriptures patterns of divine activity that indicate that God acts in ways orderly and disorderly. It is a question of theological expediency to articulate these new ways of God as the legitimation of Paul's new maps of persons.

In summary, Paul sees in Scripture and in his own experience a way in which God works that is quite different from that treasured in synagogue and Temple. Paul proclaims God's impartiality to all, his reversal of worldly patterns of order, and his freedom to act in new and different ways. To synagogue and Temple these remarks seem like disorder in the cosmos, but to Paul they form the basis for a new order.

## 3.0 Paul and New Maps

Earlier we examined Paul's typical tendency to perceive and articulate an extensive set of maps of persons, things, and times. Such maps indeed exist in Paul's letters, and they reflect a perception of an elaborate purity system of order and classification. Yet in the same letters of Paul we find a series of "new maps" whose presence and function do not cancel out the earlier maps but invite a closer look at the situations when Paul proclaims order and when he articulates disorder. Both patterns are found; but when do they occur, and how do they function in terms of the occasional character of their historical situation?

*3.1 New Maps of Things* Paul's first letter to Corinth remains the best place to observe Paul's articulation of disorder and reversal in regard to accepted perceptions of order and classification. In particular, we pay attention to the extensive list of slogans found in the document, many of which aggressively erase former Jewish classifications of things such as food and the body. Not all of the slogans function in this way, but it is good to list them all.

6:12 "All things are lawful for me."
6:13a "Food is meant for the stomach and the stomach for food."
6:13b "God will destroy both one and the other."

8:1    "All of us possess knowledge."
8:4a   "An idol has no real existence."
8:4b   "There is no God but one."
8:8a   "Food will not commend us to God."
8:8b   "We are no worse off if we do not eat, and no better off if
       we do."
10:23  "All things are lawful."

For the sake of completeness, we should include other remarks that reflect a new map of time: "One man esteems one day as better than another, while another man esteems all days like" (Rom. 14:5; see the converse in Gal. 4:10). These slogans deserve to be considered in discussions of Pauline patterns of disorder, for they are generally thought to reflect aspects of Paul's own preaching (Hurd 1983:278–280).

In general, the thrust of the slogans in 1 Corinthians focuses on the declassification of foods and on the obsolescence of moral rules for the physical body. Foods and the body, then, are taken out of the realm of "clean" and "unclean." According to the slogans, they are removed from the realm of order. Both of these topics will be discussed in detail in subsequent chapters of this book. But for the present we note that both touch upon maps that were particularly important for Jews in the second-temple period. For *maps of foods* replicate *maps of persons* (see Acts 10:10–15, 27–28). And a *map of the body* replicates maps of the social body, of which the physical body is a symbol. With new attitudes to foods and the body, we find different patterns of order, or *new maps*, that reverse previous values and structures.

It is interesting to speculate how the Pauline preaching of freedom from the Law could lead to a slogan such as "All things are lawful for me" (1 Cor. 6:12; 10:23). It appears that certain elite or pneumatic people at Corinth interpreted Paul's words to mean an end of the Mosaic Law and even all laws that make up a purity system. Such a perception would validate the disregarding of all maps—maps of persons, things, times, and places.

**3.2 New Maps of Persons**   In discussing certain patterns of God's "disorder," we cited Paul's perception of God's freedom from traditional maps of persons. God is *one*, namely, the God of Jews and Gentiles; God makes no distinctions and shows no partiality. God reverses traditional maps of persons by electing the lowly and showing favor to the less honorable. God's freedom is manifested in the surprising election of the younger son

over the elder. The perspective there was God's actions, which
served to legitimate new and different social arrangements
within the church. We now continue that investigation, but
from the specific perspective of the new map of persons and the
membership within the social body of the church that results
from this view of God. God's actions, then, erase older maps or
create new maps of persons. Three specific new maps of persons can be noted:

1. No Jew or Gentile (1 Cor. 12:13; Gal. 3:28)
2. No slave or free (1 Cor. 12:13)
3. No male or female (Gal. 3:28)

The premier classification of persons in Paul's perspective
was in terms of Jew/Gentile, which was replicated in the phrase
circumcised/uncircumcised. As Paul sees the issue, such a map,
which was once operative, no longer adequately reflects a true
classification of members of God's covenant people. Speaking
in terms of divine election and describing the liminal state of
entrants into the people of God, Paul argues that such former
maps of persons are not operative "in Christ." "For by one
Spirit we were all baptized into one body—Jews or Greeks,
slaves or free—and all were made to drink of one Spirit" (1
Cor. 12:13; see Rom. 10:12). The same idea is expressed in a
comparable expression: "Neither circumcision nor uncircumci-
sion is of any avail" (Gal. 5:6; 6:15; 1 Cor. 7:19; Rom. 2:28–
29). God is one, and the covenant family is one, both Jew and
Gentile. Such a perception attacks former maps of covenant
persons and so constitutes a new map of persons.

The baptismal formulae continue to erase patterns of classification found in the old maps. "In Christ" there are no distinctions of male and female, a statement that could strike at the
root value whereby all persons in the Mediterranean world
were classified, the values of "honor and shame" that distinguish male and female (Malina 1981:25–50). "For as many of
you as were baptized into Christ have put on Christ. There is
neither Jew nor Greek, there is neither slave nor free, there is
neither male nor female; for you are all one in Christ Jesus"
(Gal. 3:27–28; see Col. 3:11).

Modern readers tend to understand these passages in terms
of our egalitarian vision of church and society, and as such
they have become shibboleths for our modern social agenda. I
mention them here because they patently describe a new map
of persons, and they function in their limited way as illustrations of disorder in Paul's world. But a fuller treatment of them
would have to go back to the maps discussed earlier, which

stand in considerable tension with such new maps. Such formulae, which evidently reflect the liminal status of candidates
for entrance into the church, will be examined in greater detail
when we discuss rituals of status transformation and the circumscribed nature of "liminality" in rites of passage (Meeks
1983a:150–157). But these new maps exist, which erase some
of the most fundamental classifications made by Paul and his
world: Jew/Greek, slave/free, and male/female. These new
maps, moreover, function precisely as attacks on former principles of classification. Hence they are new maps of persons.

Any treatment of such phrases would be incomplete if it did
not examine places in Paul's letters where such new maps of
persons are moderated and qualified. If, as we suspect, they
were intended as descriptions of the liminal status of initiants,
did Paul expect the same absence of status among those fully
reintegrated into the world after their rite of passage? (See
Meeks 1983a:154–157.) Although Paul said "no Jew or
Greek," he continues to make distinctions of that sort in Romans when he speaks of "the Jew first and also the Greek"
(1:16; 2:9, 10). Despite his remark that in Christ there is no
slave or free, he told the slaves at Corinth to remain slaves (see
1 Cor. 7:17–24). In addition to his remarks about "no male or
female" in Christ, Paul still spoke of distinct male/female roles
in 1 Corinthians 11:3 and 14:33b–34. Without doubt, Paul can
propose new maps of persons in the church. But we would have
to study these passages more carefully to see when he urges new
maps and why, and when he reverts to old maps and why. The
answers may lie in Paul's sense of strategy and timeliness in
regard to the shifting problems of his churches. It would surely
be a mistake to claim that he completely abolished the old
maps of persons and replaced them with new maps of persons.
Both sets of maps are found in his letters! The important question then becomes, When did he propose new maps and why?
and, When did he repeat old maps and why?

**3.3 New Maps of Times**   Jews like Paul and Jesus were socialized to certain maps of time. As we noted above, Genesis 1
established the principle of such maps and so laid the foundation for a calendar. At creation God separated night and day;
after six workdays, God rested on the Sabbath. In time, Jews
came to distinguish certain fast days during a given week (Luke
18:12), as well as a full cycle of feasts, such as Rosh Hashanah,
Yom Kippur, Dedication, and Passover. Along with kosher
diet and circumcision, ancient Jews identified themselves by
their strict Sabbath observance. Jewish maps of time ordered

their own internal life and distinguished them from all other peoples.

But when Paul proclaims the end of the Law, he signals as well an end of the old maps of time and heralds a different sense of time, which we will call a *new map of time*. Paul and other early Christians no longer kept the Jewish Sabbath as it was prescribed in the old maps of time. They met on the first day of the week for Eucharist and Agape (1 Cor. 16:2; on "the Lord's day," see Rev. 1:10; *Did.* 14:1). The choice was neither accidental nor insignificant. This new map of time defined them as followers of Jesus, not as disciples of Moses.

More significantly, however, Paul reacts strongly against the Galatians' fascination with Jewish maps of time. When Paul proclaimed the end of the covenant of law, he erased specific Jewish time lines and attacked in principle the old map of time. But because of Judaizing propaganda in the Galatian churches, some members became fascinated not only with circumcision (Gal. 5:2–4; 6:12–13) and dietary concerns (2:11–13), but also the Sabbath and sacred days (Betz 1979:217–218). Paul ridicules the maps of times to which some aspire: "You observe days, and months, and seasons and years!" (4:10), a map suggestive of Sabbath, new moons, and other Jewish sacred times. By observing these sacred times, such people would organize their world according to Jewish principles of ordering, both maps of things and time. Paul argues against such maps of time. And by viewing all time as of equal importance, he has established a new map of time (Col. 2:16).

At the end of Romans, Paul discusses the same issue in a different context. As he lays out the problem, certain "strong" people disregard maps of foods, whereas "weak" people (probably Jewish Christians) favor eating vegetables in situations where a kosher diet might be compromised (Segal 1986:365–368). In addition to conflicts over diet (14:1–4), Paul notes disputes over "days": "One man esteems one day as better than another, while another man esteems all days alike" (14:5). This too is a conflict over maps of time. Some would rank days and so establish a map of time, perhaps by validating certain days as fast days; but others erase all such lines, considering "all days alike." We should probably see these two maps as reinforcing each other, so that those who eat vegetables observe fast days and those who eat meat do so any day of the week. The principle of an orderly cosmos would suggest maps both of foods (14:1–4) and time (14:5–7).

Paul's response is quite complex. On the one hand, he urges toleration on the part of "strong" and "weak." As regards dietary concern, "Let not him who eats despise him who abstains, and let not him who abstains pass judgment on him who eats" (14:3). As regards ordering of time, "He who observes the day, observes it in honor of the Lord. He also who eats, eats in honor of the Lord" (14:6). Yet the burden of toleration falls on the strong, whom Paul exhorts "to bear with the failings of the weak" (15:1). If we may compare Romans 14:5–7 with Galatians 4:10, Paul does not espouse a map of time, although in Romans he is more tolerant of those who do so than he was in the letter to the Galatians. Yet even this tolerance is a form of a new map of time, for in principle it allows for a legitimate point of view in which "all days are like." This indeed is a new ordering of time.

## 4.0 Summary, Conclusions, and Further Inquiry

*4.1 Summary and Conclusions*  What do we know if we know all this? We learned that Paul, like most Jews in his world, basically perceives the world as an orderly cosmos that is carefully mapped to give "a place to everything and everything its place." We understand how this general tendency among ancient peoples gets its specific Jewish shape from the priestly creation story in Genesis 1 and from the actual temple system in Jerusalem. Paul the Pharisee was certainly socialized to perceive the world in this way.

Yet we began to learn the more specific maps implicit in Paul's new symbolic world, which are not always carryovers from being a Pharisee. We saw how Paul's many references to "holy," "pure," and "spotless" build on his socialization as a Pharisee, his Jewish concerns with purity and the orderly patterns of that symbolic world. He perceives the world as an orderly cosmos, whether in strictly Pharisaic categories or in terms of Christ. His basic viewpoint is order.

Interesting historical questions arise from this discussion about the specific Jewish contents of Paul's orderly cosmos. How strongly and where does Paul reflect specific Jewish maps? Anthropological perspectives cannot answer this traditional question, but they invite the use of other methods and techniques in this regard (see Davies 1948; Sanders 1977).

We have, moreover, examined patterns both of order and disorder. They do not cancel each other out. Nor should readers in virtue of their own preference or bias favor one pattern over the other. Both may be found, even in the same letter. The patterns of divine disorder are essentially reworkings of the cultural maps of order, for Paul never advocates anarchy or lawlessness. Nor has he abandoned allegiance to Israel's God and Scriptures. Rather, as a reformer he sees new and different patterns, and so he sets out to rearrange maps, not to discard them entirely (Theissen 1978). Yet in examining Paul's persistent concern with order, system, and classification, a reader might be led to give more attention to Paul's penchant for order than previous scholarship has. In particular, such considerations should affect the way we perceive of Pauline talk about freedom (Malina 1978c:62–73) and ethics. Even when being "disorderly," Paul never abandons his pervasive and strong perception of an orderly universe.

The fact is that Paul perceives the world as a carefully ordered cosmos. Yet even when he tries to rearrange certain maps, we might raise a sociological concern: When and in what circumstances does Paul argue for order and system? When and in what circumstances does he favor reversals and disorder? Modern readers sensitive to the occasional quality of his letters are aware that the issues and problems at Corinth are not those in Galatia, and the circumstances that prompted the letter to Philippi are not those behind the letter to the Romans. Even within a document like 1 Corinthians, we find Paul affirming traditional orderly maps of persons, places, and things in regard to certain situations, yet reversing those maps or presenting new maps in other circumstances.

By asking this type of question we become more aware of flexibility in Paul's perceptions and remarks than of consistency (see 1 Cor. 9:19–23). Recent articles of Pauline "inconsistency" may simply be misguided, for they tend to ignore the historical specificity of the situations that Paul addressed. Thinking of Paul as a systematic theologian, such studies search for consistency of opinion. A more historical and sociological approach to the Pauline letters will surely help us see when Paul favors known patterns of order and when he suggests reformed maps. He may be consistent in his tendency to perceive and impose order on the world, but inconsistent in the specific maps he puts forth.

This first use of anthropological perspective seems convincing and productive. We learned to see the pervasive patterns and how these patterns are replicated in other areas. Maps of persons are replicated by maps of places and times. Learning to think this way, we are led to see greater coherence in Paul's symbolic world. And this in turn gives us some grounds for using these perceptions to examine more carefully other passages in Paul's letters.

***4.2 Further Projects***   This examination of purity systems and
patterns of order and disorder has been somewhat long, but
long enough to illustrate what needs illustration. In passing, we
noted other passages that a reader might consider in the light of
this model of perception. We have by no means exhausted this
inquiry into Paul's symbolic world, and we suggest other areas
and passages that might be investigated. We mention just a few
areas for further consideration.

***4.2.1 The Kingdoms of God and Satan***   Implicit in Paul's perception of the cosmos is a sense of two kingdoms, God's and
Satan's. For example, Paul speaks of Satan's realm when he
says that "death reigned" (Rom. 5:14, 17) or "sin reigned"
(Rom. 5:21, 6:12; 20). He speaks explicitly of God's kingdom
in passages such as 1 Thessalonians 2:12; 1 Corinthians 6:9–
10; 15:24, 50; and Galatians 5:21. If we risk *not* entering the
kingdom of God, this means that we are located somewhere
else on the map. Given Paul's fundamentally dualistic perspective, if we are not in the kingdom of God, then we are found in
the kingdom of Satan, where sin and death reign.

***4.2.2 Other Maps of Space***   Paul calls the church of God a holy
space, a temple. This implies a *map of space*, for only holy
people may enter that space to give God glory and praise.
Those who corrupt it will be destroyed by God. Yet Paul warns
the Corinthians of the dangers attendant on their presence in
other temples. We know that Paul first converted people to
loyalty to the one, true God of Israel (1 Thess. 1:9–10; 1 Cor.
12:5). In principle, then, Christians belong in a new map of
place, which negates an old map of place, the temple of idols.

  But the issue becomes complicated by virtue of the meals
that were regularly served in temple precincts. May Christians
continue the pattern of social relations they enjoyed before
swearing loyalty to the God of Jesus Christ? May they attend
family and civic ritual meals served in the old map of place?
Paul says that they may not eat at the table of demons (1 Cor.
10:18–22). But what of merely family or social meals eaten
there, meals that may not require any commitment to the deity
of the temple?

  The issue of *place* overlaps with concern for *things* and *persons*. Certain Christians may be harmed to see a fellow believer
in Jesus eating "in an idol's temple" (1 Cor. 8:10). Causing
scandal would impinge on the map of persons who make up the
church, and those who harm the temple of God stand in danger
of God's wrath. Christians, moreover, attempted to declassify

Jewish foods by effectively abolishing any map of things (see 1 Cor. 10:26). But the matter will not rest there, for some people are socialized to map foods in a certain way (1 Cor. 8:7–10; 10:27–29; Rom. 14:1–6). It will help us understand the problems in 1 Corinthians 8–10 if we attend to the various overlapping maps of place, persons, and things involved there.

### 4.2.3 Leaders in the Church: New Maps

Did Paul ever appoint local leaders with authority over the church in his absence? Philippians 1:1 suggests some form of local leadership, probably one based on the natural precedence of elders. But Paul seems to want to hold on to the control of his churches, despite long periods of absence. Hence, figures like Apollos move into the vacuum at Corinth, with disorderly consequences from Paul's perspective. Given this situation, a reader might carefully read 1 Corinthians 16:10–16 and tease out Paul's map of persons in leadership roles among the Corinthians.

### 4.2.4 Controversial Times

A careful reader may be sensitized by this discussion to examine other maps of time in the Pauline letters. Why, for example, is it so important to affirm in Romans 6:9–10 that "Christ being raised from the dead will never die again; . . . the death he died he died to sin, once for all"? A time line is drawn, not only for Jesus but for his followers too. But having died to sin and death, are they beyond judgment? Have they crossed a further line? Several passages (1 Cor. 10:6–13 and Rom. 11:17–24) give further refinement to Paul's map of times to answer these questions.

Time questions are raised by some apropos of the date when the dead will be raised. The map of time in 1 Corinthians 15:22–25 is phrased to undercut claims to share already in Christ's resurrection. Although in Romans 5 Paul argues that death no longer reigns, in 1 Corinthians 15:22–26 he argues that death has not been destroyed. These are two different maps of time. The difference in the two maps may be resolved in light of the claim of some in his churches that they have already passed beyond death and so are dead to all earthly laws and claims (1 Cor. 4:8; 13:8–12). To them Paul gives a map of time in which death still reigns. But to the Romans, Paul stresses the break with sin and death by virtue of the obedience of the New Adam, hence a different map of time. Furthermore, faced with a different problem altogether, Paul describes in 1 Thessalonians a scenario that indicates who will rise first (1 Thess. 4:14–17), probably in response to the death of members of the group. Paul's major map of time needed occasional adjustments.

**4.2.5 Anti-Maps?** Some Corinthians seem to espouse anti-maps. They do not propose reformed variations of maps as Paul does, but rather prefer to declassify completely certain persons, places, and things. "All things are lawful" (1 Cor. 6:12; 10:23), including illicit sexual union (5:1–2), food offered to idols and consumed in a temple, and so forth. It is a matter of scholarly debate to what extent this "disorderly" position could have been derived from Paul's preaching about the "end of the Law" and freedom from the slavery of the Law. For our purposes, however, does this tendency to reject all maps and all systems of classification reflect Paul's own point of view? From what we have seen, Paul qualifies these slogans and suggests some form of mapping, some form of ordering one's experience.

# 4

# Rituals:
# Making and Maintaining
# Boundaries

We were buried therefore with him by baptism into death, so
that as Christ was raised from the dead by the glory of the
Father, we too might walk in newness of life.

Romans 6:4

## 1.0  Rituals and Ceremonies

As we take up the study of rites in Paul, we must learn new concepts and a new language in order to have an adequate understanding of this phenomenon in his letters. What have Bastille Day, the Fourth of July, or the Queen's birthday in common? What have graduations, convictions, and divorces in common? In anthropological jargon, we call the former "ceremonies" and the latter "rituals." These are two forms of rites, the general concept that covers both.

The following chart highlights the distinguishing characteristics of rituals and ceremonies:

| Ritual | Ceremony |
|---|---|
| 1. frequency:<br>irregular pauses | 1. frequency:<br>regular pauses |
| 2. calendar:<br>unpredictable,<br>when needed | 2. calendar:<br>predictable,<br>planned |
| 3. time focus:<br>present-to-future | 3. time focus:<br>past-to-present |
| 4. presided over by:<br>professionals | 4. presided over by:<br>officials |
| 5. purpose:<br>status reversal;<br>status transformation | 5. purpose:<br>confirmation of<br>roles and statuses<br>in institutions |

**Frequency**: Our daily lives are routinely punctuated with pauses in their regular rhythms. The pauses that occur irregularly and unpredictably we call "ritual" (e.g., graduations, sickness, divorces, etc.). Those pauses that occur routinely we call "ceremonies" (meals, birthdays, anniversaries, civic holidays, etc.).

**Calendar**: Ritual pauses are unpredictable; we take them when necessary or timely. Ceremonial pauses are fixed dates on the calendar, such as Labor Day, Thanksgiving Day, Christmas, and Easter; we anticipate and plan for them.

**Time Focus**: Ritual pauses take us from present needs to future possibilities because they mark changes in our role and status. Ceremonies, however, look to the past and celebrate its influence on the present by re-presenting actions and events.

**Presiders**: Different kinds of people preside over rituals and ceremonies. Professionals (doctors, school presidents, lawyers, etc.) preside over or direct ritual pauses, the irregular breaks such as illness, graduation, or divorce. Officials (father and mother, presidents, popes, etc.) preside over or direct ceremonies such as Thanksgiving meals, Fourth of July celebrations, High Mass in St. Peter's.

**Purpose**: Ceremonies leave the lines of the maps of society in place, because they function to confirm the values and structures of society, to affirm its purity system, and to celebrate the orderly classification of persons, places, and things in the cosmos. Birthdays, anniversaries, festivals, and the like, confirm the roles and statuses of individuals in the group as well as the group's collective sense of holy space and the holy time that pertains to them. Ceremonies look to the stability of the lines of the maps of society.

Conversely, rituals attend to those lines but focus on their crossings. Many rituals are stable ways of dealing with necessary instability in the system: single people cross lines and become husband and wife; sick people cross lines and become healthy; sinful become purified, living become dead. The status of those who cross lines is thereby changed, and so rituals are often called "status transformation" rituals. If ceremonies look to the center of the map and the stable lines that make up the map, rituals look to the edges of the map, its boundaries that should be stable but may be legitimately or fraudulently crossed.

In Paul's symbolic universe, we have noted many maps. We are aware of a strong tendency to see order and clarity in the cosmos and to celebrate it. Yet we note also that Paul often disagrees with the maps of his world; he would rearrange the lines to bring to the center people usually left on the periphery. Yet he reacts sensitively when his place on the map is blurred or challenged by another. And he can act as a rancher who rushes to mend a broken fence and discern if anything has gotten out accidentally or entered unwanted. If we would examine the social dynamics of Paul's symbolic world, we must be aware of the difference between ceremony and ritual. Then we must ask which is more important to Paul, rituals or ceremonies? And which takes up his attention more frequently? My hypothesis is that Paul's letters reflect both ceremonies and rituals, but he focuses the bulk of his energy and attention on rituals, namely, crises on the boundaries and lines of his cosmos.

***1.1 Ceremonies in Paul***   Ceremonies serve to confirm values and structures in the institutions of a society. The primary institutions of Paul's world were politics (local and imperial government) and kinship (families and households) (Malina 1986a:92–95). Because ceremonies function to confirm the social institutions that structure life shared in common, they tend to confirm the respective statuses of persons in those institutions and demonstrate unity and solidarity among all those who gather for these ceremonies.

A study of specific ceremonies in Paul's letters would necessarily include meals, the collection for Jerusalem, letters, and visits to Jerusalem. These four do not exhaust the list of ceremonies of concern to Paul, but they adequately indicate many of the major ones.

1. Meals: (a) Idol meat: 1 Cor. 8:1, 7–13 and 10:23–11:1 (see Acts 10:9–16; 11:3–9; 15:20, 29)
       (b) Eucharist: 1 Cor. 10:14–22; 11:17–34 (see Acts 20:7–12)
       (c) Community-shared Meals: Gal. 2:11–13
2. The Collection: Rom. 15:25–29; 1 Cor. 16:1–4; 2 Cor. 8–9; Gal. 2:10 (see Acts 11:27–31)
3. Letters: all of Paul's letters, including 1 Cor. 5:9 (see Acts 15:23–29)
4. Pilgrimage to Jerusalem: Gal. 2:1–10 (see Acts 15:1–21; 20:16)

The most prominent ceremony in Paul's churches was the meal, not simply the community's Eucharist or the agape meal, but also the private meals eaten with friends in their homes or in the local temple. The collection Paul takes up regularly constitutes a ceremony that affirms the centrality of the Jerusalem church and its leaders (Johnson 1977). Let us not overlook the phenomenon of sending letters as another important ceremony, which aims to confirm Paul's role as leader of the local church. Finally, Paul's journey to Rome to consult with the "pillars" at Jerusalem (Gal. 2) might profitably be viewed as a pilgrimage ceremony.

If ceremonies are intended to confirm values as well as

roles and statuses in a group, Paul's letters record a continu-
ous history of problems surrounding them in his churches.
*Meals*: His accounts of meals tell a story of disharmony and
division: there is disunity over what is eaten (1 Cor. 8:7–13;
10:23–11:1; Rom. 14:1–4), as well as over when it is eaten (1
Cor. 11:21–22, 33–34) and with whom (Gal. 2:11–13). *Collection*: The popularity of the collection seems problematic, nor
was its offering always met with success (Rom. 15:25–29).
*Letters*: Paul wrote his letters to churches that contested his
leadership and authority (1 Corinthians; 2 Cor. 10:9–11; Galatians). *Pilgrimage*: Paul himself seems ambivalent about
the ceremonial importance of his visit to Jerusalem, for he
seems to pride himself on a certain independence of it (Gal.
1:16–24). Stable roles, statuses, and unity may have been
important goals for Paul and the early church, but there
was not much to celebrate. The ceremonies were beset with
crisis.

Certain rituals which were acceptable in Judaism Paul declares unacceptable to the followers of Jesus. The map of times
alluded to in Galatians 4:10, if celebrated ceremoniously,
would imply affirmation of living a Jewish way of life. Because
in Paul's eyes this violates the way Jesus' followers should live,
he censures such ceremonies. The same might be said of the
celebration of temple sacrifices that are now unacceptable ceremonies for new Christians (1 Cor. 10:14–22).

These observations about ceremonies in Paul should leave us
with a sense that the lines of the maps in Paul's churches were
quite unstable. Unity and harmony were fragile; structures
were brittle. In Paul's letters, proportionately less time was
spent on ceremonies than on rituals, for the occasions of the
letters tended to be a crisis about the blurring of internal lines
within a group or trespassing on the periphery of the group's
boundaries.

**1.2 Rituals in Paul** Rituals generally function in terms of status reversal or status transformation. Sinners are cleansed, outsiders are included, and people on the periphery are drawn to
the center. Just as rituals assist people to cross lines and so
enter (baptism, circumcision), they function to mark the exit of
people as well (funerals, excommunications, anathemas). Line
crossings in most cultures are ambiguous and dangerous times
that require the assistance of professionals such as teachers and
prophets.

Again, we attempt to list some but not all of the specific
rituals in Paul's letters:

1. Entrance Rituals: (a) baptism (Rom. 6:1–11; Gal. 3:27–28); (b) circumcision (Gal. 5:1–11)
2. Exit Rituals: (a) excommunication (1 Cor. 5; 2 Cor. 10–13; Gal. 4:30); (b) anathemas (Rom. 9:3; 1 Cor. 12:3; 16:22; Gal. 1:8–9)
3. Marriage: (a) whether to get married (1 Cor. 7:1, 8, 25–35); (b) divorce (1 Cor. 7:10–16); (c) remarriage (1 Cor. 7:39–40)
4. Enthronement Rituals: 1 Cor. 15:20–28
5. Judgment: Rom. 2:4–11; 5:6–11; 8:31–35; 14:10–12
6. Resurrection and Status Transformation: 1 Thess. 4:13–17; 1 Cor. 15:42–57; 2 Cor. 5:1–5
7. Fences Breached/Fences Mended: (a) turf violated (2 Cor. 10:13–18; Gal. 2:12); (b) status and role challenged (2 Cor. 10:12; 11:5, 21–33; Gal. 1:1; 2:4; 6:17); (c) heresy discovered (2 Cor. 11:3–4, 13–14; Gal. 1:6–8; 3:1)
8. Jesus' Status Transformation Rituals: Phil. 2:6–11; Rom. 6:3–4, 9–11
9. Emancipation of Slaves: Philemon
10. Vocation and Transformation: Gal. 1:13–16; 1 Cor. 15:3–11

Rituals in Paul encompass those that apply to Jesus, to converts, and to Paul himself. Individually they all experienced a change in status, which may be analyzed in terms of ritual process either as enthronement, baptism, or vocation rituals. Other ritual considerations have to do with crossing from single to married status and vice versa, from slavery to freedom, or from guilt to judgment. All such rituals are orderly crossings of lines that leave the maps intact and confirmed. But Paul's experience and his symbolic world were filled with disorder that was created by surreptitious crossing of boundaries and lines. The rituals dealing with unwarranted trespassing occupy much of Paul's energy and time, and so ours as well.

*1.3 Rituals and Paul's Symbolic Universe* When we introduced the major elements of an anthropological investigation of Paul's symbolic universe, we noted that Paul and others in his world typically attend to the boundaries of their world. Considerably more time is spent in rites of making and maintaining boundaries than in ceremonies that confirm the internal order and structure of the group. This appears so because people like Paul perceive their cosmos as a world under attack. Indeed, they sense that a polluting evil is already in their midst, and so energy and attention are rallied to the perimeter to repair the breach and to discover the covert evil in their midst so as to expel it. Yet all their efforts to purify the organism seem not to succeed. Paul and others in his world, then, typically focus on boundaries of the social and physical body that are perceived to be under attack.

Although we read of many ceremonies in Paul's letters, they all seem to be unsuccessful as rites that confirm the group's values and structures. According to Paul's letters, the lines marking role and status are constantly threatened, not confirmed by these ceremonies. Both external boundaries and internal lines remain precarious. For this reason, this chapter will focus more on rituals that make and maintain boundaries than on ceremonies. The focus reflects both the theoretical appreciation of Paul's world as a universe under siege and the pervasive emphasis in the letters on boundary and line disputes.

## 2.0 Making Boundaries: Rituals of Entrance and Exit

It is a hypothesis of this chapter, easily verified, that Paul spends proportionally more time and energy on rituals than ceremonies. His attention focuses on the external boundary of the church as well as on certain specific internal lines that are meant to separate and divide. Paul both makes boundaries and struggles to maintain them.

***2.1 Rituals of Boundary Definition*** Readers will recall from the previous chapter the map of persons in the church. In distinguishing the followers of Jesus from those of Moses, Paul makes a boundary that is unmistakably clear and absolute (Gal. 5:2–4). In his perception, the covenants of promise have nothing to do with the covenant of law (Gal. 4:21–31). And from the perspective of this former Pharisee, clean has nothing to do with unclean. A fence around holiness is necessary; a boundary must be erected. We turn our attention now to several examples of Paul as a boundary definer.

***2.1.1 Clean Separated from Unclean*** From synagogue and Temple, Paul the ex-Pharisee transfers to the church his acute sense of holiness. The church comprises "the saints," the holy ones; by God's favor and grace they have been "washed . . . sanctified . . . justified" (1 Cor. 6:11). Those baptized into Christ are "freed from sin" (Rom. 6:6–7). Because the church must be holy and completely separate from any sin, stain, or uncleanness, Paul demands that the man in an illicit sexual union be expelled outside the boundaries of the holy church (1

Cor. 5:1–8, 13). Conversely, he exhorts "the saints" to remain spotless and sinless for the day of judgment: "guileless" as to what is evil (Rom. 16:19), blameless and innocent (Phil. 2:15), irreproachable (1 Cor. 1:8), and faultless (Phil. 2:15; 3:6; 1 Thess. 2:10; 3:13; 5:23). Thus he makes an absolute boundary between the holy followers of Jesus and all others, who are not holy (Meeks 1979).

That boundary, however, proved to be unrealistic to the urban members of Paul's churches. So he draws a more realistic boundary:

> I wrote to you in my letter not to associate with immoral men; not at all meaning the immoral of this world, or the greedy and robbers, or idolaters, since then you would need to go out of the world. But rather I wrote to you not to associate with any one who bears the name of brother if he is guilty of immorality or greed, or is an idolater, reviler, drunkard, or robber—not even to eat with such a one.
>
> 1 Corinthians 5:9–11

They cannot, like the Essenes at Qumran, "go out of the world." But they can separate themselves from church members ("any one who bears the name of brother") who are sinful and stained with immorality.

In the document called the Second Letter to the Corinthians we find a passage that has exercised scholars, namely, 2 Corinthians 6:14–7:1. The language sounds non-Pauline when compared with his authentic letters, but the perception is not. The hands may be the hands of Esau, but the voice is definitely Jacob's.

> Do not be mismated with unbelievers. For what partnership have righteousness and iniquity? Or what fellowship has light with darkness? What accord has Christ with Belial? Or what has a believer in common with an unbeliever? What agreement has the temple of God with idols? For we are the temple of the living God; as God said,
>> "I will live in them and move among them,
>> and I will be their God,
>> and they shall be my people.
>> Therefore come out from them,
>> and be separate from them, says the Lord,
>> and touch nothing unclean;
>> then I will welcome you,
>> and I will be a father to you,
>> and you shall be my sons and daughters,
>> says the Lord Almighty."

> Since we have these promises, beloved, let us cleanse ourselves from every defilement of body and spirit, and make holiness perfect in the fear of God.
>
> 2 Corinthians 6:14–7:1

Paul erects an absolute boundary: "Do not be mismated with unbelievers." Those in the church have no partnership or fellowship with the non-Christian world, because in Paul's perception, the world is divided into irreconcilable opposites:

| | | |
|---|---|---|
| righteousness | vs. | iniquity |
| light | vs. | darkness |
| Christ | vs. | Belial |
| Temple of God | vs. | idols |

Hence, "believers" have nothing whatsoever in common with "unbelievers" (6:15). As the song says, "Two different worlds, we live in two different worlds."

Paul's perception reflects a view of God's holiness that cannot abide anything unclean, sinful, or polluted (Neyrey 1988c). As God is completely separated from evil, so concerning God's people Paul quotes from Isaiah: "Come out from them, and be separate from them . . . and touch nothing unclean" (2 Cor. 6:17//Isa. 52:11). On the basis of this Scripture, he commands them: "Let us cleanse ourselves from every defilement of body and spirit, and make holiness perfect" (7:1). Thus Paul erects a formidable boundary to fence in and protect the holy people of God. In subsequent chapters of this book we will examine Paul's perception of sin, which indicates why he is so intolerant of evil in the church. And inasmuch as he perceives the world dualistically divided into the kingdoms of God and Satan, Paul sees no gray area, no neutral zone: one is either holy in God's realm or one belongs to the kingdom of the Evil One. A boundary is made that must be maintained.

### 2.1.2 Abraham Separated from Moses

The boundary wall may be built on the basis of the separation of holy from sinful, light from dark, and Christ from Belial. Such a wall serves to separate God's saints from Gentiles. Paul, however, needed to erect another boundary, this time between church and synagogue and between the followers of Jesus and those of Moses. The bricks for this wall come from the familiar language of covenants.

Particularly in Galatians Paul compares and contrasts two kinds of covenants—the covenant with Abraham and that with Moses. This very act of rhetorical contrasting itself erects a boundary line that definitively separates the followers of Jesus, who are the offspring of Abraham, from those of Moses. The language event itself erects the boundary.

According to Paul's radical perception, the Scriptures record two mutually exclusive covenants—one with Abraham and another with Moses. The following diagram teases out in abstract terms the radical differences between the two covenants as understood by Paul.

| Covenant with Abraham | Covenant with Moses |
|---|---|
| 1. God's action: promise given as free gift | 1. God's action: law issued as reciprocal contract |
| 2. Response expected: belief in the promise (faith) | 2. Response expected: keeping the contract (works) |
| 3. Result: blessing | 3. Result: curse |

Turning to Galatians 3:6–13, we can flesh out this diagram by attending to the details of Paul's argument. He contrasts two quotations from Scripture to distinguish the different ways in which the two covenants operate. Concerning the covenant with Abraham, he cites Habakkuk 2:4: "He who through faith is righteous shall live" (3:11). But apropos of the covenant with Moses, he cites Leviticus 18:5: "He who does them shall live by them" (3:12). Although both are concerned with "life," the way to that life is contrasted: life comes either "through faith" or by "doing them."

Paul further contrasts the covenants in terms of their results—blessing or curse. Earlier Paul legitimated God's blessing to Abraham with the citation from Genesis 15:6: "Abraham believed God and it was reckoned to him as righteousness" (3:6); blessing-through-belief identifies those "men of faith" (3:7, 9), even the Gentiles and "all the nations" (3:8). In contrast, the second covenant operates on the basis of works; but Paul characterizes it as curse: "Cursed be every one who does not abide by all things written in the book of the law, and do them" (3:10//Deut. 27:26). Blessing follows faith, which Paul labels as righteousness or holiness; but curse follows failure to do "all things written," which means sinfulness.

Paul continues the distinguishing of the two covenants in Galatians 4:21–31, where he compares and contrasts them by means of an "allegory," which is the story of Hagar and Sarah.

| Covenant with Abraham | Covenant with Moses |
|---|---|
| 1. Sarah, the free woman = Jerusalem above | 1. Hagar, the slave woman = Mount Sinai, present Jerusalem |

2. Isaac, the free son
3. Born according to the Spirit
4. Remained in the house because he was the heir

2. Ishmael, the slave son
3. Born according to the flesh
4. Was cast out of the house because he does not inherit

Paul's presentation of the allegory typifies his tendency to perceive reality in sharp, dualistic terms. Of such perceptions does Paul make boundaries.

If the comparison of the two covenants in Galatians 3:6–12 stressed blessing/curse, faith/works, and righteousness/sinfulness, the allegory in 4:21–31 emphasizes freedom/slavery, inheritance/dispossession, remaining/being cast out, and spirit/flesh. The distinctions are emphatically sharp so that the lines might be drawn as clearly as possible.

One cannot belong to both covenants. The covenants, moreover, are incompatible. Symbolizing this, Paul concludes his allegorical contrast with the citation of Genesis 21:10: "Cast out the slave and her son" (4:30). As with 1 Corinthians 5:9–11 and 2 Corinthians 6:14–7:1, a separation must take place; a boundary has been erected. Hagar, Ishmael, and all those of the covenant with Moses have no share in the inheritance that God gives Isaac and his spiritual kin. They belong outside, separated, walled off from the tents of Abraham.

**2.1.3 Scripture Makes Boundaries** When possible, Paul draws from the Scriptures the convenient boundaries that are needed to separate the followers of Jesus from those of Moses. Obviously, the process is highly selective, and the principles of reading the Scriptures would certainly be different for synagogue Jews and temple priests, but the process is clear and its function evident. From a Christocentric reading of the Scriptures, Paul perceives how the covenant represented by Abraham is distinguished from that of Moses. Thus Scripture makes a boundary.

In Romans 4, Paul stitches together fragments of the Abraham story to outline the shape of the process whereby God's righteousness is revealed in the world after the desert of sin and just judgment described in the early chapters of Genesis. Citing Genesis 15:6 three times, Paul clearly states the principle in Romans 4:3, 9, and 22: "Abraham believed God, and it was reckoned to him as righteousness." Paul then interprets the key terms of this foundational principle to indicate the structure of right relationship with God, thereby building a boundary be-

tween church and synagogue, the descendants of Abraham and
the followers of Moses:

| | |
|---|---|
| *Abraham* | = Abraham is blessed with God's promise *before* he was circumcised (4:10–11). |
| *believed* | = Abraham is canonized because of his faith: "trusts him who justifies the ungodly" (4:5); "he did not weaken in faith" (4:19). |
| *God* | = How does God act? " . . . in the presence of God in whom he believed, who gives life to the dead and calls into existence the things that do not exist" (4:17, see vv. 19–21). |
| *reckoned* | = God gives freely, not according to a contract: "to one who works, his wages are not reckoned as a gift but as his due. And to one who does not work but trusts him who justifies the ungodly, his faith is reckoned as righteousness" (4:4–5). |
| *to him* | = To Abraham alone or to his offspring through Jesus? "But the words, 'it was reckoned to him,' were written not for his sake alone, but for ours also. It will be reckoned to us" (4:23–24). |
| *as righteousness* | = God makes holy, gives grace, and extends mercy: " 'Blessed are those whose iniquities are forgiven, and whose sins are covered; blessed is the man against whom the Lord will not reckon his sin' " (4:7–8). |

Paul perceives Genesis 15:6 as a fundamental organizing text
to explain God's dealing with us. But in the careful, even mid-
rashic interpretation of each word of Genesis 15:6, Paul sees
how Scripture makes a boundary, both clearly defining the true
nature of the covenant with Abraham and distinguishing it
from the way he perceives the covenant with Moses to function. God blessed Abraham with a promise *before* he was circumcised, that is, before the covenant with Moses, before any
works were demanded. Abraham became holy by faith and
trust in God, not by his deeds. Holiness was "reckoned" to
him, that is, given freely by God, not merited or contracted for
by law observance. This very Scripture, then, makes the fundamental boundary separating the covenant with Abraham,
which includes not just Abraham but his descendants in faith,
from the covenant with Moses.

## 2.2 Entrance Rituals

We commonly read of two entrance rituals in the Bible, one particular to the followers of Jesus (baptism) and another characteristic of the followers of Moses (circumcision).

### 2.2.1 Baptism

Paul's most characteristic activity, then, is making boundaries. As a Pharisee, Paul understands them as fences around what is holy, protecting and guarding what is enclosed. But with all boundaries, there must be gates for legitimate entrance; so there are rituals that carefully define the process of who may enter and who may legitimately cross the boundaries. Paul's most noted entrance ritual is baptism.

The New Testament frequently speaks of "entering the kingdom of God." Baptism in particular is the ritual whereby outsiders legitimately enter the realm of God: " 'Unless one is born of water and the spirit, he cannot enter the kingdom of God' " (John 3:5). Paul likewise understands baptism as the only valid way to cross the radical boundary separating God's holy realm from the kingdom of sin and death. In a number of places Paul speaks of baptism (Rom. 6:1–11; 1 Cor. 6:11; 10:1–4; Gal. 3:27–28), although he seems infrequently to have acted as the ritual elder presiding at the ritual (1 Cor. 1:14–17).

We do not intend to rehearse Paul's remarks on baptism, but rather to call attention to his perception of baptism in terms of boundary making and boundary crossing. In this regard, we may conveniently borrow from the analysis of baptism as ritual by Wayne Meeks (1983a:150–157). A complete analysis of baptism in terms of ritual process would describe its three stages: separation, liminality, and reaggregation. Neophytes are separated from their former pagan world, its temples and gods, its alleged life of vice, and its allegiance to Satan and his kingdom (see Eph. 4:17–5:20; 1 Peter 4:1–6). In their liminal state, neophytes are betwixt and between, still in the process of separating from the old, but not yet within the new. With the actual rite of washing, however, they cross that boundary; and legitimated by that ritual, they enter the holy temple of the church and are aggregated into God's society as saints and kin.

Let us focus on the language patterns by which Paul describes the boundary that must be crossed by baptism. Typical of Paul's dualistic perspectives, the language explaining the ritual of baptism is expressed in pairs of opposites:

| dying and death | vs. | life and rising |
| descending | vs. | ascending |
| burial | vs. | enthronement |

| flesh | vs. | spirit |
| vice | vs. | virtue |
| sin, stain | vs. | holiness, purity |
| idols, demons, | vs. | the living God and Jesus Christ, |
| and rulers | | the Lord |
| of this world | | |

Neophytes once were slaves of sin and death, under the dominion of Satan or other cosmic powers of evil. By baptism they are freed from such slavery to become servants of the living God and of the Lord Jesus. They were once sinful and stained with vice, but by baptism they are "washed . . . sanctified . . . justified" (1 Cor. 6:11). Instead of walking in vice and living fleshly lives, they are led by the Spirit and live spiritual lives of virtue (Gal. 5:16–25). Neophytes accomplish this transfer from the kingdom of Satan to that of God by imitating the ritual of Jesus himself—his death, burial, and resurrection. They die to sin and death, descend into the tomb, and are buried with Christ but rise with him to new life (Rom. 6:3–4). From being slaves in the realm where "death reigned" (Rom. 5:14, 17) and where "sin reigned" (Rom. 5:21; 6:12), they become servants in God's realm (Rom. 6:12–22).

In short, candidates for baptism leave one world, cross a boundary, and enter another world. The difference between the two worlds is itself expressed in terms of dualistic expressions that describe the irreconcilable differences between the before-and-after state of the entrance ritual of baptism:

| Former World | | New World |
| --- | --- | --- |
| darkness | vs. | light (Rom. 1:21; 2:19; 11:10; 1 Thess. 5:4–5; Eph. 4:17–18) |
| ignorance | vs. | knowledge (Eph. 4:18) |
| deceit | vs. | truth |
| drunkenness and sleep | vs. | sobriety and wakefulness (1 Thess. 5:6–7) |
| lust | vs. | holiness (1 Thess. 4:3–7) |
| blindness | vs. | sight (Rom. 2:19) |

Baptism, then, functions for Paul as a foundational boundary line, separating God's "saints" from the rest of the world.

**2.2.2 Circumcision** The premier entrance ritual in the synagogue was circumcision. By it an infant boy or an adult male was physically marked as a member of God's people and as a sharer in God's covenant. With it came the rights and duties of full members of Israel. We look at circumcision, however, through Paul's eyes. From his perspective, circumcision of Gentile Christians was not a ritual of entrance but of exit. This, of course, represents a radical change in perspective for Paul the Pharisee (Phil. 3:5–7).

After sharply drawing the boundary between synagogue and church, Paul reevaluated circumcision in the light of this perspective. Although Jews still practiced circumcision as an entrance ritual, Paul sees it as a ritual of exit, apostasy, when practiced by followers of Jesus. The crisis of Judaizing preachers in the Galatian churches galvanized Paul's perception. If a follower of Jesus were to be circumcised, "Christ will be of no advantage to you" (Gal. 5:2). Not only would the transfer noted above cease to operate, but those baptized would find themselves back across the boundary they thought they had crossed by baptism. Using a pun on the word *cut*, which makes up the word "circum*cision*," Paul says that if anyone baptized into Christ then "cuts" around the foreskin, they are themselves "cut off" from Christ: "You are severed from Christ" (Gal. 5:4). Judaizers proclaimed that glory comes from a circumcised penis; they want to make a good showing in the flesh of the hearers (Gal. 6:12–13). But Paul says that glory comes, not from circumcised flesh, but from the cross and from the crucified flesh of Christ (6:14). He glories in different marks on his flesh, not circumcision, but the wounds of Christ, which he shares by sharing Christ's rite of passage from death to life (6:17).

Neophytes, therefore, cannot participate in two entrance rituals—baptism and circumcision. Only baptism, the imitation of Christ's death and resurrection, constitutes the valid entrance ritual into Christ's body and God's new temple. Circumcision means entrance into the covenant of Moses, where "every man who receives circumcision . . . is bound to keep the whole law" (Gal. 5:3). One cannot enter two covenants. One cannot be both a follower of Moses and a follower of Je-·sus. To be circumcised, then, means to be "cut off" from Christ. Circumcision, then, becomes an exit ritual for Christians.

### 3.0 Maintaining Boundaries

Paul is intent on maintaining the boundaries he makes. They are necessary and vital defenses around the people whom God has separated from evil and sin; they are intended to guard and protect the holy flock of God. But boundaries, once erected, require maintenance. Guards must be posted to screen out trespassers. The householder does not know at what hour of the night the thief will break in and rob, so he must watch and be ready always (Matt. 24:42–44). But when he discovers a trespasser or thief, he must take appropriate ritual steps to expel the intruder and repair the breach in his walls. We turn now to consideration of the exit rituals that Paul talks about in terms of maintaining boundaries: God's judgment and the church's excommunication.

**3.1 Exit Ritual: Judgment** Many parables and sayings attributed to Jesus describe divine judgment as a separation ritual. Sheep are separated from goats, wise from foolish maidservants, and profitable from unprofitable servants (Matt. 25:1–46). Wheat is separated both from chaff (Matt. 3:12) and from weeds (Matt. 13:24–30); good fish are separated from bad ones (Matt. 13:47–50). Those without wedding garments are separated from those appropriately dressed; they are then bound and cast into the outer darkness (Matt. 22:11–13). Judgment, then, is an act of separation—that is, a ritual whereby a boundary is maintained—and what does not belong is expelled.

Not all who successfully perform the required entrance ritual may remain within. They may be forced to exit, both now (1 Cor. 5) and in the future. Twice Paul warns: "The unrighteous will not inherit the kingdom of God" (1 Cor. 6:9; Gal. 5:21), not meaning pagans, but sinful Christians. A more formal warning was given in 1 Corinthians 10:6–13 to those baptized, that they beware of lapsing from holiness (Meeks 1982b). Paul compares the Exodus generation to the church. Like the followers of Jesus, the generation that Moses led out of Egypt was "under the cloud" and "passed through the sea"; that is, its people were "baptized into Moses in the cloud and in the sea" (1 Cor. 10:2). After their entrance ritual, they participated in the group's ceremonial: they ate pneumatic food (manna, 10:3) and drank pneumatic drink (water from the rock, 10:4). But they lapsed from grace and were subject to subsequent exit rituals.

Interpreting Exodus 32:4 and 6 to the Corinthians, Paul tells how "the people sat down to eat and drink and rose up to dance" (1 Cor. 10:7//Ex. 32:6). Despite baptism, God was not pleased with them, and they were overthrown in the wilderness. Because of their immorality, twenty-three thousand fell in a single day (10:8); they put the Lord to the test and were destroyed by the Destroyer (10:9–10). In these verses, Paul describes a process in which the holy God judged that generation and discovered that they had lapsed from holiness into sin. Appropriately, God instigated an exit ritual, or status degradation ritual, whereby they were removed from the holy group and its boundary was repaired. Divine judgment, then, functions as an appropriate exit ritual.

In other places, Paul describes God's judgment as a trial in a courtroom. All must stand before the *bēma*, the judgment seat of the ruler (Rom. 14:10–12; 2 Cor. 5:10). They will render an account of all they have done, and "[God] will render to every man according to his works" (Rom. 2:6–11). Christ will act then as their advocate or defense lawyer (Rom. 8:33–34; see 5:9). He will "deliver [them] from the wrath to come" (1 Thess. 1:10).

Trials and judgment mean rituals of status transformation. The just will enter God's holy presence. The righteous will experience a status transformation ritual. Mortality will put on immortality, and their mortal, perishable nature will be clothed in imperishability (1 Cor. 15:53–54). For them, judgment becomes another entrance ritual as their status is transformed into glory and holiness. But those who do wickedness will not inherit the kingdom of God (1 Cor. 6:9; Gal. 5:21). Their status will be transformed from insider to outsider. Instead of another entrance ritual, they will be separated from the saints in an exit ritual.

**3.2 Exit Ritual: Excommunication**   The chapters in this book dealing with witchcraft accusations will examine in considerable detail rituals of excommunication. There is no need to repeat that material here. But readers should not think that, because our treatment of excommunication here is brief, it is insignificant in Paul's mind. The phenomenon may be found behind whole documents (Galatians; 2 Cor. 10–13), parts of letters (1 Cor. 5), or in passing remarks (Rom. 9:3; 1 Cor. 16:22).

Like judgment, excommunication is an exit ritual. Whereas judgment occurs at the end of time and before the throne of God, excommunication rituals happen now in the life of the church. The process is basically the same: when unholy and sinful persons are found within the holy church of God, a boundary has been breached. Excommunication rituals identify the culprits and demand their removal from the group, thus maintaining the group's boundaries. Like judgment, excommunication is a status transformation ritual: an insider is processed to become an outsider, with consequent loss of status.

Whatever the specific sin was, a certain man in the church at Corinth was found in an illicit sexual union. Although there have always been warnings against adultery and sexual immorality (1 Cor. 6:9), this particular sin is of a different magnitude: " . . . of a kind that is not found even among pagans" (1 Cor. 5:1). It is, moreover, scandalous in that it is corrupting the church. Some are arrogant about it, seeing no evil in it but maybe a demonstration of transcendence of earthly norms and rules (5:2). But Paul has labeled this sexual union as an exceptional sin that violates his Pharisaic sense of purity in regard to sexual unions (see 1 Thess. 4:3–7). From this perspective, then, radical action is warranted.

The ritual process of excommunication takes the form of a trial scene. The community must be assembled; even though Paul is absent in body, he is present in spirit, at least in this letter, which contains his "presence" and his explicit command. Together they must remove the public sinner from within the circle of the saints (1 Cor. 5:3–5). Why excommunication? Paul likens this sin to leaven fermenting dough. Recall that at Passover, Jews gathered all leaven and leavened products, threw them out of their houses, and burned them. Why? Because they perceive leaven as something that corrupts. Thus they celebrate their great holiday of freedom by symbolically becoming free from evil, corruption, and pollution. Paul applies these culturally specific ideas to this present situation, reminding the church that they too are celebrating a Passover ("Christ, our paschal lamb, has been sacrificed," 5:7b). Correspondingly, they must celebrate as well the Feast of Unleavened Bread, and "cleanse out the old leaven that you may be a new lump, as you really are unleavened" (5:7). As all know, even a little leaven will corrupt the whole lump (5:6).

In this scenario, intolerance is a fitting response; excommunication is appropriate. Paul cites a formal command of God as his warrant for acting this way: "Drive out the wicked person from among you" (5:3//Deut. 17:7; 19:19; 22:21, 24; 24:7). By excommunicating this person, the evil within is labeled as such and expelled. The boundaries that were breached are mended; a vigilant defense can continue.

## 4.0 Trespassing and Boundaries

Both heavenly judgments and earthly excommunications exemplify exit rituals and the maintenance of boundaries. In a striking number of places Paul discusses the same problem in terms of trespassing.

**4.1 Trespassing and Overextending Oneself**  According to Galatians 2:7–9, Paul perceives the world as divided into two mutually exclusive spheres. He works among the uncircumcised, while Peter labors as the apostle to the circumcised. By these remarks Paul indicates a strong spatial perception of his mission and territory, namely a sphere which is mentally fenced in and whose sovereignty must be respected.

To say the least, Paul makes it his boast *not* to intrude on the territory of others. His proposed journey to Rome might be the single exception to this (compare Rom. 1:11–13 with 15:18–29). The issue, however, might be more correctly stated by noting that Paul bitterly resents others coming into his territory. In 2 Corinthians 10–13 Paul responds in alarm and panic at *Because he regards* the arrival of "superlative apostles" on his turf (11:5). We will *them heretics* discuss the incident more in detail under the rubric of "witchcraft accusations" in the final chapter of this book. But here we note the Pauline perception of the church as his turf, which is now invaded by deceiving and polluting powers. The boundaries of his *map of apostolic space* are once more threatened.

The following translation of 2 Corinthians 10:13–16 highlights the spatial elements of Paul's language and thus brings out his sense of turf.

> v. 13 But we do not boast *beyond measure* (*eis ta ametra*) but [we remain] according to the *measure* (*metron*) of the rule/space (*tou kanonos*) which the God *of measure* (*theos metrou*) *divided* to us (*emerisen*) to *reach* even to you (*ephikesthai*).
>
> v. 14 For we did not *overextend* ourselves (*hyperekteinomenoi*) as though we did not *reach* as far as you (*ephiknoumenoi*), for we *arrived* [first] to you with the gospel of Christ (*ephthasamen*).
>
> v. 15 We do not boast *beyond measure* (*eis ta ametra*) in the labors of others, but having a hope that the growth of your faith [will mean] an increasing of our *space* (*kata ton kanona*), to a vast extent,
>
> v. 16 for the preaching of the gospel [in places] *beyond* you (*hyperekeina*), not in the *space* of another (*kanoni*) boasting of others' [achievements].

The resources of the present study will help us to discern Paul's perceptions here.

Paul envisions God as the Sovereign Orderer who "allots" (*merizein*) specific portions of territory to specific people (2 Cor. 10:13; 1 Cor. 7:17; Rom. 12:3). Accordingly, God "divides" the portions. In this context the exact proportion, or limit, of God's "measure" is important. Twice Paul remarks on *not* boasting "beyond measure" (10:13, 15). According to the perceptions of a purity system, the exact measure is sacred and should neither be augmented nor diminished; too much or too little distorts boundaries and renders something unclean. Yet the "measure" Paul envisions is not a quantity of something (e.g., Matt. 7:2), but area or space. We know this from the context of the passage: Paul speaks about "reaching" and "arriving [first]" at Corinth (10:13–14). And his concern is with those who are "overreaching" certain territorial boundaries, namely, the superlative apostles who arrived lately in Corinth.

In this light, we note how the Greek word *kanōn* in 10:13 and 15 has spatial connotations, which are clearly evident in its use in verse 16. For in 10:16 Paul compares and contrasts his behavior with that of his rivals: they boast "beyond measure," but he does *not* boast beyond measure; they have "overextended" themselves by coming onto the turf of another, but he will never expand by working in the space of another. In 10:13–16, then, Paul understands a map of apostolic space, a "land grant" from God. All should respect it because God apportioned it thus, but in Paul's eyes, that is not the case. The boundaries are clearly marked as Paul's turf, but they are breached, and no small harm is occurring as a result. In Paul's eyes, the rival preachers are trespassing.

This is no minor matter for Paul, for in several places he expresses displeasure with trespassing on his turf (Phil. 1:15–18; 1 Cor. 3:5–9, 10–15). In other situations, however, Paul attacks the trespassers by labeling them as agents of Satan (2 Cor. 11:3, 13–15) or as witches (Gal. 3:1). These examples suggest, then, a strong Pauline perception of a map of apostolic space. He stands on guard constantly to defend his turf.

Thus far we have visualized the crisis in terms of trespassers raiding Paul's pastures. Paul uses a second metaphor in this regard when he describes the church as a building rising on a foundation. He describes himself as a master builder who "laid a foundation, and another man is building upon it" (1 Cor. 3:10). The remark is not devoid of a sense of proprietorship and even of anger and threat. Paul deeply resents the idea of another building on his foundation, to judge from the warnings and threats that follow (3:11–17). At the end of Romans we find a similar remark in which Paul boasts that he, at least, has not poached on the territory of other apostles: " . . . making it my ambition to preach the gospel, not where Christ has already been named, lest I build on another's foundation" (15:20). The "lest" implies that such intrusion is wrong, and Paul for one is not guilty of this breach. The metaphor is again spatial, and the perception is of a violation of territory. Boundaries are clear and should be observed, but they are not! People are not only trespassing on forbidden turf, but builders are arrogantly distorting the architect's plans for the new temple.

When Paul perceives that trespassers have entered his turf and threaten the church (as temple, body, or bride), his characteristic ritual is to sound the alarm and rush to the breach in the boundary. He must identify the trespasser and then demand his expulsion back across the fence. In short, he demands an exit ritual that will purify his pasture and rebuild its fences.

**4.2 Trespassing in the Sacred Space of the Church** When we studied the various maps whereby Paul and others classify persons, things, and times in their world, we noted that they tend also to make maps of places. For Jews the symbolic geography of Genesis 1 and the architecture of the Temple adequately embody this mapping of spaces. Yet Paul and others in his world explicitly reject the map of places represented by the Temple; for him there seems to be no fixed sacred space, no sacred mountain to which pilgrimage is made, no sacred grove or spring. Jerusalem retains symbolic importance for Paul, not because of the Temple, but because of the presence there of the "pillars of the church" (Johnson 1977). The collection is not simply alms to the Christian poor, for the poor are with us everywhere. Rather, Paul's alms for the Christian poor of Jerusalem indicate a centripetal movement acknowledging the central authority of the group (Malina 1986b:106–110). But like the remarks in John 4:21: "Neither on this mountain nor in Jerusalem will you worship," there is no fixed sacred space.

This does not mean that Paul and others have no sense of a map of place. Although they declassify certain Jewish maps, they retain a keen sense of space that is carefully mapped. Paul focuses his attention both on internal geography of the group and on its external boundaries, namely, the frontiers, walls, fences around it. Let us examine some of these patterns.

Turning first to the external boundaries of the church, we can identify three dominant metaphors for it. They all imply a sense of space with exact and precise boundaries. The church may be a temple (1 Cor. 3:16–17; 2 Cor. 6:16), a body (1 Cor. 12:14–25; Rom. 12:3–8), or a bride (2 Cor. 11:3, 13). Although such metaphors might also invite comment about their internal patterns and order, Paul's use of them tends to focus on their boundaries, especially as these are under attack. These metaphors, then, express Paul's sense of boundary maintenance.

*[handwritten margin note: This is not the point of these metaphors]*

***4.2.1 The Church as Temple*** According to 1 Corinthians 3, Paul maps the church as a temple. This metaphor replicates a conflict over another map of considerable importance to Paul, the map of persons whereby he and Apollos are evaluated and ranked by the church. Paul perceives considerable support for Apollos, which he typically interprets as diminishment of his own status. The accomplishments of Apollos are evident to all, accomplishments that Paul appears to lack: wisdom, eloquence, strength, and power. At first, Paul seems to make light of any rivalry between himself and Apollos: they are both servants of God laboring in God's field. "I planted, Apollos watered, but God gave the growth" (3:6). "He who plants and he who waters are equal" (3:8). But this does not solve Paul's problem of loss of honor and status; and he certainly is not content to remain in second place, although the exact formula for stating this will have to be carefully nuanced. If the church is a "field," Paul's status vis-à-vis Apollos is hinted at in the map of time applied to the two of them: Paul is first in that he "planted"; Apollos is second in that he "watered" what Paul planted.

*But see also 1 Cor 3:5.*

The metaphor of the church shifts from field to building: "You are God's field, God's building" (3:9). At this point Paul can more openly assert his claim to precedence in 3:10–12. His claim rests on his authorization: "According to the [commission] of God given to me." That commission was to be "a skilled [wise] master builder"; he notes: "I laid a foundation, and another man is building upon it" (3:10). As in the case of the field, Paul's place on the map of persons in the church is grounded on his temporal precedence as the first builder, who laid the foundation, as well as his authorization as a wise master builder. He is, moreover, quite confident about the quality of his work, but demands that other work on the building be carefully judged (3:12–15). Yet his remarks are clearly judgmental; he is perturbed about the building that is rising on his foundation (3:12–15).

As the one who first planted and who laid the foundation, Paul continues to speak. As "first" and as master builder, he claims ultimate responsibility for his field and building. Yet this building is no shed for housing animals, no silo for storing grain, not even a home for people, but a temple. Temples must be pure and clean; hence the warning that follows: "Do you not know that you are God's temple and that God's Spirit dwells in you? If any one destroys God's temple, God will destroy him" (3:16–17a).

The verb *destroy* (*phtheirein*) can mean "to corrupt" or "to seduce (virgins)." Hence it connotes pollution, the loss of purity. And how is a temple corrupted but by the presence within its boundaries of someone or some thing that is unclean. This might be a pig sacrificed on the high altar (Mark 13:14//Dan. 12:11), Roman army standards in Jerusalem (Josephus, *Antiquities* 18:55–59), or Gentiles entering the sacred courts (Philo, *On the Embassy to Gaius* 212; Segal 1989:70). The perception is spatial; something unclean has crossed the boundary meant to protect pure space, and pollution occurs. In the case of 1 Corinthians 3:16–17, the space is not just any mapped territory, but the holiest of spaces, a temple where God's Spirit dwells. *Corruptio optimi est pessima!* Given this perspective, exit rituals are an appropriate response.

**4.2.2 The Church as Body** In two letters Paul speaks of the church as a "body" (1 Cor. 12:12–26; Rom. 12:3–8). As in the case of church-as-temple, a map of place is implied in the metaphor of church-as-body. Just as the boundary walls define and protect temples, so bodies too enjoy a natural shape with clear external boundaries (skin, clothing). The cultural perception of the body will be specifically examined in the next chapter, but for the present we note that a body's purity is related to two aspects: (1) what enters and leaves its orifices (e.g., food, semen, menses, tears, etc.) and (2) its integrity or wholeness. Bodies are pure when whole. An unwhole body is unholy; it may not come into the presence of God to offer a gift (Lev. 21:16–20); an animal that is not whole (i.e., that is blemished) may not be offered in sacrifice. Hence, the wholeness of the physical body is essential to its holiness; the loss of an eye, a foot, a hand, or sexual organs renders a body unwhole and so unholy.

Yet Paul fears just such mutilation in regard to the church-as-body at Corinth. As we noted earlier in regard to 1 Corinthians 12:12–27, the wholeness of the body of Christ is threatened when some say: "I do not belong to the body" (12:15, 16). It is equally threatened when some say: "I have no need of you" (12:21). If both voices were true, the body would be radically diminished, first by the loss of those who feel that they do not belong, and second by the amputation by those who find certain parts unnecessary. Mutilation would result, and with loss of wholeness, a corresponding loss of holiness. Thus Paul perceives any threat of division and loss of unity in the body as an attack on the boundaries of holy space (1 Cor. 1:10, 13; 3:1; 11:18; 12:25; Gal. 5:20). Yet according to Paul's map of space, the group's boundaries are threatened, and so attention and energy are focused there.

***4.2.3 The Church as Bride*** Much is implied in this metaphor of the church in 2 Corinthians 11:2–3. Presumed here is the positive value of female "shame," the virtue of women in Paul's world, whereby they are sexually exclusive (Malina 1981:42–47). A bride must be a virgin, pure and spotless (2 Cor. 11:2; see Eph. 5:26–27). As the spouse of "one husband," she must be guarded against the seductions of other men. Yet such maidens are eminently desirable and so the object of deceit, seduction, rape, and the like. Of course, this perception evokes a sense of boundaries both guarded yet attacked.

*[margin note: "one husband" is Christ, not Paul.]*

Paul, then, perceives the church in spatial terms, as a pure young woman, which is an extension of his metaphor of church-as-body. Moreover, the holiness of this body is not simply its limbs, but its orifices; and in particular, the sexual orifice, which is guarded by a membrane of skin, the hymen. Paul states that he feels "divine jealousy" on behalf of the church, as befits the father of a bride (2 Cor. 11:2). Jealousy here means defense of what belongs to Paul, that is, the holiness of the church. He fears for her that she is being seduced by suitors who preach a new gospel or a different doctrine (2 Cor. 11:3–4). Paul compares the situation to the seduction of Eve by Satan, which intensifies his perception of the situation at Corinth as a tragic threat to holiness and a definitive loss of primal innocence and purity. In short, a map of the physical body serves as a map of space for the church. But that space is threatened by uncleanness. A boundary, the hymen, is besieged and must be defended.

In summary, the three metaphors of the church all express maps of place that separate holy space from its secular surrounding. They imply that boundaries have been made and must be maintained. Yet in Paul's perspective, those boundaries seem constantly under attack by evil. He sees the temple in danger of being "corrupted," the body threatened with "mutilation," and the bride being "seduced." There is correspondingly little interest in mapping out the internal space, such as we find in maps concerning the Jerusalem Temple (see *m. Kelim* 1:6–9). Paul focuses intensely on the boundaries of the map, which are always precarious and in a state of threat.

## 5.0 Maintaining Internal Lines: Challenge and Rivalry

Thus far we have examined Paul's persistent effort to make and maintain the external boundaries that define, separate, and guard the church. But in his perspective, there are internal lines within the church that likewise need to be made and maintained. Certain internal lines map out positions of authority, rank, and status among the members of the church. It is surely an understatement that Paul experiences challenges to his own position in the church, his authority and status. In his view, these boundary lines are attacked, just like the external boundaries of the group. Therefore, Paul labors to maintain them.

***5.1 Authority Problems*** This material will not be new to the reader. In Chapter 2 we examined two sets of maps: maps of heavenly persons and maps of church persons. In regard to Paul's map of heavenly persons, he labored to clarify the nature of the heavenly hierarchy. God ranks above all, followed by Christ and then by the Spirit. We suggested that Paul's purpose in describing such maps lay in settling internal disputes in the church. Paul perceived some people promoting pneumatic gifts and powers so that they seemed to replace Jesus with Spirit under the rubric of freedom. Moreover, some celebrated their sharing in Christ's resurrection as a denial of all authority, certainly in heaven and desirably on earth. Paul's response was a map of divine hierarchy in the macrocosm, which legitimates comparable maps in the microcosm on earth. Paul's maps, then, served to make boundaries where none might have existed before and to maintain them when threatened.

***5.2 Challenge/Riposte*** In regard to the internal workings of the church, Paul articulated many maps of church persons. He affirms his legitimate place on the map of apostles to whom Christ appeared and whom he commissioned (1 Cor. 15:6–11). In regard to factions favoring one leader over another, he argued for his rightful place as father (4:14–15), planter (3:4–9), and master builder of the church at Corinth (3:10). In regard to disputes about spiritual gifts, which are disputes about the ranking and prominence of persons in the church, Paul affirmed a map that confirmed his premier gift as apostle and so his precedence as the leader of the group (12:28; 9:1). In each of these three arguments, Paul perceived the lines of the maps of internal space in the church threatened and attacked; he labored to maintain them.

Paul's efforts to make and maintain both sets of maps are further illustration of the argument of this chapter. Paul would gladly presume such maps and enjoy their confirmation in ceremonies that celebrate such arrangements. This is done regularly by ceremonies such as the celebration of the birthdays of past American presidents, reigning monarchs, bishops, and so forth. But such ceremonies never took place in Paul's experience, with the exception of his own pilgrimage to Jerusalem (Gal. 2:1–10). Instead, Paul experienced challenges to such maps of authority and status (1 Cor. 1–4).

## 6.0 Summary and Further Investigation

Paul's perception of the universe as an orderly cosmos is confirmed by our examination of both ceremonies and rituals. Ceremonies function to confirm patterns of order and classification. Rituals likewise presume patterns of order and systems of social lines that define space, time, and roles. These patterns and lines are not innocently crossed, and so elaborate rituals exist to make the transition orderly.

Yet as we study Paul's letters, we note not only his perception of and desire for order and clear structures in the church, but his acute sense of a world whose external and internal lines are threatened. Internally, divisions and rivalry threaten the unity of the church; lines demarking role and status are being crossed by unauthorized persons. Externally, the boundaries of the church are attacked by disguised seducers (2 Cor. 11) and by bewitching teachers (Gal. 3:1). Polluting sin is being found within the temple-church (1 Cor. 5). The more valued the boundaries, the more intense Paul's sense of their vulnerability.

In regard to rites, then, Paul may be said to give more attention to rituals than to ceremonies. His attention is focused on boundaries, external and internal. He labors either to make them when necessary or to maintain them when threatened or attacked. Although ceremonies are known and celebrated in his churches, they seem unable to confirm the unity and stability needed for the group. Status transformation rituals, either entrance or exit rituals, dominate Paul's perception. Given his perception of an orderly universe under attack, this focus is neither unreasonable nor unpredictable. Paul's defensive behavior, then, should be seen for what it is—a pervasive and consistent reaction to perceived attack on every side.

Given this information, readers might well continue this investigation of Paul's sense of rites. We identified several ceremonial actions (meals, the collection, and letter writing). These ceremonies presume an elaborate system of maps of persons, places, and things. Each of them deserves to be considered more carefully in terms both of systems of order and elements of ceremony. Similarly, Paul speaks of many more rituals than were noted here. In particular, one might study the status transformation rituals of Jesus, his cross and his enthronement in heaven (Gal. 3:13; Phil. 2:6–11; 1 Cor. 15:22–28). In regard to specific exit rituals, one might pay closer attention to Paul's use of the term *anathema* (Rom. 9:3; 1 Cor. 12:3; 16:22; and Gal. 1:8–9).

# 5

# Perceiving the Human Body:
# Body Language
# in 1 Corinthians

The body is not meant for immorality, but for the Lord, and the Lord for the body.

1 Corinthians 6:13

So glorify God in your body.

1 Corinthians 6:20

## 1.0 Introduction

Marcel Mauss once observed that there is no such thing as natural bodily behavior. Every kind of action carries the imprint of learning (Mauss 1973:70–76). Bodily behavior, it is argued, is learned behavior; and if learned, it reflects the values, expectations, and customs of those from whom it is learned. This may sound strange to Western ears, in light of the fact that one of the most recent popular books is *Our Bodies, Our Selves*. It argues that the human body should *not* be subject to the controls of someone else. But even so, its argument admits what this chapter is all about: we learn to think of our bodies and govern and control them according to norms given us by our culture. People in Paul's world were group-oriented people who were strongly shaped by their peers; people in North America and Northern Europe are individualists who argue for the right to choose for themselves what norms or laws bind them.

Therefore, we are led right back into the area of a symbolic worldview, purity systems, and social perceptions. These concepts can aid us in appreciating the way New Testament people, Jesus, the early church, and Paul perceived their world and comparably perceived and regulated the physical body. Moreover, anthropologists like Marcel Mauss and Mary Douglas can offer us concepts and models to learn to perceive the physical human body as a cultural artifact, that is, as an object perceived and regulated according to the norms and values of the social body. With these new lens, we will study the way Paul perceives and regulates the human body in 1 Corinthians.

## 2.0 The Model: Perceiving the Physical Body

*2.1 Social Body/Physical Body*  In a series of studies, Douglas put forth a hypothesis about the physical human body as a symbol of the social body. In *Purity and Danger* she focused on issues of purity and pollution, and in that context she sought to explain how for ancient Jews pollution was associated with contact with bodily excreta (spittle, menses, semen, excrement). In explaining this, she advanced the idea of the symbolic correspondence between society and physical body as macrocosm to microcosm. Speaking of the social body, she noted:

> The idea of society is a powerful image. . . . This image has form; it has external boundaries, margins, internal structure. (Douglas 1966:114)

Highlighting these three aspects of society (boundaries, margins, and structure), Douglas then suggested that the human body symbolizes the social body and may be studied also in terms of these three aspects:

> The body is a model which can stand for any bounded system. Its boundaries can represent any boundaries which are threatened or precarious. The body is a complex structure. The functions of its different parts and their relation afford a source of symbols for other complex structures. We cannot possibly interpret rituals concerning excreta, breast milk, saliva and the rest unless we are prepared to see in the body a symbol of society, and to see the powers and dangers credited to social structure reproduced in small on the human body. (Douglas 1966:115)

In *Purity and Danger* her analysis focused on bodily margins and bodily exuviae, inasmuch as the book concerned itself with the issues of purity and pollution. But the basic elements of a more comprehensive theory were advanced: (a) symbolic correspondence between social and physical body and (b) analysis of structure, boundaries, and margins.

In a subsequent book, *Natural Symbols*, Douglas explained the demise of ritual in modern society. In this context she developed in greater detail her characteristic interest in social control, which in her jargon she calls "group," that is, group pressure to perceive reality in certain shared ways and to conform one's behavior to such shared perceptions. Enlarging on the importance of shared social norms in regard to bodily behavior, she summarized the insight of Marcel Mauss: "Mauss saw that the study of bodily techniques would have to take place within a study of symbolic systems" (Douglas 1982a:65). How the body is perceived, then, relates to how the cosmos is perceived.

Building on the insight that there is a correlation between the social body (culture, system) and the physical body, Douglas stated her theory more clearly:

> The social body constrains the way the physical body is perceived. The physical experience of the body, always modified by the social categories through which it is known, sustains a particular view of society. There is a continual exchange of meanings between the two kinds of bodily experience so that each reinforces the categories of the other. (Douglas 1982a:65)

Therefore, she advanced the key concept that governs her investigation, the influence of social control on bodily control:

> Consequently I now advance the hypothesis that bodily control is an expression of social control—abandonment of bodily control in ritual responds to the requirements of a social experience which is being expressed. (Douglas 1982a:70–71)

At this point we may draw heavily on the previous chapters of this book, for in them we have attempted to sketch the symbolic system and the patterns of order and classification of the world as Paul and his contemporaries perceived them. From our study of various maps shared by Paul and other Jews, we gained quite definite ideas about Paul's perception of the social body, what it accepts or does not accept, and how it constrains or controls.

Control, then, is the key concept. But what is being controlled in regard to the physical body? Just as society has boundaries, margins, and internal structure, so has the physical body. And these are subject to varying degrees of social control.

The human body is always treated as an image of society and

... there can be no natural way of considering the body that
does not involve at the same time a social dimension. Interest in
its apertures depends on the preoccupation with social exits and
entrances, escape routes and invasions. If there is no concern to
preserve social boundaries, I would not expect to find concern
with bodily boundaries. The relation of head to feet, of brain
and sexual organs, of mouth and anus are commonly treated so
that they express the relevant patterns of hierarchy. (Douglas
1982a:70)

Although this triple aspect of the body first mentioned in *Purity and Danger* returns, Douglas now gives formal attention to
(1) internal structure ("the relation of head to feet . . . patterns
of hierarchy"), (2) boundaries, and (3) margins ("exits and entrances").

In summary, the physical body may be viewed as a symbol of
the social body. Like the social body, it has three specific areas
to which we must attend: (1) structure—the relationship of its
parts; (2) boundaries—defenses around it; and (3) margins—
entrances, exits, and their exuviae. The social body and physical body are related as macrocosm to microcosm. Controls operative in the social body tend to be replicated in control of the
physical body.

**2.2 Control and Noncontrol: Suggested Patterns**  In trying to
show the replication of attitudes between physical and social
bodies, Douglas suggests a series of contrasting terms: (a) for-
mal/informal, (b) smooth/shaggy, (c) structured/unstructured,
and (d) ritualism/effervescence.

**Formal/Informal:** A controlled physical body may be described as *formal*. In social terms this means "social distance,
well-defined, public and insulated roles" (1982a:71). An uncontrolled physical body is *informal*, which means "role confusion, familiarity, intimacy" (Douglas 1982a:71).

**Smooth/Shaggy:** These terms express much the same as *for-
mal/informal*. *Smooth* is appropriate where group ideals are
clear, where roles are defined, and where ladders of authority
or pyramidal structures exist. *Shaggy* denotes individualism,
criticism of the system, less commitment to role or structure
(1982a:72).

**Structured/Unstructured:** These terms are borrowed from
Talcott Parsons (1956:236). In highly *structured* situations
there is a minimum of possible responses other than the ones

required by the norms of the situation. Conversely, the less highly structured situations are, the more informality is valued, the greater the tendency to abandon reason and follow crazes, and the more license for bodily expressions of abandonment (1982a:73).

**Ritualism/Effervescence:** The final pair of labels describing social control or its absence is *ritualism* (strong control) and *effervescence* (uncontrol) (1982a:73–74). According to Douglas, the conditions for *ritualism* occur when (a) there is an articulated and controlled social structure, (b) interpersonal relationships are subordinated to public patterns of roles, and (c) society is differentiated and exalted over the self. *Effervescence* occurs when (a) there is a lack of articulation in social structure and weak control, (b) little distinction is recognized between public and interpersonal relations, and (c) society is not differentiated from self. *Ritualism* is symbolized in differentiation of roles, sacramental attitudes to rites, distinctions between inside and outside, and a high value placed on control of consciousness. *Effervescence* is expressed in diffused symbols, preference for spontaneity, absence of interest in magic or sacraments, and the absence of control over consciousness.

These four pairs of contrasting concepts capture in their own ways the major factor that Douglas advances for perceiving the body in cultural perspective, namely, control or noncontrol.

| **Control** | **Noncontrol** |
|---|---|
| Formal | Informal |
| Smooth | Shaggy |
| Structure | Unstructure |
| Ritualism | Effervescence |

**2.3 Correlation: Social Control/Body Control** In *Natural Symbols*, Douglas developed a model for assessing the degree of control or noncontrol over a social body. Social systems exert varying pressure on their members to conform to societal norms. Where there is strong group pressure, the body is imaged as a controlled or bounded system; entrances and exits are guarded; order and discipline are valued; personality is not individualistic; and group values predominate. Where group pressure is weak, the body is not perceived as a controlled system; entrances and exits to the body are porous; norms and discipline are not valued; and personality is very individualistic.

Social groups have cosmologies, that is, particular views of the world and one's place in it. Because the physical body is controlled in ways that replicate the way the social body is perceived and structured, let us briefly suggest the typical attitudes of both strong and weak controlled groups. Understanding these, we may better see what type of body control or its lack is consonant with such cultural viewpoints.

**2.3.1 Cosmology of a Controlled Body**  We are, of course, using here the basic anthropological categories that we employed earlier in this book for understanding Paul's cosmology or viewpoint.

**Purity:** In a strongly controlled social group, we tend to find a correspondingly strong concern for the purity of the social and physical body. As we saw, purity refers to the ordering, classification, and structuring of the social world; it means an avoidance of all that violates that sense of order. In terms of the physical body, it means identification of and distancing of oneself from "dirt" (spittle, feces, menses), which socially means concern over persons and events that do not fit the group's ideals and sense of order (i.e., whatever violates its rules).

**Ritual:** There are fixed rituals for determining where the lines and boundaries of the ordered system lie and who is properly within the body and who is not (i.e., concern over boundaries of the body). And there are ritual symbols that express the internal classification system of the group. Every body has a place and knows where it is; hence, boundaries that define location are carefully drawn, and entrances into and exits from carefully defined space are guarded. Authority, status, and roles are clear and clearly expressed.

**Personal Identity:** Identity here is nonindividualistic and group oriented. One's role and place in the group is assigned and learned.

**Body:** Social and physical bodies are strongly controlled. Along with a strong sense of purity goes a protection of the body from threatening pollutions.

**Sin:** This is defined not simply as violation of rules but as pollution that invades the body and threatens to pollute its pure insides. Moral norms are well defined and are sociocentric, that is, learned from the group and measured in those terms.

### 2.3.2 Cosmology of an Uncontrolled Body

**Purity:** There is a reactionary or weak concern for purity. This implies considerable tolerance for diversity and plurality.

**Ritual:** Again, there is a rejection of strong entrance rituals into the group or of clear boundaries around it. There tends to be a weak internal classification system, implying fluid social status. Effervescence and spontaneity are valued here.

**Personal Identity:** Society is seen as oppressive; assigned roles are rejected. Personal and social control are devalued; therefore, individualism is pronounced.

**Body:** The body is not perceived as a bounded system, and there is no sense of protecting its orifices and its purity. The body is not a symbol of life, for life is spiritual.

**Sin:** This is a matter of personal ethical decisions and interiority, rather than a violation of sociocentric norms.

**2.3.3 Cosmology and Body Control** From these contrasting cosmologies we can describe contrasting attitudes to the body. Where there is strong pressure to conform to social norms, the body is perceived as a bounded system, strongly controlled. It is considered as a "holy" or "pure" body, and so it guards its orifices (eyes, ears, genitals) and maintains firm and clear boundaries. Its concern for order and clarity makes it fear unconsciousness, fainting, or any loss of control. It will tend to take a negative view of ecstasy or spirit possession. It is a regulated and harmonious body whose individual parts are disciplined and coordinated for group action, as in the case of an athlete.

Where social control and pressure are weak, the body is not perceived as a bounded system, nor is it strongly controlled. There is no fear of pollutants around the body, and so there is no control over its orifices and boundaries, namely, what it sees or hears, to whom it is joined in marriage or sexual union. Porosity to its environment is accompanied by a celebration of freedom of movement and spontaneity of individual members of the body. Trances and spirit possession are looked upon favorably.

Thus, as we approach 1 Corinthians, we are aware of an intense concern with the body, yet of contrasting points of view in the church. The conflict may be about specific rules governing this or that bodily action, but at stake is a larger conflict about how the world works and how individuals fit into it. The physical body is a microcosm of the macrocosmic symbolic universe.

**2.4 Bodily Structure, Boundaries, Margins**   As social bodies are perceived to have boundaries, internal structures, and margins, so it is with physical bodies.

**2.4.1 Internal Structure**   Just as well-regulated societies have clearly assigned roles, so too there will tend to be a corresponding replication of this in the way the physical body is perceived. Hierarchy of social roles is mirrored in a hierarchy of bodily parts: eyes over ears, hands over feet (1 Cor. 12). Right is preferred to left (Needham 1973) and higher to lower (Schwartz 1981). Rulers of society may be described as "heads" of the body (Eph. 1:22–23), with other roles corresponding to other bodily parts (Eph. 4:11–12, 16). Such metaphors were commonplace in antiquity (Nestle 1927; Conzelmann 1975:211).

**2.4.2 Boundaries**   Boundaries may be the external perimeter that defines and guards, or the series of internal lines that map out proper identity and place. The external boundary of the physical body is its skin and, by extension, clothing and hair, which replicate it. Because clothing denotes gender classification, women should wear women's clothing and men men's (Deut. 22:5). Certain clothing, moreover, indicates social location or special classification, such as priestly garments (Ex. 28). Observant Jews, for example, wear clothing that tells of this concern, namely, phylacteries (Matt. 23:5) and tefillin. Nudity removes social classification and so blurs the map of persons that it signifies; hence nudity is pollution and shame (Gen. 3:9–11; Ezek. 16:39). Corresponding observations can be made about hairstyles that are appropriate to men and women; certain hairstyles are masculine, others feminine. For men to wear their hair in the fashion of women or women in the style of men would be a pollution (Murphy-O'Connor 1980).

There are also internal boundary lines that distinguish and define the proper place of persons and things. A strict classification system in the social body is intended to bring clarity and ensure that persons, things, places, and times are fully in their right place. Ideally, there should be no bulges or dents in these lines; there should not be too much or too little.

In regard to the physical body, "too much" means that something spills over into areas where it does not belong. Six fingers on a hand is "too much" (2 Sam. 21:20). Similarly, bodies might have "too little" and so be defective and unclean. Eunuchs, those with damaged testicles, and those without a penis lack adequate sexual organs to be classified as males (*t. Meg.* 2:7). Thus bodies have boundaries: (a) external boundary lines such as skin, clothing, and hair, and (b) internal boundary lines such as cultural definitions of male and female or ideas of physical wholeness.

**2.4.3 *Margins and Orifices*** The boundary of the body, moreover, is punctuated at fixed points by orifices that are gateways into and out of it, just as walled cities have gates with guards and countries have ports of entry with customs checkpoints. Because they are gates to the interior, the bodily orifices must screen out what does not belong and guard against an enemy or a pollution entering. The guarded orifices are the eyes, ears, mouth, and genitals.

Great scrutiny is given to the margins of the body and its orifices in terms of what enters or leaves them. For example, the *eye* is "the lamp of the body"; if it is sound, the whole body will be full of light; but if not, the whole body will be filled with darkness (Matt. 6:22–23). In Jewish culture, the *mouth* is strictly guarded against unkosher foods, for unclean foods render the whole body unclean (Acts 10:14). In regard to the *sexual orifice*, we find rules for intermarriage that prescribe and proscribe who may cross the sexual orifice and who may marry whom (Lev. 18:6–23; Neh. 13:23–28; *m. Kid.* 4:1; Jeremias 1969:271–274). Moreover, danger and pollution are attached to semen and menses, which flow from the sexual orifice. Attention, then, is given to the exits and entrances of the body, its margins and their orifices.

**2.5 *The Body and Purity Perceptions*** Physical bodies not only are perceived in terms of structure, boundaries, and margins; they can be labeled "pure" and "polluted." We cannot read the Jewish or Christian documents from the time of Jesus and Paul without being aware of how such categories figured in their perceptions. Leviticus contained an elaborate grammar of bodily pollutions that would be developed later in the Mishnah and rabbinic literature. The priestly caste and those who shared their perspective, that is, the Pharisees, already attended to such concerns in the time of Jesus and Paul. As a perfect Pharisee, Paul would have been socialized to concern himself with bodily purity and pollution (e.g., the washing of hands, kosher foods, etc.). What constitutes purity and pollution in regard to the physical body?

The earlier chapter on purity systems and order treated in detail the importance Paul and others gave to labels such as "clean" and "unclean," "pure" and "polluted." We will draw upon that material in this study of the purity of physical body (Douglas 1966:118–127; see Malina 1981:122–137; Neyrey 1988c). In general, purity and pollution in regard to the physical body have to do with completeness and wholeness. But how are these understood?

**2.5.1 Completeness** Completeness is an abstract idea that may be visualized in specific ways. Were we studying the actions of Jesus in the Gospels, we would pay considerable attention to the bodily boundary, which is its skin, because what peels off the body (leprosy) is incomplete in that it has separated from its proper place, the body (Pilch 1981). We recall the abstract definition of purity and pollution: what is in place is clean, but what is out of place is unclean. The definition depends on knowing what a given culture perceives as "in place" or "out of place." In regard to Paul the Pharisee, skin flaking off the body surface is matter that is out of place (likewise pus or fluids from a blemish on that surface).

As we saw, boundary lines exist not just on the external perimeter of something but within an organism as well. They are intended to define and locate things exactly. What resides completely within its defining lines is clean. But what bulges, dents the lines, or crosses them is unclean: it is "too much." Likewise, what does not completely fill the lines is "too little," and so unclean. For example, a hermaphrodite is too much in that it is both male and female (*t. Meg.* 2:7). The boundary lines distinguishing both male and female are blurred here. In a similar vein, effeminate males and masculine females are too much, affecting both male and female behaviors (Murphy-O'Connor 1980:482–500).

Completeness has to do also with bodily margins, that is, with bodily orifices and exuviae from them (e.g., tears, spittle, menses, semen, excrement). Such things, when they exit from the body, are perceived to be out of place, and therefore dangerous and polluting. Contact with them renders one unclean. One need only recall the crisis created with the touch of Jesus by a menstruating woman (Mark 5:25–34) or with the tears and kisses of a sinner woman (Luke 7:38–39). Leviticus already provided Jews with an elaborate catalog of such pollutions. And subsequent generations would later create *maps of uncleanness* related to bodily exuviae, such as the following:

1. There are things that convey uncleanness by contact (e.g., a dead creeping thing, male semen).
2. They are exceeded by carrion . . .
3. They are exceeded by him who has connection with a menstruant . . .
4. They are exceeded by the issue of him who has a flux, by his spittle, his semen, and his urine . . .
5. They are exceeded by [the uncleanness of] what is ridden upon [by him who has a flux] . . .
6. [The uncleanness of] what is ridden upon [by him who has a flux] is exceeded by what he lies upon . . .
7. [The uncleanness of] what he lies upon is exceeded by the uncleanness of him who has a flux . . . (*m. Kelim* 1:3).

One aspect of bodily purity, then, is completeness. Something must be *completely* in place to fulfill its category. What is incomplete, what does not fulfill a cultural definition, and what seeps out of the body's orifices is out of place, and so unclean or polluted.

### 2.5.2 Wholeness

Cleanness and purity are also related to what is whole and physically perfect. In a new sense, the body must not be too much or too little. We can illustrate this simply by asking, What kind of animal was fit to be offered to God in sacrifice? Only clean animals (by definition), and then only those whole and unblemished (Lev. 22:20–21; Num. 19:2; Deut. 15:21). Correspondingly, certain people were prohibited from offering bread to God in the Temple, namely, those whose bodies were not physically perfect:

> "Say to Aaron, None of your descendants throughout their generations who has a blemish may approach to offer the bread of his God. For no one who has a blemish shall draw near, a man blind or lame, or one who has a mutilated face or a limb too long, or a man who has an injured foot or an injured hand, or a hunchback, or a dwarf, or a man with a defect in his sight or an itching disease or scabs or crushed testicles."
>
> Leviticus 21:16–21 (see 1QSa 2:3–10; 1QM 7:4–7)

Lack of bodily wholeness, however it occurred, was perceived as a lack of holiness and purity.

It follows, then, that any attempt to blemish the body physically or to sever even a small part of it would be perceived as rendering it unclean. Josephus illustrates this clearly when Antigonus mutilated Hyrcanus's body, thus disqualifying him for the role of high priest:

> Hyrcanus threw himself at the feet of Antigonus, who with his own teeth lacerated his suppliant's ears, in order to disqualify him for ever, under any change of circumstances, from resuming the high priesthood; since freedom from physical defect is essential to the holder of that office. (*Jewish War* 1:269–270; see *Antiquities* 14:366)

How threatening, then, is the situation in Mark 9:42–48, when mutilation of the body, which renders it unclean, is preferred to eternal consignment in Gehenna.

In short, using the most abstract definition of the anthropologists, purity and cleanness in regard to the physical body have to do with completeness, wholeness, and physical perfection (Douglas 1966:51). More concretely, we have noted numerous examples of the specific Jewish definitions of purity and cleanness that were known by Paul the Pharisee and other observant Jews. It is simply a fact that Jews in the world of Paul and Jesus were attentive to issues of bodily purity (Neusner 1973a, 1975; Neyrey 1986a:93–99; 1988b:71–74, 81–89).

Our model for perceiving a physical body is complete. Now let us turn to one of Paul's major letters and examine his perception of the body in the light of the various lenses with which we have learned to see.

### 3.0 Conflicting Attitudes to the Body at Corinth

We turn now to 1 Corinthians, a document that deals more extensively with the physical body than any other Pauline letter. But before we use our model to learn how Paul perceives the physical body, we can help ourselves by attending to some of the specific aspects of 1 Corinthians that have to do with bodily issues.

*3.1 1 Corinthians: Focus on the Physical Body*    Of all Paul's letters, 1 Corinthians is thoroughly and intensely concerned with the physical body. (1) There is great concern for bodily orifices: (a) chapters 5–7 deal with the genitals, a major bodily orifice, (b) chapters 8–11 are concerned with another orifice, the mouth, for eating, and (c) chapters 12–14 are likewise concerned with the mouth, for speaking. (2) Bodily surface is discussed in 11:2–16, whether this refers to veils on the head or to hairstyles. (3) The body as the prime image of the church is developed in chapter 12. (4) Head and feet are used to describe the relational position of God to Jesus (15:25–28); head also describes Jesus' relation to members of his body (11:3). (5) Discipline of an athlete's body serves as a model for Paul's advice in 9:24–27. (6) Whether in the resurrection there will be a body and what that body will be like are questions that are treated in chapter 15. The body, then, is a constant topic of discussion in 1 Corinthians.

Yet in that letter there are two levels of issues. Particular bodily issues are discussed: whom one may not marry (ch. 5), with whom one may not have sexual intercourse (ch. 6), whether to marry and stay married (ch. 7), what foods one may eat (chs. 8–10), how the surface of one's head must be covered and which "heads" one should obey (ch. 11). Besides these particular bodily issues, 1 Corinthians is concerned with more general issues relative to the social body. The designation of the group as a "body" implies many things about membership, roles, structure, order, and authority in that same body. It is important, then, that we attend to the specific issues affecting the physical body as well as the more social view of the group implied by its designation as a body.

**3.2 Paul vs. Others: Control vs. Noncontrol**   Our understanding of the body in 1 Corinthians is complicated because some Christians at Corinth did not share Paul's position on specific body issues. The following brief synopsis indicates the range of diversity on specific, practical issues concerning body in that group.

| Issue | Non-Pauline Position | Pauline Position |
|---|---|---|
| 1. incest | boast (5:2) | horror (5:6–7) |
| 2. fornication | freedom (6:12–13) | pollution (6:15–19) |
| 3. idol meat | freedom (8:1; 10:23) | restraint (10:24, 28–29) |
| 4. head surface | no restraint | restraint (11:16) |
| 5. tongues and prophecy | no restraint | restraint (14:26–32) |

This synopsis indicates that Paul's position inclines to bodily control; it reflects a sense of traditional group norms for governing the behavior of individuals (e.g., 1 Cor. 5:1; 14:33–34). In contrast, the non-Pauline position favors little bodily control and considers itself independent of traditional norms (e.g., 1 Cor. 6:12; 10:23).

Whether in fact at Corinth Paul's opponents on one issue are the same as his opponents on another issue is a problem that cannot be addressed here. We know, however, Paul's own reaction to the series of issues and problems noted above. And, as I hope to show, it is coherent and consistent. The same claim can be made in regard to the opponents' position—at least from Paul's perception of it. Two attitudes to body, then, are found in 1 Corinthians, attitudes that are antithetical in terms of the degree of control deemed appropriate to the body.

## 4.0 The Model Applied to 1 Corinthians

The concepts and the model developed above provide us with a valuable way of examining Paul's perceptions of the physical body in 1 Corinthians. At this point we can state our hypothesis quite clearly.

1. There are two different views of physical and social body at Corinth, Paul's and his opponents'.

2. Paul's viewpoint of the physical body is that of a highly controlled body:

> It is a bounded system, to be strongly controlled; it is a pure or holy body and so must guard its orifices. Its concern for order and clarity make it fear unconsciousness or loss of control; it takes a negative view of spirit possession. It is a regulated and harmonious body whose parts are clearly differentiated and co-ordinated for the good of the whole body. No individual member is allowed to disrupt the body's disciplined functioning.

This view of the physical body replicates a view of the social body marked by strong social control, formality, smoothness, structured features, and ritualism.

3. Some of Paul's opponents view the body as an uncontrolled organism:

> Fearing no pollutants around the body, they see no need for control of the bodily orifices. Accordingly, the bodily boundaries are porous. Porosity is accompanied by celebration of freedom of movement and spontaneity. Trances and spirit possession are looked upon favorably.

This view of the physical body replicates the perception of the social body as marked by weak group pressure, informality, unstructured features; here effervescence flourishes.

4. The contrasting attitudes to control of the body in 1 Corinthians are an important source of information about the conflict in Corinth and offer a clearer window into the issues that divided Paul and his adversaries there. The attitude toward the physical body, moreover, affords a source of consis-

tency and coherence in evaluating the perspective of Paul and his adversaries.

**4.1 The Sexual Orifice**   Paul's paramount concern was with the body's orifices, both the sexual orifice and the mouth, whether the issue is eating, speaking, or kissing. In 1 Corinthians 5–7, Paul is concerned with sexual problems and issues, that is, with the sexual orifice of the body and with the proper/improper crossing of that orifice.

**4.1.1 Illicit Sexual Union (1 Cor. 5:1–8)**   The first issue Paul deals with is the problem of a prohibited form of marriage (Conzelmann 1975:96). Two attitudes are immediately evident: (1) some are "puffed up" approvingly over it (5:2a), but (2) Paul recoils in horror at it (5:1, 2b). Bodily control is scorned by some, but expected by others.

Paul expresses his point of view in 5:6–8 through the metaphor of leaven. He likens the incestuous marriage in the Christian group to leaven, which is perceived as a pollutant threatening the body. Leaven means "the old leaven of malice and evil" (5:8); if it enters the pure batch of flour it will "leaven the whole lump" (5:6), that is, pollute it. On the contrary, Christian believers are called to be a new lump—holy, pure, and unleavened in virtue of Christ's Passover sacrifice (5:7–8). No polluting impurity should be found in the midst of the Corinthian saints. Paul, then, perceives the matter from the standpoint of purity and pollution, and from this perspective there can be no tolerance or compromise.

He perceives the illicit marriage as a pollution of such magnitude that it is "not found among the pagans" (5:1). This pollution threatens the social body, as the leaven metaphor in 5:6–8 makes clear. It also pollutes the Christian partner; for, when a man joins himself to a woman, "the two become one flesh" (6:16). If one partner is impure and polluting, the other partner will be corrupted. This corrupting sexual union, therefore, represents an illicit crossing of the sexual orifice; the holy social body of the church and the individual Christian body are threatened.

Paul's strategy in this crisis is clear. The threatened social body must expel the pollutant by excommunicating him (5:2b–5, 7, 13). As Douglas predicted, concern to regulate the sexual orifice replicates concern for the integrity of the social body's boundaries and entrances. Implied in this strategy is the expectation that excommunication from the group may pressure the offending Christian partner to break off the incestuous marriage. The "one flesh" (the marriage) must be destroyed; the individual must reestablish the holiness of his own body and guard his sexual orifice. The depolluted Christian may then reenter the holy group (5:5; see 2 Cor. 2:5–7). The control of individual bodily orifices, then, replicates the group's concern with its social boundaries.

**4.1.2 Fornication (1 Cor. 6:12–20)**   In the treatment of fornication in 6:12–20 we discover that two views of the body are again operative. According to some, the body is uncontrolled: "All things are lawful for me" (6:12). For them, the body is neutral; it is not a bounded structure whose inside is pure and must be guarded. This is brought out in the analogy made between eating food and fornicating. "Food is meant for the stomach" (6:13); that is, any food may cross the orifice of the mouth and enter the stomach; eating is a neutral action that has nothing to do with purity concerns. Likewise with fornication, the sexual orifice is neutrally perceived; anything may pass across it; any sexual union is permitted. In the eyes of some, carnal intercourse, like eating, has nothing to do with purity or boundary violations (Murphy-O'Connor 1978a:393–395; 1979:297).

For Paul, however, two different principles are operative. First, the physical body of the believer is not neutral but holy: "The body is not meant for immorality, but for the Lord, and the Lord for the body" (6:13). The body, in fact, is a "member of Christ" (6:15). Like the Christian social body (3:16), the physical body is expected to be a container of holiness: "Your body is a temple of the Holy Spirit within you" (6:19). Second, the body is a bounded and controlled system. All is not "lawful" for it, for some things may "enslave" it (6:12), and so bodily control is an appropriate strategy. Paul is concerned with the body's purity and so enunciates rules controlling the orifices of the body and regulating what crosses them.

As we saw in 5:1–8, when a holy person is joined to an unclean partner, the resulting "flesh" becomes corrupted. In the case of sexual commerce with a prostitute, the resulting "flesh" is polluted (6:16). The example of prostitution serves to explain the evil of fornication; it is a sexual union that is seen as polluting the Christian partner. Alternately, when a person is joined to the Lord who is holy, the resulting union is holy (6:17). Fornication, like prostitution, is perceived as a pollution, for the resulting body cannot be holy; its pollution makes impossible a holy union with Christ.

The concern in 6:12–20 is with the pure interior of the body.

Every other sin is committed "outside" the body, that is, on the outside of the boundary that maintains the purity of the inside. Such sins, although evil, are not called pollutions or abominations. But sexual sins are perceived as attacking one's own body (6:18); that is, they cross the boundary or orifice and threaten the holy inside. This implies that illicit sexual commerce is a pollution that occurs *within* the "one flesh," which results from the joining of the two. In the case of fornication, prostitution, and incest, the sexual orifice and the organism's boundary should be vigorously guarded and not illicitly crossed. The result will be a pollution of the body's interior.

Paul, moreover, considers rules for the body and its orifice appropriate, because for him individual bodies are not neutral or free but controlled. "You[r body is] not your own; you were bought with a price" (6:19). Freedom, even freedom for the body, may be the shibboleth of some at Corinth, but that is not Paul's viewpoint. He prescribes control of the body and its orifice in 5:1–8 and 6:12–20, a view in keeping with his perception of the body as a holy system that needs to be guarded (Malina 1978c).

**4.1.3 Marriage (1 Cor. 7:1–9, 25–40)** The issue of marriage in chapter 7 has further bearing on the sexual orifice of the body. Paul repeatedly states the ideal: absolute noncrossing of the sexual orifice is highly desired either in virginity or celibacy.

1. "It is well for a man not to touch a woman" (7:1; see Hurd 1983:154–163).
2. "It is well . . . to remain single as I do" (7:8).
3. "He who refrains from marriage will do better" (7:38).

Implicit in this posture of guarding the sexual orifice lies a view of sex as somehow inherently polluting, which is not far removed from the biblical prohibition of sexual intercourse before engaging in war or offering sacrifice.

Paul hints at his rationale for this in 7:32–35. He perceives the unmarried person as joined to the Lord, totally concerned "how to please the Lord" (7:32) and "how to be holy in body and spirit" (7:34). Married persons are "divided" in concern for the Lord and their spouses (7:34b). Dividedness is inherently destructive of a body, a point that will be made evident in the discussion of 1 Corinthians 12, which follows. And it is implied that loyalty is a "limited good" (Foster 1965; Malina 1978b). There is only so much loyalty available; as much as is given to a spouse, that much cannot be given to the Lord. Married persons may be holy in spirit, according to Paul, but being holy in body as well is problematic for them (7:34–35).

Paul's permission for sexual intercourse is but a pragmatic concession. He will allow a lesser evil to avoid a greater pollution: "Because of the temptation to immorality, each man should have his own wife" (7:2). Or, if a man's "passions are strong, and it has to be, let him . . . marry" (7:36). The ideal would be to remain celibate and virginal so as to be wholly concerned with the Lord and to be holy in body and spirit.

Paul's ideal of sexual abstinence, however, cannot be maintained. Hence, sexual union is permitted. But it is wrapped in controls and subject to numerous regulations. First, there will *not* be promiscuous crossing of boundaries or orifices: "Each man should have his own wife and each woman her own husband" (7:2). Second, sexual relations are themselves subject to control: "The wife does not rule over her own body, but the husband does; likewise the husband does not rule over his own body, but the wife does" (7:4). According to a third rule, it is not permitted to refuse sexual intercourse "except perhaps by agreement for a season," in this case to do something truly holy, such as devoting oneself to prayer (7:5–6). Paul's reason for this concession is fear of pollution, that is, "lest Satan tempt you through lack of self-control" (7:5). Purity concerns lead to guarding of bodily orifices and to regulating the proper crossing of that orifice; that is what self-control means in this context. Such protection is appropriate to a body perceived in this way.

### 4.1.4 Divorce (1 Cor. 7:10–16)

Paul's teaching on divorce repeats much of his concern for orifices and his perception of the body as a bounded, holy system. On the one hand, he categorically prohibits divorce (7:10–11, 27–28). When two bodies join and become one flesh, that "one flesh" is a whole and holy body. Like all bodies, it must resist unwarranted entrances into it as well as the threat of being rent asunder, for any mutilation renders it unclean. The rule prohibiting divorce, although ascribed to the Lord (7:10), is coherent with Paul's viewpoint of a regulated body.

Even in the case of exogamous marriages (where two pagans married and one subsequently became a Christian), Paul does not act according to the prescriptions in Ezra 9:1–2, 11–15 in attempting to break those marriages (7:12–13). Divorce is perceived as a worse pollution than the mixed marriage. But pollution is the appropriate concept here, for the issue is one of purity and pollution. Why not break this marriage? Paul says that the pagan (unholy) partner may be made holy by the holy partner, and so the "unclean" children become "holy" (7:14). This reverses the image of unclean leaven that corrupts (see 5:6–8), but clearly indicates that pollution concerns govern Paul's perception of marriage and divorce.

Yet, as great a pollution as divorce is for Paul, he permits it (7:15–16). Why? The unbelieving partner—the partner who is unholy—desires to separate. The holy inside of this "one flesh" is already polluted in some way; the union is already split. In that situation Paul attempts to preserve the holiness of the believing member: "Let them separate" (7:15). A higher law of purity operates: a lesser impurity (divorce) is tolerated in fear of a greater pollution (apostasy, loss of Christian membership). As in the case of the offending eye, hand, or foot in Matthew 5:28–30, let the boundaries be redrawn to exclude the offending pollutant. In this case, the divorcing person is seen as amputated from the holy divorced person; and the body's holiness, although impaired, is maintained.

### 4.2 The Mouth (for Eating)

A second orifice, the mouth, becomes the focus of Paul's remarks in 1 Corinthians 8–11. The problem concerns eating—what may or may not cross the orifice of the mouth. To appreciate Paul's perspective, let us first examine 10:14–22, where he states his viewpoint regarding body and mouth most clearly.

### 4.2.1 Holy Food/Demon Food (1 Cor. 10:14–22)

It is important to note the principle Paul lays down in 10:14–22. He gives rules concerning eating: some food is prescribed (10:16–18), and some food is proscribed (10:19–22). Paul regulates the orifice of the mouth, but what principle determines the food that may or may not pass across the oral orifice?

The prescribed food is the "holy" food of the Eucharistic meal. The cup of blessing that Christians drink is "participation in the blood of Christ," and the bread that they break is "participation in the body of Christ" (10:16). The Eucharistic food is permitted to cross the boundary of the mouth and to enter the body; in doing so it reinforces the body's purity. The Eucharistic food functions here as leaven did in 5:6–8. If what goes in is good, it renders the body holy and does not contaminate; so it is prescribed. But if what is ingested is corrupting, like leaven, it pollutes the holy inside of the body, and so it is proscribed.

Paul, however, proscribes another kind of food, as he notes: "You cannot drink the cup of the Lord and the cup of demons.

You cannot partake of the table of the Lord and the table of demons" (10:21). Foods sacrificed to idols certainly are not holy. In view of Paul's view of the body as a bounded system threatened by pollution, such foods constitute a pollutant that will corrupt the individual because they will mean being "partner with demons" (10:20). Paul once more perceives the issue on the basis of purity and pollution, and so demands control of the body accordingly.

The logic here resembles that in chapters 5–7. By eating and drinking at a cultic table, a person has *koinōnia* with the cultic lord (10:16, 20) and becomes "one body" with this lord (10:17). This perception corresponds to the one body that is formed in sexual commerce: the two become "one flesh" (6:16). Even with virginity, those who join themselves to the Lord form a new unity with the Lord (6:17). This one body may be holy or unclean depending on whether the partner to whom one joins oneself is clean or unclean (see 6:15–16). Incest and fornication involve a *koinōnia* that corrupts; Christian marriage results in a *koinōnia* that sanctifies. So with foods. Sharing the body and blood of Christ means *koinōnia* with the holy Lord; and this one body is holy. But sharing the cup and table with demons means *koinōnia* with an unholy demon; this union is polluting. Paul's metaphor manifests the same analogy Douglas suggested between the social and physical body:

| Collective social body | Individual physical body |
|---|---|
| *koinōnia* with cultic lord | *koinōnia* with spouse |

Just as in marriage there cannot be two husbands, so there cannot be two lords of the covenant, Jesus and demons. Hence, one cannot eat at both tables. The pure and the polluted are mutually exclusive realms.

### 4.2.2 Eucharistic Foods (1 Cor. 11:17–34)

Issues relating to food and eating continue to occupy Paul's attention in 11:17–34, the discussion of behavior at the Eucharist. For Paul, the Eucharist should mean the holiest of times, things, activities, and persons. *Time*: Paul operates with a map of time, indicating that the time when the group gathers to celebrate its holiest rite is the most important time for them. Violation of this map of time is as much a pollution for him as was Jesus' violation of the Sabbath for the Pharisees. *Objects*: The Eucharist, because it is the body and blood of the Lord (10:16–17) is the holiest of objects and must be treated with utmost purity. *Activity*: The celebration of the Eucharist expresses the group's identity, cohesion, and boundaries (Meeks 1983a:159–162). It is the premier ceremony of ordering and classifying this group of people, and so its proper celebration requires absolute holiness among its participants, who must themselves be in a state of holiness.

But holiness is threatened on two fronts. First, Paul locates the problem in regard to the orifice of the mouth and the foods, secular and holy, that are being consumed. Second, Paul understands that the problem of the physical body represents a problem in the social body. When the church assembles, it is presumably to express the unity of the body, the union among the participants and between themselves and their holy Lord. But it is reported in 11:18–20 that the body that gathers is *not* holy. "Divisions" are occurring in the body (11:18); any "division" of a body constitutes a violent threat to its wholeness and hence to its holiness. We remember the perception of uncleanness that is associated with bodily deficiencies or mutilation (Lev. 21:16–20); wholeness is a prerequisite for holiness.

The bodily problem, insofar as it is expressed, deals with the divisiveness created by intemperate eating and drinking at the Eucharist: "In eating *each one* goes ahead with *his own* meal, and one is hungry and another is drunk" (11:21; see Gal. 5:20–21). This deregulation of the oral orifice is compounded by some becoming drunk, which is itself an evil (see 6:10), for excessive wine pollutes (see Gen. 9:20–21; Philo, *On Noah's Work as a Planter* 142–148). Such behavior is typical of pagan meals and cultic practices.

The crisis over the orifice of the mouth reflects a crisis over the boundaries of the social body. Discriminatory eating and drinking manifest distinctions among the social levels of those present, thus establishing artificial boundaries within the group to exclude the poor, the hungry, or the weak: "Do you despise the church of God and humiliate those who have nothing?" (11:22; see Theissen 1982:124–132, 153–162). Paul perceives the breakdown in table manners (i.e., the deregulation of the oral orifice) as a threat to the boundaries of the social body. Lack of control of the orifice of the body manifests a serious disregard of the social body's integrity and purity.

There is probably great irony in the remark that "there must be factions among you in order that those who are genuine among you may be recognized" (11:19). This means that those causing the factions and divisions are perceived as doing so for the purpose of distinguishing themselves as "genuine" or elite members of the group. Some, such as those who are puffed up at the incestuous marriage (5:2) and who boast of freedom to eat anything (10:23), would see no harm in their unregulated eating and drinking at the Eucharist; on the contrary, it may distinguish them as the strong in the group as opposed to the weak, the foolish, and those easily offended. Eating and drinking in their minds have nothing to do with pollution. Not so with Paul, who is concerned with the division in the holy body of the Lord caused by intemperate eating and drinking: "Do you despise the church of God and humiliate those who have nothing?" (11:22). What threatens the unity and health of a body is a pollution. Unsocial eating threatens; it is a pollution; it is proscribed.

This behavior pollutes the Eucharist itself as well as the holy group. "When you meet together, it is *not* the Lord's supper that you eat" (11:20). This is so, not because they are using the wrong formula, but because they are *desanctifying* the rite. Receiving it when drunk or in a disorderly fashion means profaning the holy Eucharist: "Whoever, therefore, eats the bread or drinks the cup of the Lord in an unworthy manner will be guilty of profaning the body and blood of the Lord" (11:27). Those who do so bring "judgment," not holiness, upon themselves (11:29; see 3:17). They are thereby liable to condemnation (11:32–34), that is, being publicly rendered unclean and barred from God's presence. The holy Eucharist that is received in an unholy person is rendered ineffective; it loses its holiness. It is profaned.

Rules, then, must be laid down to guard more closely the orifice of the mouth and so to protect the holiness of the Eucharist itself and the social body whose cohesion and holiness are threatened. Rules proscribe certain food and drink and regulate the consumption of others. No drunkenness is allowed (11:21). Consumption of food at the feast must be done all at the same time: "When you come together to eat, wait for one another" (11:33). Lest intemperate eating cause a problem, "If anyone is hungry, let him eat at home" (11:34). By regulating the orifice of the mouth, Paul's rules aim at restoring the health of the social body by healing divisions (11:18) and by eliminating humiliations (11:22). Other rules enjoin self-examination on the offending parties to see if their interior is holy enough to receive the Eucharist worthily (11:27–28) and to discern whether they are the cause of any harm to others. In other words, the proper governing of the orifice of the mouth at the Eucharist is the prime way to guard both the holiness of the Eucharist and the wholeness of the group receiving it.

When we approach the issue of eating idol meat in chapters 8–10, several of Paul's principles should be clear:

1. The physical body is constantly threatened by pollutants

that attempt to cross its oral orifice and that, when ingested, work to divide the body.

2. On the basis of Paul's perception of purity and pollution, there are appropriate rules for regulating the orifice of the mouth: certain foods are proscribed, others prescribed. The manner of eating may also be regulated.

3. The rules guarding the oral orifice likewise guard the boundaries of the social body.

However we evaluate Paul's remarks concerning the eating of idol meat, it should be clear at this point that he can and does regulate the orifice of the mouth in the interest of bodily wholeness and purity.

### 4.2.3 Idol Meat (1 Cor. 8 & 10)

The issue of idol meat in chapters 8–10 is more complicated than that of the Eucharist, for the Eucharistic food can be argued to be intrinsically holy. Rules for its proper reception are appropriate. But the early church desacralized food in its abolition of Jewish dietary laws (Mark 7:19; Acts 10:8–15; 11:5–9; 1 Cor. 10:25–26; see Neyrey 1988b:84–89). Yet Paul makes no appeal in 1 Corinthians to this ecclesial decision as the basis for the eating of idol meat. As we shall see, such an appeal to authority is totally out of character for those who urge that idol meat be eaten. On the contrary, the arguments in favor of eating it seem to reflect a view of the body that is radically different from Paul's, a view that was described earlier under the cosmology of an uncontrolled body.

Among the arguments urged in favor of eating idol meat, the dominant one seems to be based on a sense of radical freedom from laws and taboos. Paul twice cites the slogan "Am I not free?" in regard to the validity of eating (10:23; see 6:12 and 8:9). Although Paul admits the legitimacy of this "freedom" to eat (10:29), he indicates that it is not the overriding value here. By arguing in chapter 9 that he himself relinquished his rights and freedoms, Paul indicates that freedom is not the absolute value for him, as it is for others at Corinth.

A second argument for eating comes from the individualistic claim to have "knowledge" (8:1, 10). The claim to special insight serves to redraw boundaries within the group, dividing the elite who have this knowledge from those who do not have it (8:7, 11). The knowledge claimed has to do with a judgment on the neutrality of foods; that is, how they are no longer evaluated according to old Jewish laws and maps of things. Inasmuch as some claim that "food is made for the stomach and the stomach for food" (6:13), food is neutral. To eat it may even be a way of demonstrating that one is beyond old legal and purity concerns.

The nature of Paul's remarks in chapters 8–10 indicates his sensitivity to the strong individualistic claims made by those who eat but who disregard any consequences that such eating might have on the weaker members (8:7–13). No holiness, no group concerns, no regulation of freedom colors their thinking. Paul understands these arguments, but they do not represent his viewpoint at all.

The gist of Paul's position lies in the rules he enunciates to regulate the orifice of the mouth so as to protect the holiness of the body. Under certain circumstances eating is proscribed: "You may not eat" (*mē esthiete*, 10:28). Under other circumstances eating is permitted. One may eat when invited out: "If one of the unbelievers invites you to dinner . . . eat whatever is set before you" (10:27). In what appears to be an instance of legal casuistry, Paul enumerates the specific circumstances when one may or may not eat. Nevertheless, one may not eat if eating would scandalize a fellow Christian, that is: (1) if someone sees you at table in an idol's temple (8:10) and (2) when a weak-conscienced member explicitly says, "This has been offered in sacrifice" (10:28).

Not only the regulations but the arguments that support them resemble what we have seen in regard to Paul's regulation of the oral orifice in 10:14–22 and 11:17–34. Paul acts on the basis of strong purity concerns. First, he labels even the weak-conscienced member of the church as holy in virtue of Christ's purifying death (8:11). His paramount concern in chapters 8–10 is to prevent this weak but holy member from being "defiled": "Some . . . eat food as really offered to an idol; and their conscience, being weak, is defiled" (*molyntai*, 8:7). Second, Paul repeatedly concerns himself with the interior space of the persons involved, especially the threatened "weak conscience" (8:7, 10, 12; 10:28–29). Just as Paul worried about polluting leaven entering a pure batch of flour, so he guards lest the holy interior of a member be defiled by the sight of another eating idol meat or by actual ingestion of it. Conscience, then, speaks to the holy interior, which is threatened with defilement. So Paul concludes: "If food is a cause of my brother's being scandalized, I will never eat meat, lest I scandalize my brother" (8:13). "To scandalize" means to cause the loss of interior holiness in the affected person, that is, to pollute them (see Matt. 18:6–9).

Paul's argument implies the same concern articulated in

7:12–14; 10:14–22, and 11:17–34, namely, to protect the social body from division. Paul perceives a lack of concern for the integrity of the social body in the position of those who would eat ("the strong"), and so disregard the divisive effects of their eating on "the weak." Such behavior becomes a stumbling block to some (8:9); "sinning against your brethren . . . you sin against Christ" (8:12). This "sin against Christ" is none other than an attack on the body of Christ, the church (Murphy-O'Connor, 1978b:563–564). Paul's concern with the guarding of a bodily orifice once more communicates his concern for the boundaries of the social group.

In Paul's argument in chapters 8–10, we find other elements of the cosmology of a controlled body, which arguments are radically different from those urged by "the strong."

1. *Freedom*: Although freedom to eat is nominally endorsed, Paul proceeds to wrap that freedom in constraints and to circumscribe it with regulations. He does not consider freedom as an absolute or overriding value. For example, Paul claimed for himself a series of individual rights (9:3–15), which he sees as circumscribed by the needs of the social body. He affirms that he is indeed free: "Am I not free? . . . Have I not seen Jesus our Lord?" (9:1). But that freedom is controlled by what is good for the social body: "For though I am free, . . . I have made myself a slave to all" (9:19) for the benefit of the body of Christ (9:20–23; see Malina 1978b).

2. *Personal Identity*: In Paul's eyes, a certain individualism describes those who claim knowledge and would eat; they are concerned basically with themselves and their rights. Paul, however, attends to what is good for the group: "Let no one seek his own good, but the good of his neighbor" (10:23), and again: "I try to please all men in everything I do, not seeking my own advantage, but that of many, that they may be saved" (10:33). The knowledge of the strong only "puffs them up" (8:1); it yields no advantage for the group.

3. *Ethics*: The ethical norm of those who would eat springs from a sense of individualistic freedom: "All things are lawful for me" (10:23; 6:12). For Paul, however, the ethical principle is what "builds up" the group. "Love," or concern for the group's unity, "builds up" (8:1); it surpasses knowledge, which puffs up (see 1 Cor. 13:2). Although all things are lawful, "not all things build up" (10:23). Therefore, Paul rates what strengthens group boundaries as a higher value than the freedoms of the strong individuals.

Paul's regulation of the eating of idol meat and the reasoning that underpins it sharply contrast with the behavior and attitudes of those who would eat in freedom. We can conveniently sketch the differences in the cosmologies of Paul and his opponents, which will summarize the discussion thus far:

| Opponents | | Paul |
|---|---|---|
| no pollution concerns | Purity | strong pollution concerns |
| porous boundaries | Ritual | strong concern for what crosses boundaries |
| not a bounded system and no protection needed; no concern with bodily orifices and boundaries | Body | bounded system strongly defined and strongly guarded; concern with bodily orifices and boundaries |
| individualistic, freedom unrestrained | Personal Identity | strong group orientation, freedom restrained |
| personal decisions | Sin/Deviance | group norms |

**4.3 The Mouth (for Speaking)**   In 1 Corinthians 12–14, Paul continues to focus attention on the orifice of the mouth. As we shall see, he establishes rules for controlling this orifice. But it is important to note the reasons accompanying his regulation of it. The question here is not like that of eating idol meat—what crosses the mouth and enters the body—but rather what comes out of the mouth and enters the ears of the assembled body. Paul's regulation will concern the mouths of speakers.

**4.3.1 Tongues: Pneumatics vs. Paul**   We find in 1 Corinthians 14 two different views of the body and of tongues. Certain pneumatics at Corinth highly valued the gift of tongues as a symbol of effervescent spirit possession: "One who speaks in a tongue speaks not to men but to God; . . . he utters mysteries in the Spirit" (14:2). In anthropological terms, Mary Douglas would consider speaking in tongues a form of trance. Apropos of this, she remarked: "Where trance is not regarded as at all dangerous, but as a benign source of power and guidance for the community at large, I would expect to find a very loosely structured community, group boundaries unimportant, social categories undefined" (1982a:79). Spirit possession indicates a lower degree of social structure and control, as well as strong individualism. In this context, freedom *must* prevail, for one should never "quench the spirit" (1 Thess. 5:19). Nor would one ever consider governing the orifice of the mouth or structuring this gift in the life of a community: "Where the Spirit of the Lord is, there is freedom" (2 Cor. 3:17). The cosmology of those who prize speaking in tongues is highly individualistic and freedom oriented; no rules are appropriate for this uncontrolled body (Neyrey 1988d:180–185).

In contrast, we know that Paul views the body as a highly structured and strongly controlled organism. In this context, other remarks by Douglas about spirit possession prove useful: "We tend to find trance-like states feared as dangerous where the social dimension is highly structured, but welcome and even deliberately induced where this is not the case" (1982a:74). Let us, then, examine Paul's viewpoint on speaking in tongues in this light.

Paul's argument for regulating speaking in tongues lies in his sense of group identity. On the basis of what benefits the whole body, he makes a value judgment on the relative importance of tongues and prophecy. Those who speak in tongues "edify themselves," but those who prophesy "edify the church" (14:4). "He who prophesies is greater than he who speaks in tongues" because prophecy edifies the group (14:5). Edification emerges as Paul's persistent value: "Let all things be done for edification" (14:26). Eating idol meat disedifies, abstinence edifies (8:1, 10); seeking one's own good may disedify another, so "let no one seek his own good, but the good of his neighbor" (10:23–24). Edification, then, indicates that one's personal identity and behavior is group, not individualistically, oriented. Edification, moreover, denotes purity concerns. Disedification causes scandal and pollutes the conscience (8:7); edification strengthens the wholeness and holiness of the individual conscience and the group. Paul expresses a purity concern, then, when he tells the congregation to "be babes in evil" (14:20). This means, be innocent of disedifying behavior that is consequent to unregulated speaking in tongues. Edification, then, becomes Paul's code word for the cosmology of a controlled body; it serves group identity, emphasizes purity concerns, and regulates personal freedoms. Prophecy edifies, but tongues do not.

### 4.3.2 Prophecy over Tongues/Mind over Spirit

Besides valuing prophecy for its edification of the group, Paul correspondingly devalues speaking in tongues. That phenomenon is fundamentally unintelligible (14:9) and unfruitful (14:14): "If I pray in a tongue, my spirit prays but my mind is unfruitful" (14:14). For, "five words [spoken] with my mind" are worth more than "ten thousand words in a tongue" (14:19). By this, Paul clearly values consciousness and clarity; he favors group-edifying and group-regulated behavior. Speaking in one's "mind" betokens these values. But praying in one's "spirit" is unconscious and unintelligible; it is highly individualistic and uncontrolled behavior.

Mary Douglas evaluated just these terms, *mind* and *spirit*, in view of their relationship to the social body (1969:69–72). She argued that "philosophical controversies about the relation of spirit to matter or mind to the body be interpreted as exchanges of condensed statements about the relation of society to the individual" (1969:69). In her argument, the body, or the flesh, represents society; mind and spirit stand for the individual. She then articulates a theory of the relation of society to individual, body and mind to spirit.

> To insist on the superiority of spiritual over material elements is to insist on the liberties of the individual and to imply a political program for freeing him from social constraints. In the contrary view, to declare that spirit works through matter, that spiritual values are made effective through material acts, that body and mind are separate but intimately united, all this emphasis on the necessary mingling of spirit and matter implies that the individual is by nature subordinate to society and finds his freedom within its forms. (Douglas 1969:69)

Paul's preference for praying "in mind" expresses his view of personal identity as group oriented, not individualistic. It implies respect for societal restraints and regulation of freedoms. Those who glory only "in the spirit" may be said to be individualistic people who reject societal restraints and for whom freedom has become an absolute, unrestrained value.

Paul's final evaluation of speaking in tongues takes into account its consequences. As we noted above, prophecy edifies the group; speaking in tongues does just the opposite. Speaking in tongues, like intemperate eating and drinking at the Eucharist, plays havoc with the body's unity. When someone speaks in unintelligible tongues, an artificial but deleterious redrawing of boundaries within the group results: "I shall be a *foreigner* to the speaker and the speaker a *foreigner* to me" (14:11). From Paul's perspective, speaking in tongues betokens spirit possession and is seen as a sign of elite status by some; its unregulated practice disrupts the unity of the body, causing factions and divisions (see 12:21). Speaking in tongues, then, jeopardizes the wholeness of the social body, as happened in 11:18–22. And if outsiders and unbelievers observe this unregulated practice, "they will say that you are mad" (14:23). They will be confirmed as outsiders and lose the chance to be made holy by membership in the holy body of Jesus. Although not positively polluting, speaking in tongues can function to redraw boundaries within and around the group, preempting God's prerogative to say who is in or out of it. Thus, the wholeness of the body is harmed and its holiness threatened.

Paul's regulation of the oral orifice is consonant with his view of the church as a controlled body. He establishes clear rules for the governance of the mouth. As regards speaking in tongues, only two or three at most may speak in tongues during any meeting. Even this rule he phrases so as to avoid loss of control: "If any speak in a tongue, let there be only two or at most three, and *each in turn*" (14:27). Paul mandates the complete shutting of the orifice: "But if there is no one to interpret, let each of them keep silence in church and speak to himself and to God" (14:28).

Those who prophesy are likewise regulated: "Let two or three prophets speak" (14:29). And, "if a revelation is made to another sitting by, let the first be silent" (14:30). As with the rules for speaking in tongues, Paul permits no loss of control. The principle emerges that even if a regulated body is filled with a free and uncontrollable spirit, order and control are *not* to be sacrificed: "The spirits of prophets are subject to prophets" (14:32). Control is never to be sacrificed in regard to the body.

## 5.0 Control of Bodily Boundaries and Surfaces

A discussion of bodily surfaces and their control emerges in 1 Corinthians 11:2–16. In this I am following the study of Murphy-O'Connor (1980:482) that the issue was over hairdos: men wearing unmasculine hairdos and women wearing unfeminine ones.

As with the case of incest and fornication, two contrasting views of body are operative in the discussion. The primary fact seems to be that some men were wearing their hair long and coifed in an unmasculine fashion and some women were wearing their hair loose, unbraided, and unbound, which was contrary to societal customs. Long and coifed hair for men denoted effeminacy and possibly homosexuality; uncoifed hair for women suggested freedom and perhaps sexual license. At least, the novel hairdos tended to blur conventional sexual identity and to confuse sexual and societal roles assigned to men and women. This, of course, would not be objectionable to those who saw that in Christ there is no male or female (Gal. 3:28) and to those who proclaimed that in Christ "we are all free"—from Torah, law, and custom (see 1 Cor. 6:12; 10:23). The blurring of sexual roles and identity because of unmasculine/unfeminine hairdos is but the external symbol of a view of the body as a free organism, without clear boundaries, and without concern for purity and rituals to maintain that purity. For certain people, no sense of dishonor (i.e., pollution) threatening the individual or the social body attends the blurring of sexual roles and distinctions by novel hairdos.

Inasmuch as Paul's view of the body is quite different, let us see what he makes of the issue of novel hairdos. Women's hair should be plaited, braided, and wrapped around their heads. Paul notes that such hairdos are lacking (11:5, 6, 15). Plaited hair that is wrapped around the head in orderly fashion symbolizes control over the surface of the body, the part of the woman in direct contact with the social world. Plaited and braided hair denotes a clear social role and clear sexual differentiation; the braiding of hair exemplifies the social concern for matronly chastity and for modesty (Derrett 1977:171–175). This type of hairdo is appropriate where the body is perceived as a controlled structure, where boundaries are guarded, where roles are clear, and where purity is prized. For those with this view, then, uncoifed and unbound hair suggests just the opposite view of body: freedom, loss of control, and blurring of clear sexual roles. Loose hair suggests loose morals and therefore takes on the appearance of a pollutant.

Where the physical body is perceived as a system requiring control, a man's hair must be short and natural. Thus he will be perceived in masculine terms and not confused with women, whose hair is customarily long (see 11:6). Nor should the man dress his hair, curl it, or make it resemble a woman's hairdo (Murphy-O'Connor 1980:485). Such hairstyling suggests confusion of sexual identity and/or loss of bodily control, and so is seen as a pollutant, that is, a danger to the social order. Hair rules replicate social rules dealing with sexual differentiation and roles; such rules are appropriate to a bounded body.

Paul expresses his perception of the issue of unacceptable hairdos in terms of purity and pollution. The offending man "dishonors" his head (11:4, 14), as does the offending woman (11:5). He labels this irregularity a "disgrace" (11:6). Because such hairdos blur the lines that define masculine and feminine roles and status, they are a pollution. They are doubly offensive at a worship service, where "praying and prophesying" occur (11:4–5, 13) and where holy time demands holy behavior and

holy attire. Paul consciously refers to this in 11:10, when he
expresses his reason for prescribing and proscribing hairdos—
"because of the angels." Joseph Fitzmyer (1957:55–56) explained this remark in terms of the cultural perception of the
worship ceremony taking place before the angels and mediated
by them (Ps. 137:1 LXX and Rev. 8:3). As a participation in
the heavenly liturgy at which the holy angels presided, human
worship demanded that unclean, or polluted, members be excluded, "for holy angels are present," as the following text from
Qumran indicates:

> Nor shall anyone who is afflicted by any form of human unclean-
> ness whatsoever be admitted into the assembly of God; nor shall
> anyone who becomes afflicted in this way be allowed to retain
> his place in the midst of the congregation . . . for holy angels are
> [present] in their [congre]gation. . . . Let him not enter, for he is
> contaminated. (1QSa 2:3–11)

In summary, just as eating and drinking at a Eucharist were
matters of purity and pollution (11:17–34), so also were
hairdos. Paul clearly intends to regulate the surface of the
body, the hair. He prescribes that women should wear their
hair long, braided, and coifed; men should wear their hair short
and undressed. Hairstyles that confuse gender roles and status
are proscribed.

## 6.0 Control and Bodily Structure

The discussion in 11:3–16 centered around hairdos, that is,
control of the body surface. Yet Paul saw in that issue the larger
issues of role differentiation and authority in church and society. As Mary Douglas indicated, where formality, smoothness,
and ritual are valued in one's cosmology, people will also value
well-defined roles, social control, and a strong commitment to
a structured system. Where informality, shagginess, and effervescence are prized, there tends to be less role differentiation,
little control, and loose adherence to a structured system.
Where personal identity is group oriented, roles will be clearly
defined; where individualistic, a weak internal classification
system emerges.

*6.1 Head and Body*  Role and status differentiation, moreover,
are frequently expressed in terms of the relationship of body
parts, head to body, head to feet, and so forth. In two places, 1
Corinthians 11:2–16 and 15:20–28, Paul speaks of a differentiation in role and status in terms of the relationship of head to
body.

**6.1.1 Head (1 Cor. 11:2–16)**   The liminal description of baptismal neophytes, in Christ "there is neither male nor female" (Gal. 3:28), stands in considerable tension with Paul's remarks in 1 Corinthians. For in the latter letter he argues for differentiation of the sexes. People in rituals of status transformation frequently experience a liminal state in which all former marks of social differentiation are absent during their rite of passage. One need only look at boot camp training for the military or at the novitiate socialization of religious orders. Yet when the rite of passage is completed, these same people leave the liminal, undifferentiated state and return to their former society invested with their new role and status. Previous absence of differentiation and classification, which was appropriate during the liminal state, yields as people return to their ordered and structured worlds. Such seems to be the case with the liminal remarks in Galatians 3:28. They do not describe the state when neophytes are reaggregated into society, but the undifferentiated, liminal state. First Corinthians describes life in the group after the ritual of status transformation is completed and the newly baptized resume their normal living in the world to which they were socialized from birth.

Alluding to the original order of creation, Paul points out in 1 Corinthians how even then the sexes were differentiated: "Man was not made from woman, but woman from man" (11:8, 12a); "[man] is the image and glory of God; but woman is the glory of man" (11:7). We are reminded here of the strong influence on Paul the Pharisee of the map of persons found in Genesis 1 and replicated in the temple system. Yet, in the new creation in Christ, Paul affirms some changes: "In the Lord woman is not [different (*chōris*) from] man nor [is man different (*chōris*) from] woman" (11:11; see Kurzinger 1978:270–275). Two contrary things are being said: differentiation of sexes and nondifferentiation. Which one predominates? Which one controls behavior in the church?

According to Paul, sexual differentiation is by no means totally abolished in the new creation (Barton 1986). For he states at the beginning of the passage a principle that undergirds the hierarchical differentiation of man and woman:

> The head of every man is Christ,
> the head of a woman is her husband,
> and the head of Christ is God.
>                                         1 Corinthians 11:3

This points to differentiation according to gender and role. We know abstractly that men and women are both chosen by God and both are recipients of grace and gift—both "pray and prophesy" in the church (11:4–5). This parity, however, which is appropriate to household settings, stands in considerable tension with other statements in 11:3–16, which envision public settings where the gender roles characteristic of Paul's society remain in force. Paul states that "a woman ought to have authority (exousia) over her head" (11:10) because woman was made from man for man (11:8–9). For Paul the sexes remain clearly differentiated in the public forum; and so totally different hairdos are appropriate to the respective sexes (11:13–15).

Returning to 11:3, the term *head* (*kephalē*) is not devoid of importance. Although Murphy-O'Connor insists that it not be translated as authority or supremacy (1980:491–493), perhaps that modern reading needs to be revised in the light of the present discussion. Despite the freedom slogans found in the letter ("Am I not free?" 9:1; "All things are lawful for me," 6:12, 10:23), Paul by no means sees authority abolished in the new creation (see 16:15–16). The reader is reminded of the map of heavenly persons in the second chapter. God's authority is beyond question, as is Paul's. Paul never abolishes the place of authority in his churches. Hence, a metaphorical reading of "head" as authority is fully in keeping with the argument of 1 Corinthians.

From the point of view of body symbolism, "head" denotes high position, rank, and authority (Schwartz, 1981:51–52). So when Paul says that "the head of a woman is her husband" (11:3), "head" denotes status and rank appropriate to husbands. He repeats this in 11:10, where woman, who is from man and for man, ought to have authority (*exousia*) over her head. She is situated "lower" than man: she is "from" man and "for" him; he has *exousia* over her. Every man, too, is subject to authority, for "the head of every man is Christ"; even Christ has a "head" over him—God (11:3). All people, therefore—Christ, husbands, and wives—have authority over them. Taking our clue from Paul's comment on the headship of Christ, we conclude that he uses the bodily image of "head" as a synonym for role and status, that is, for authority. Man and woman or husband and wife are differentiated in terms of social role and status, not an improbable statement in the light of Paul's tendency to present a complete map of persons.

**6.1.2 Head and Feet (1 Cor. 15:20–28)**  Body imagery affords still another clue to social rank and authority. Even Christ is said to have a "head" over him: "The head of Christ is God"

(11:3). In 1 Corinthians 15:20–28 Paul speaks of Christ as the new Adam—the new head/source. On one level the argument simply states that as all die in Adam, so all rise in Christ (15:21–22; see Rom. 5:12–21). But the passage says much more; like Adam, Christ has dominion and rule over all creation (15:24; Gen. 1:26–28). As head, he is first in time and first in precedence. Like other Christians, Paul visualizes Christ's headship by stating that "all things are put in subjection *under his feet*" (15:25, 27; see Heb. 1:13; 2:6–8). Christ is head, both as source and as sovereign.

Yet Paul perceives even Christ-as-head to be in a structured relationship with God:

> When all things are subjected to him [Christ],
> then the Son himself will also be subjected to him
> who put all things under him,
> that God may be everything to every one.
> 1 Corinthians 15:28

On one level, this serves as an answer to the Corinthians who espoused an overly realized eschatology: the last enemy, death, has not yet been subjected. But terms such as "head . . . feet" and "subjected" are body language suggesting role differentiation, structural relationships, even authority and hierarchy. I suggest that this language in 1 Corinthians 15:20–28 serves other purposes: (1) to reassert concepts of control where pneumatic freedom threatens communal order, (2) to support authority where it is weak, and (3) to affirm structure where it is blurred. If Paul perceives Christ truly risen and genuinely free, as "subjected to him who put all things under him," then the free and spirit-filled Corinthians can see a model for their own structural relationship to Paul's authority and that of other leaders of the group (see 16:16). "The head of Christ is God" (11:3) implies that even Christ has a structured relationship to God; he himself is not absolutely free of authority and control.

**6.2 *Eyes and Ears/Hands and Feet*** Body imagery may express differentiation of role and status within the body beyond the simple head/body metaphor. This sense of differentiated status, rank, and authority occurs in the description of the body of Christ in 1 Corinthians 12. "Feet" are said to complain that they are not "hands": "Because I am not a hand, I do not belong to the body" (12:15). "Eyes" lord it over "hands" and "heads" over "feet": "I have no need of you" (12:21). Yet in spite of the problems reflected in the discourse in 12:14–21,

Paul does not abolish distinctions of rank and status in the body: "If all were a single organ, where would the body be?" (12:19). No, in the body there will be head and eyes, hands and feet. And Paul the Pharisee bases this on God's creative ordering in Genesis 1: "But as it is, God arranged the organs in the body, each one of them, as he chose" (12:18).

Earlier in 1 Corinthians, Paul called upon the members of the church to remain in their ascribed social positions: "Let every one lead the life which the Lord has assigned to him, and in which God has called him (7:17). And "in whatever state each was called, there let him remain with God" (7:24). Slaves maintain their same status and role of slaves; Jews are still Jews; Gentiles remain Gentiles. Again in chapter 12, Paul reminds the church that there is no radical blurring of roles in the body of Christ: "If all were a single organ, where would the body be?" (12:19). "If the whole body were an ear, where would be the sense of smell?" (12:17b). Differentiation of bodily organs is expected and desired.

Douglas's model suggests that where there are strong purity concerns, there will be a correspondingly strong classification system that clarifies precise roles and statuses. In the case of the body of Christ, the superior bodily parts are perceived as higher ranked and as possessing greater honor and authority in the anatomical hierarchy. And in chapter 12, Paul sees the anatomy of the body as a clear cipher for the taxonomy of the social body. In his perspective, moreover, this configuration is God's doing: "But as it is, God arranged the organs in the body, each one of them, as he chose" (12:18).

The issue is hardly a minor concern for Paul, for after establishing a hierarchy of roles and statuses in the physical body, he comments on a similar structure in the social body. Far from blurring the differentiation of roles and status within the social body, Paul clearly articulates them: "First apostles, second prophets, third teachers, then workers of miracles, then healers, helpers, administrators, speakers in various kinds of tongues" (12:28). We studied this passage carefully in Chapter 2, under the rubric of maps of church persons. We note clearly the correlation of structure between the social body and the physical body.

**6.3 Body of Christ**   Paul speaks at great length about the body of Christ, which is the church. The social body of the church is a holy body, the body of Christ (12:12; 6:15). Its holiness consists, moreover, in being filled with a "holy" Spirit (12:4–11, 13; see 3:16 and 6:19). But the holiness of the body is likewise perceived in terms of its wholeness, namely, its unity. Paul indicates in 12:4–11 that one of the functions of the Spirit is to unify the cornucopia of gifts given to the body's diverse members. It is through "the *same* Spirit" that wisdom is given to one, knowledge to another, and prophecy to still another (12:8–10). Not only is diversity of gifts unified in "the same Spirit," but diversity of races and roles is unified in "the *one* Spirit": "By one Spirit we were all baptized into one body—Jews or Greeks, slaves or free—and all were made to drink of one Spirit" (12:13). Unity is touched upon in the remarks that indicate that the "same" Spirit, Lord, and God dispense different gifts (12:4–7). All of the gifts, moreover, have a unifying purpose; they are "for the common good" (12:7), that is, for the "building up" of the body (see 1 Cor. 14:3–5, 12, 26). The body, then, is holy in virtue of its "holy" Spirit, and its holiness is perceived in terms of its wholeness. As wholeness is a mark of the purity of the physical body, so unity manifests the holiness of the social body.

The greatest threat to a holy body is pollution; comparably, the most dangerous threat to a whole body is unwholeness, that is, a bodily defect or mutilation. Paul repeatedly expresses concern with "divisions" in the church at Corinth (1:10; 11:18; 12:25). At times they derive from members preferring different "heads" over them: "I belong to Paul . . . I belong to Apollos . . . I belong to Cephas . . . I belong to Christ" (1:12; 3:4). Divisions, moreover, are made between strong and weak (1:18–29), wise (knowing) and foolish (8:10–13), and sated and hungry (11:18–22). Jealousy and strife are rampant (11:11; 3:3). Some even "puff themselves up" against others (4:6, 18–19; 5:2; 8:1). Some look only to their own good and not to the good of their neighbor (10:24, 29). The premier unifying event is the Eucharistic meeting: "Because there is one bread, we who are many are one body, for we all partake of the one bread" (10:17). But even this unifying event is "divided" by factions (11:18–19). The body at Corinth, then, is threatened with its most dangerous pollutant—division and disunity.

In the description of the body of Christ in 12:14–26 the threatening pollutants are already within the body. Two different sets of anatomical parts speak in 12:15–16 and 21. The first set speaks from a sense of inferiority, sensing that it is not welcome in the body. The foot, because it is not the hand, says, "I do not belong to the body" (12:15); and the ear, because it is not the eye, says, "I do not belong to the body" (12:16). The second set speaks from a sense of superiority and boasts that it is the only honorable member of the body. The eye says to the hand, "I have no need of you," and the head speaks likewise to the feet (12:21). Both of these postures threaten pollution because they would corrupt the body for the same reason; they attack its basic wholeness, and so its holiness. Inferiority attitudes make that person an outsider to the rest of the group (recall 14:11). And superiority attitudes, which foster individualism and elitism, humiliate others (recall 11:22). If left unchecked, the social body will be tragically divided by these attitudes. A divided body is unclean and polluted.

The view of the church as a body expresses other important aspects, such as differentiation of roles and statuses. There is no doubt that the organs and parts of the body are in fact differentiated: "If the whole body were an eye, where would be the hearing? If the whole body were an ear, where would be the sense of smell?" (12:17). As it is, there are head, hands, and feet as well as eyes, ears, and nose. This differentiation, moreover, is part of the way things should be; it is ordained by God in creation (12:18). God, then, has drawn the official *map of the physical body*.

The differentiated parts of the body are also ranked. The head is greater than the feet; the eye is more important than the ear; the hand is above the foot. Paul even admits that in the body there are honorable and less honorable parts, presentable and inferior parts, stronger and weaker members (12:22–24). For Paul, moreover, the ranking of the differentiated parts corresponds to the different roles ascribed to the members of the church (12:28). This, too, is God's doing, for "God has appointed" them (12:28). God has also drawn the *map of the social body*. Even the charismatic gifts can be differentiated and ranked: apostleship over prophecy, prophecy over tongues, and charity over all (12:31; 13:13).

Paul, then, perceives the body of Christ as a structured and differentiated body. He sees it, moreover, as a holy body whose wholeness is threatened with polluting division. In chapter 5 his remedy for such a threatening pollutant was to expel it; but that is not appropriate here, for it would cause the very thing Paul wants to prevent, namely, a divided body. The remedy proposed by Paul has to do with a changed sense of personal identity that is appropriate for a controlled body. As we noted in regard to chapters 8–10, individualism in regard to eating idol meat denoted a sense of identity contrary to Paul's group-oriented viewpoint. On the other hand, "building up the body" and not seeking one's good but the good of others (10:24) represent behavior commensurate with a sense of identity that is group oriented.

So with the body of Christ in chapter 12, Paul urges the members who most clearly tend to individualism to be more group oriented and to seek the good of others. He exhorts the honorable parts of the body to invest with greater honor those parts they consider less honorable; likewise the presentable and unpresentable parts, the superior and the inferior parts (12:23–24). Although God ascribed distinct role and status to certain body parts (12:18), this same God has "composed the body, giving the greater honor to the inferior part" (12:24b). This remark seems to contradict what was said in 12:18, where differences of status and role were affirmed. But that is not surprising when we consider that Paul seeks to be "all things to all people." He confirms both differentiation and control. Yet his overriding concern is with the unity of the social body of the church, which he expresses in terms of a concern for the wholeness of the physical body: "That there be no discord in the body, but that the members may have the same care for one another" (12:25). Thus a sense of group identity supercedes a sense of individualism; bodily wholeness is thus maintained.

**6.4 A Body, Even in Heaven**   One final question interests us: "With what kind of body" are the dead raised? (15:35). We will view this question from an anthropological perspective; questions of Gnosticism or the Greek background of the Corinthian argument against resurrection (15:12) cannot be addressed here. Rather, we are interested in the reasons why Paul emphatically insists on "body" as the appropriate characteristic of the risen state: "It is raised a spiritual *body*. If there is a physical body, there is also a spiritual *body*" (15:44). Why the insistence on "body"?

From the perspective of this chapter, one suspects that there might be two contrasting views of the resurrection, views that perhaps are compatible and consistent with the Pauline and non-Pauline positions discussed here. And in fact, critical scholarship has suggested a coherent reconstruction of the non-Pauline viewpoint of the Corinthian pneumatics. Briefly, then, the elites at Corinth are (1) credited with espousing an overly realized eschatology (4:8), (2) whereby they are beyond the body, which is at best neutral (6:12–13), and value only things spiritual. (3) This results in the abolition of all control and the celebration of radical freedom: "All things are lawful!" (6:12; 10:23). (4) A denial of social and sexual differentiation logically follows (5:1–2; 11:2–16). (5) In this perspective, resurrection would be perceived as a spiritual condition unrestrained by and unrelated to the physical and social body. Hence, the elitist

view of the social body is replicated in its perception of the
physical body.

Such a perspective is reflected in 15:45–49. A radical contrast is made between Adam and Christ, which would imply
that in the final time, when Christ and his followers are resurrected, what results is spirit and not body.

| **First Adam** | **Second Adam** |
|---|---|
| 1. The first Adam became a "living being" (*psychēn*) (15:45a). | 1. The last Adam became a "life-giving spirit" (*pneuma*) (15:45b). |
| 2. The physical (*to psychikon*) came first (15:46). | 2. Then came the spiritual (*to pneumatikon*, 15:46). |
| 3. As was the man of earth, so are those who are of dust (15:48a). | 3. As is the man of heaven, so are those who are of heaven (15:48b). |

A radical distinction is made between what is (1) a "living
being . . . physical . . . of earth" and (2) "a life-giving spirit
. . . spiritual . . . of heaven." Whatever the background of this
conception, it is certainly capable of being co-opted by the
pneumatics (see especially 15:45, where it says that "the last
Adam [the risen Jesus] became a . . . *spirit*").

Historical questions aside, our interest lies in what correlation there might be between one's view of body and of resurrection. In the case of Paul's opponents, it would seem that
resurrection as spirit would adequately express their eschatological perspective and reflect their typology of a noncontrolled
body. The Pauline perspective on eschatology differs on every
point from that of the pneumatics at Corinth. (1) Eschatology
is realized in one sense, but not overly; for death still reigns
(15:23) and all things are not yet under Christ's feet (15:24–28);
judgment remains (4:5; 5:13; 6:2, 9–10). (2) Christians are not
beyond the body, for "[it] is not meant for immorality, but for
the Lord" (6:13). (3) Even when baptized and gifted with the
Spirit, Christians are subject to rules and authority; their freedom is not absolute. (4) Therefore, social and sexual differentiation is expected and appropriate (11:3; 12:14–21). (5)
Resurrection, then, is appropriately expressed as resurrection
of the body, not escape from body into spirit. Control is never
sacrificed, even when describing the final state of those baptized into Christ.

Paul's discourse on what kind of body occurs in the resurrection is governed by a basic purity principle: "Flesh and blood
cannot inherit the kingdom of God" (15:50); it must be
"changed" (15:52). This is based on a map of heaven that

indicates that God is radically different from humankind. God is imperishable and immortal, and can never know corruption. What is perishable and mortal will corrupt (Jeremias 1955:151–154), and so does not belong in the presence of God who is immortal and imperishable. It must be changed by putting on "immortality and imperishability" (15:53–54). Yet what comes into God's presence is ultimately body, albeit a transformed body.

Paul presents the substance of his argument in 15:35–44 with a series of three contrasts. First, he contrasts dried and dead seeds with living plants (15:36–37); then terrestrial bodies with celestial bodies (15:39–41); finally, unresurrected bodies with resurrected bodies (15:42–44). The common denominator in the analogical argument is the fact that *living* plants, *celestial* phenomena, and *resurrected* persons are all described in somatic language as "bodies":

1. "What you sow is not the body which is to be, but a bare kernel" (15:37).
2. "There are celestial bodies and there are terrestrial bodies" (15:40).
3. "It is sown a physical body, it is raised a spiritual body. If there is a physical body, there is also a spiritual body" (15:44).

How is this so? As God gave bodies at creation, so God will also allocate bodies in heaven: "God gives it a body as he has chosen" (15:38). The holy, immortal, and imperishable God himself gives an appropriate body to what is mortal and perishable so that it may come into God's holy space.

Commentators often remark that Paul's idea of a spiritual body contains the sense of "a total person controlled by God's spirit" (Sider 1975:434). Control is the operative concept here, for just as Paul envisions a charismatic body on earth acting orderly and in control (14:32), so should a spiritual body in heaven. He communicates the value he places on order and control in his affirmation that what is raised is a body.

Paul's insistence on "body" even in the resurrected state replicates his general body typology. The bodies that are described in 15:36–41 are differentiated bodies that may be ranked hierarchically. On earth, bodies are differentiated and classified as human, animal, bird, and fish:

> For not all flesh is alike, but there is one kind for men, another for animals, another for birds, and another for fish.
>
> 1 Corinthians 15:39

This, of course, reflects God's work at creation (Genesis 1 once more). Concerning celestial bodies, Paul speaks of a corresponding hierarchical classification system: sun, moon, and stars.

> There are celestial bodies and there are terrestrial bodies; but the glory of the celestial is one, and the glory of the terrestrial is another. There is one glory of the sun, and another glory of the moon, and another glory of the stars; for star differs from star in glory.
>
> 1 Corinthians 15:40–41

This type of perception and language is fully consonant with Paul's Pharisaic sense of an exact purity system—a place for everything and everything in its place. Just as the macrocosm is differentiated in terms of glory, likewise the microcosm. As there are bodies on earth, so are there bodies in heaven.

We should see this alongside other remarks about Christian resurrection where there is order, pattern, and differentiation: "In Christ shall all be made alive. *But each in his own order*: Christ the first fruits, then at his coming those who belong to Christ" (15:22–23). In heaven Paul expects a distinct hierarchy among its inhabitants: God, Christ, then Christians. In the risen state in God's presence, moreover, there will not be a total abolition of authority and structure. "Every rule and every authority and power" will be put under Christ's feet (15:24), and then Christ will be under God's feet (see 15:28). For the head of Christ is God. As it is on earth, so it will be in heaven.

According to Paul, then, the order and structure of the heavenly macrocosm should be replicated in the earthly microcosm. But after the end of the earthly microcosm, the heavenly macrocosm will endure, with all its order and patterns. Earthly persons who enter the heavenly world must confirm its maps. As there is a hierarchy of heads and authority on earth (11:3), so in heaven Christ will be subject to God even when the end comes and all is put under his feet (15:24–28). As God differentiated on earth the parts of the physical and social body (12:18, 24), so "God [will give] it a [risen] body as he has chosen" (15:38). As there was a body on earth, which implied order and control, so Paul maintains that there will be a body in heaven as well, with the same symbolic import. The order of God's creation will not be abolished in heaven.

**6.5 *An Athlete's Body*** Paul's attitude to the physical body and its replication of the social body is never clearer than in the athletic metaphor he uses in 9:24–27. As far as the metaphor goes, the physical body is subject to strong regulation. Every athlete "exercises self-control in all things" (9:25); an athlete regulates his body and "subdues" it (9:27). No individual member of the body escapes this control: the legs do not run aimlessly nor do the fists box the air (9:26). This points to strong coordination of the individual members toward a common goal, for the common good.

The metaphor serves as the final point in Paul's argument to the knowledgeable ones who proclaim freedom to eat idol meat. He has shown in chapter 9 that he himself is as free as anyone in regard to specific items, such as support; he has a right (*exousia*, 9:4, 6, 12), which is validated in tradition, Jesus' words, and the Law. Yet Paul voluntarily regulates this right and foregoes its privileges (9:15, 17) for the sake of the common good, namely, the preaching of the gospel (9:23). Paul seeks not his own good, but the good of others: "I have become all things to all men, that I might by all means save some" (9:22). He presents his own behavior as a model for those who would eat idol meat—restraint of freedom (vs. exercise of rights) for the sake of communal cohesion (vs. individualism).

The athlete metaphor reinforces this argument by showing circumstances where discipline, self-control, regulation of the body, and group-oriented behavior are appropriate. Paul's use of the athlete metaphor implies that it is appropriate in his life as a general principle, not just in regard to his rights and freedoms. And so, Paul implies, life is an athletic contest and the discipline, regulation, self-control appropriate to athletic training are perennial norms structuring one's life. This, of course, is the predictable attitude to the body from the viewpoint of a strong group or controlled body cosmology.

## 7.0 Conclusions and Further Inquiry

Mary Douglas's remarks on "body" and her anthropological model prove to be an accurate and useful heuristic device for evaluating the contrasting attitudes to body in 1 Corinthians. In particular, Paul's viewpoint in the letter may be accurately described according to the cosmology of a controlled body, whereas the position attributed to Paul's opponents in 1 Corinthians corresponds to the cosmology of an uncontrolled body. Valuable also is the insight into the correlation of physical body and social body, namely, how attitudes to the physical body are replicated in the way the social body is perceived. Douglas's model, moreover, suggested a coherent interpretation of Paul's perspective by indicating the cultural cosmology of the author and how consistently interrelated Paul's remarks are in regard to freedom, authority, rules, and roles. According to Douglas's model, Paul perceives the world through a dominant value—holiness, or purity—which structures the way the social and physical bodies are perceived and regulated. Alternately, the chief evil in Paul's world is pollution, which likewise is expressed in both social and physical terms.

**7.1 Body Language in Other Pauline Letters**  One might ask, however, how typical of Paul is the perspective found in 1 Corinthians? It is beyond the scope of this study to pursue this important question in detail. But a quick glance at the Pauline corpus suggests places to test the model in other Pauline letters and to ascertain whether the perceptions found in 1 Corinthians are typical of Paul elsewhere. For example: (1) Paul's concern in 1 Corinthians with the holiness of the body should be compared with his remarks on bodily holiness in Romans 12:1–2; 13:12–14, Philippians 1:20, and 1 Thessalonians 4:1–8. (2) His concern with regulating the bodily orifices in 1 Corinthians might be compared with remarks about eating found in Romans 14–15 (esp. 14:21), and about marriage found in 1 Thessalonians 4:4–7 and 2 Corinthians 6:14–7:1. (3) The understanding of the church as a body in Romans 12:4–8 could be compared with the use of that metaphor in 1 Corinthians 12 and 2 Corinthians 6:16. (4) Paul's control of the sexual orifice in 1 Corinthians has a bearing on how we understand the description of the church as a virgin betrothed to Christ (2 Cor. 11). Calling attention to the bride's virginity legitimates a strict guarding of the female sexual orifice. (5) Paul accuses certain people in the church at Corinth of being "puffed up" (4:6, 18–19; 5:2; 13:4). This might profitably be studied in terms of bodily wholeness, that is, in terms of something being "too much" (see 2.5.1 and 2.5.2 above).

**7.2 Controlled Body Perspective in Other Letters**  Besides these specific body issues, a comparison could be made of Paul's attitudes to related topics in 1 Corinthians and his other letters. If his perception of a body is that of a controlled body that favors formality, smoothness, structure, and ritualism, these values should be evident even when the physical body is not being discussed. For example: (1) The value given to roles, rank, and status within the church and in the secular world might be assessed; one thinks immediately of Romans 13:1–7, but also of Philippians 2:19–20. (2) The contextualized understanding of freedom in 1 Corinthians might profitably be compared with the language of "slaves of God . . . and of righteousness" in Romans 6:13–22, especially in light of the diatribal false conclusion that Christians might be lawless. Galatians 5:1 and 13–15 deserve to be assessed in this light as well. (3) The perception of pollution threatening the group could also be investigated, whether this means pollution as seduction (see 2 Cor. 11:1–3, 12–15) or as threat to unity (see Gal. 5:15, 22; Phil. 3:1–11, esp. 6–7). (4) The personal identity of members of the church as group oriented might be tested in Philippians 2:1–5, 14–18 (esp. 2:3–4), and in 1 Thessalonians 1:3 and 4:9–12.

# 6

# Sin and Deviance
# in Paul's World

This persuasion is not from him who calls you. A little leaven leavens the whole lump.

Galatians 5:8–9

## 1.0 Introduction

In this chapter we begin to examine the last part of Paul's symbolic universe. We must ask about his attitudes to sin and deviance, his view of the way the universe operates, and his explanation of suffering and misfortune. These matters are of considerable importance, for the way sin is perceived implies a strategy for dealing with it, either tolerance or intolerance. If the cosmos is perceived as a battleground of warring forces, this will affect how one views enemies and opponents. And

*147*

one's attitude to suffering and misfortune in the world depends on whether one perceives the world as a just place with stable laws.

Concerning these three areas, we suggest the following hypothesis about Paul's point of view. Paul and most others in his world viewed sin in two ways, either as formal violation of rules and laws or as corruption and disease. Both perceptions are found in Paul's letters. The importance of this lies in the radically different social strategies for dealing with sin that are implied in these perceptions. Like most others in Paul's world, he perceives the cosmos in radically dualistic terms. He sees all forces and powers in it anthropomorphically, that is, personified in terms of God and God's agents, or Satan and demons. He perceives, moreover, this dualistic cosmos as a battleground for warring forces of Good and Evil. Finally, because the cosmos is peopled with personified forces of Good and Evil at war, Paul perceives suffering and misfortune as a personal attack on him or his kin. Suffering is unjustly deserved! Yet, because Evil always attacks Good, one expects such assaults. With these general ideas in mind, let us examine more closely the specific forms these perceptions take in Paul's letters.

As in the Gospels, so also in Paul's world sin and deviance are viewed in two fundamentally different ways. Sin can be understood both as the violation of formal rules and laws, as well as a disease or corruption that has entered the bodily and social organism. Both attitudes are present in the Pauline letters, and in all fairness to him we must recognize these two perspectives.

## 2.0 Sin as Rule Breaking

When Jesus' opponents attack him, they tend to accuse him of the violation of laws, rules, and traditions. How often one reads that his opponents accuse him of violating the Sabbath (Mark 2:23–3:6; Luke 13:10–17; 14:1–6; John 5:9–10, 16–17; 7:21–23; 9:14–16), thus transgressing one of the foundational commandments given to Moses: "Remember the sabbath day, to keep it holy" (Ex. 20:8). At his trial before the Sanhedrin, Jesus is accused of "blasphemy" (Mark 14:63–64//Matt. 26:65–66; see John 19:7). Other criticisms of Jesus include failures to fast (Mark 2:18) or wash his hands before meals (Mark 7:2), as well as eating with sinners (Mark 2:16). All of these are violations of known and accepted customs. We often read in the Gospels that Jesus' opponents listened carefully to every word he spoke and observed all his actions in detail to find something with which to accuse him. Such a perspective presumes the existence of laws, such as the Ten Commandments, and revered traditions and customs.

**2.1 Commonly Shared Moral Norms** People in Paul's world were not uncertain about the moral rules of their culture. At least, Paul claims that this is so: "Ever since the creation of the world [God's] invisible nature, namely, his eternal power and deity, has been clearly perceived in the things that have been made. So they are without excuse" (Rom. 1:20). It was, after all, an orderly cosmos with a clear and extensive classification system. Every thing and every person had their proper place and a clear set of cultural norms governing them.

Let us not presume the clarity of those cultural norms. A quick survey of our New Testament documents reveals the many forms in which the moral rules of that cultural world were clearly communicated:

1. The Ten Commandments (Rom. 13:8–11; Mark 10:19; Matt. 19:18; 1 Tim. 1:8–11; see also Matt. 5:21–37 and Mark 7:21–22)
2. Lists of virtues and vices (Gal. 5:19–23; 1 Cor. 6:9–11; Col. 3:5–17; James 3:13–18)
3. Tables of household duties (Eph. 5:21–6:9; Col. 3:18–4:1; 1 Tim. 2:11–5:22; 1 Peter 2:13–3:7)
4. Specific rules (1 Cor. 5:1; 9:8–10; 1 Thess. 4:3–8)

These are not the only citations of those rules, nor is the list of rules itself complete. The point is that people were socialized to know what their culture expected of them. The laws, traditions, rules, and customs were clear. Therefore, as Paul said, "They are without excuse." *For Paul the law is God's law. It reflects his will*

As in the Gospels, so also in Paul's letters we find sin often perceived as the violation of laws and rules, such as the Ten Commandments. The clearest example seems to be the remarks to the Corinthians:

> Do you not know that the unrighteous will not inherit the kingdom of God? Do not be deceived; neither the immoral, nor idolaters, nor adulterers, nor sexual perverts, nor thieves, nor the greedy, nor drunkards, nor revilers, nor robbers will inherit the kingdom of God.
>
> 1 Corinthians 6:9–10

The language is clear and uncompromising. God's will in the Scriptures gives us a clear catalog of sins to avoid.

**2.2 God's Just Judgment**  This perception of sin implies a sense of justice and fairness in God, upon which the Jewish norm of judgment, the *lex talionis*, was based (see Ex. 21:23–25; Lev. 24:18–20; Deut. 19:21). In the first part of Romans, Paul develops this notion extensively as part of his argument that all people stand rightly condemned of sin and in need of the saving death of Jesus Christ. Paul's opening remarks in Romans 1:24–28 tell a triple story of sin and its just retribution based on a clear *lex talionis*.

> They exchanged the glory of the immortal God
> . . . and God gave them up. (Rom. 1:22–24)
> They exchanged the truth about God
> . . . and God gave them up. (Rom. 1:25–27)
> Since they did not see fit to acknowledge God,
> God gave them up. (Rom. 1:28)

The law in this case is none other than the first of the Commandments, the basic obedience and loyalty owed to God. It should come as no surprise to us that Paul, the ex-Pharisee, is quite knowledgeable about the law of the covenant. Concerning his perfect observance of this law, Paul says in all candor: "As to righteousness under the law blameless" (Phil. 3:6).

The God of Israel judged justly and rendered to each according to his or her deeds (Ps. 62:12; Sirach 16:14). Hence, Paul speaks of the "righteous judgment" of God, according to which God "will render to every [person] according to his [or her] works" (Rom. 2:5–6). For according to Paul's perception: "We must all appear before the judgment seat of Christ, so that each one may receive good or evil, according to what he has done in the body" (2 Cor. 5:10). Hence, God is justified in his judgment of sin (Rom. 3:4–6). God's judgment, moreover, will produce no surprises. Rather, it will confirm the obvious. As one lives, so shall one reap (2 Cor. 9:6; Gal. 6:7–8). The principle is most clearly articulated in Romans: "There will be tribulation and distress for every human being who does evil, . . . but glory and honor and peace for every one who does good. . . . God shows no partiality" (2:9–11).

God's clear laws, his just judgment, and a sure quid pro quo retribution are characteristic features of Paul's understanding of sin (see Käsemann 1969:66–81). For example, he expresses this norm of judgment against those who pollute God's temple: "If any one destroys God's temple, God will destroy him" (1 Cor. 3:17a). Even in regard to lesser rules, such as women speaking in public, Paul shapes this custom in terms of a *lex talionis:* "If any one does not recognize this, he is not recognized" (1 Cor. 14:38).

Three ideas, then, cluster into a coherent argument: (1) There are commonly acknowledged laws, norms, and customs (2) whose violation constitutes sin, (3) which will be requited by a God who judges justly.

## 3.0 Sin as Disease or Corruption

Paul, however, perceives sin not only as the formal transgression of law, but often as an insidious corruption that threatens to pollute the integrity of the whole organism.

*3.1 Sin as Leaven* Paul regularly likens sin to leaven, which he sees as a symbol of an irresistible power of corruption. Like other Jews, his cultural perception of leaven comes from his socialization in terms of the Feasts of Unleavened Bread and Passover. At the Feast of Unleavened Bread, the leaven of the last year, which was perceived as a form of evil, pollution, and corruption (e.g., fermentation), must be cast out of the house and burned. Only in this state of purity can Passover be correctly celebrated. Leaven, then, implies corruption; even a bit of it will corrupt and ferment a whole batch of flour.

Readers must be cautious about Jesus' parable describing the kingdom of heaven as leaven (Matt. 13:33//Luke 13:20–21). The point of that parable may lie in the shocking use of something culturally viewed as "unclean" as a metaphor for God's kingdom. The traditional cultural meaning of leaven is better expressed in Jesus' remark: "Beware of the leaven of the Pharisees and Sadducees" (Matt. 16:6, 11). By this he meant their teaching (16:12), which he labeled as a virulent corruption that would completely pollute what is pure. Leaven, then, was culturally perceived by Jews as a corruption, a tiny pinch of which could ferment a whole bowl of pure flour.

We find a similar metaphor for sin in 2 Timothy 2:17, where false teaching is compared to "gangrene." This corruption, unless dealt with immediately and radically, threatens the life of the organism. Whether leaven or gangrene, sin can be perceived as something life threatening because it implies an inevitable process of corruption or fermentation of the organism in which it is found. Its presence calls for radical action, even intolerance. In this vein, one thinks of the saying in the Gospels about plucking out one eye and cutting off one hand or foot to save the whole body (Mark 9:42–48//Matt. 5:29–30; 18:6–9; Luke 17:1–2).

In two instances Paul describes the sin that he finds in the community as leaven. In both cases he appreciates the intense threat to the holy church posed by the presence of this corruption and disease. He perceives a certain illicit sexual union as an intolerable evil and prescribes its treatment in terms of what Jews do with leaven at Passover: "Do you not know that a little leaven leavens the whole lump? Cleanse out the old leaven that you may be a new lump, as you really are unleavened. For Christ, our paschal lamb, has been sacrificed. Let us, therefore, celebrate the festival, not with the old leaven, the leaven of malice and evil, but with the unleavened bread of sincerity and truth" (1 Cor. 5:6–8). Examining the illicit union as leaven, we note first of all that even "a little leaven" will corrupt the whole batch. Second, Paul perceives leaven as evil and sin, "the old leaven, the leaven of malice and evil." The church is called to be holy, that is, "unleavened," and so to celebrate the Passover totally free from corruption and pollution.

Given the perception of leaven as a threat of total corruption, Paul considers an intolerant response to this sin as appropriate: "Cleanse out the old leaven!" These remarks reinforce the command in 1 Corinthians 5 that the man involved in the illicit union be excommunicated from the holy church (1 Cor. 5:5, 11, 13).

Paul uses the example of leaven a second time in Galatians 5:2–12 in regard to the adoption of circumcision by some in the community. He perceives circumcision by a follower of Jesus as a sin, but not as a breaking of a rule, which circumcision clearly was not, according to the Scriptures. As a Pharisee, Paul viewed circumcision as obedience to God's law (Gen. 17:9–14); he himself was "circumcised on the eighth day" (Phil. 3:5) as part of his perfect obedience to God's law. But once baptized, Paul considers circumcision deviance from the covenant made in Christ. In this context, he labels circumcision a corruption that will destroy Christians. Paul argues that if a disciple of Jesus is circumcised, "Christ will be of no advantage to you" (Gal. 5:2) in terms of forgiveness of sins and participation in God's grace and righteousness. In fact, to be circumcised is to be "[cut off] from Christ" (5:4): that is, there is loss of the benefit of the Spirit and the adoption that come with being "in Christ." Circumcision, then, implies for Paul a total loss of holiness, separation from Christ, and hence uncleanness and death.

Having said this, Paul clarifies his understanding of this sin in terms of leaven: "A little leaven leavens the whole lump" (5:9). If his understanding of circumcision as a corruption was not clear before this, it should be now. This small cut on the male body, then, is life threatening. Ignored, it will destroy the whole organism. Therefore, Paul demands intolerant action toward those who urge it: cast them out, or to continue the metaphor, let them be "cut off" (5:12). In 1 Corinthians and Galatians, then, certain sins are perceived as corrupting pollutions, even as "leaven."

**3.2 Gangrenous Doctrine**  Although terms such as *leaven* are not used regarding the alleged deviant doctrine of the seductive Superapostles in 2 Corinthians 11, Paul's perception of their preaching suggests that he considers it a type of poison and corruption. The same would apply to the Judaizing doctrine of "another gospel" in Galatians. After all, in 2 Timothy 2:17 erroneous doctrine is explicitly called "gangrene." One might draw the conclusion that in certain circumstances, Paul perceived his churches as infected with evil, which is not simply the violation of a law, but appears to be a corruption threatening the life and holiness of the church. Like leaven, gangrene acts as a threat to the well-being of the whole organism; even a little will eventually corrupt a healthy body. We will have more to say on this in the chapter on witchcraft accusations, where sin-as-leaven is described as a poison given by a sorcerer to work harm.

### 4.0 Strategies for Dealing with Sin

Do the two understandings of sin affect the behaviors of those who perceive it in different ways? Most definitely, the contrasting perceptions warrant quite different responses.

**4.1 Tolerance and Forgiveness**  When sin is perceived as the violation of a known rule, then God in justice will deal with the sinner and the sin in good time. The sin is not necessarily perceived as life threatening to the community and does not necessarily warrant the intolerance of excommunication or immediate punishment.

In fact, the owner of the fig tree may manure it and give it another year to produce its fruit before it is cut down (Luke 13:6–9). God's slowness in judgment is often interpreted as the gift of time for the repentance of a sinner (Rom. 2:4–5). Therefore, there may be no sense of urgency on God's part to deal with the threat to the individual and the community. The delay of the parousia may be a gift of time for repentance (2 Peter 3:9). When sin is perceived as the violation of formal rules, then one might legitimately look to strategies that contain prayer for sinners, allowance of time for repentance, even an exhortation to forgive sinners (Matt. 18:21–22, 23–35; 1 John 5:16). The all-knowing and just-judging God remains in control of the orderly world. Therefore, no radical action is necessarily required by the orderly community of God.

**4.2 Intolerance**   If, however, one perceives of sin as corruption (leaven or gangrene), then one will tend to respond quite differently. The situation is typically perceived as life threatening: gangrene unchecked will kill the whole body; leaven, once introduced, will ferment the whole batch. Death, corruption, loss of holiness, and separation from God are issues of the utmost seriousness. Immediate action, not delay, is required. Hence, if your hand causes you to sin, cut it off! Likewise an offending eye and foot (Mark 9:43–48; Matt. 5:29–30). In this context, intolerance becomes a virtue—in fact, the only sensible strategy for dealing with the crisis. Thus, bodily mutilation (Mark 9:43–48) and excommunication (1 Cor. 5:13; Gal. 4:30), which might otherwise be condemned for rendering a whole body unclean because of its subsequent unwholeness, preserve the holiness of the organism. From this perspective, they are appropriate strategies for dealing with sin.

**4.3 Paul's Spotless Church**   Which strategy do we find in Paul's letters? Because both perceptions of sin are found in his letters, it is not surprising to find both strategies for dealing with sin—tolerance and intolerance. In Romans, where Paul seems not to be addressing a crisis in a church he founded, he takes a more tolerant view of sin and judgment. Although consigning all people under sin (3:9, 23), he still speaks of God's just and impartial judgment. In this context he notes God's kindness, which is meant to lead to repentance (Rom. 2:4). God has evidently given humankind time for repentance; but they ought not to "presume upon the riches of [God's] kindness and forbearance and patience" (2:4a). In his letter to the Romans, then, Paul articulates a strategy of repentance from sin in connection with a view of God's merciful judgment. Again, he does not address a crisis in the church, an invasion of false teachers or false doctrines.

Yet, after finding this passage in Romans and understanding it in its context, we must be careful lest we promote it as Paul's dominant or characteristic strategy for dealing with sin. A qualifying question is in order: What is Paul's characteristic reaction to sin and forgiveness in the church? Or to phrase it more cogently, when Paul finds sin or evil in his churches, how does he tend to label it? As rule breaking? Or as corruption and leaven? In short, do we find Paul urging forgiveness of sins and toleration in his letters?

Modern readers have to remind themselves that when they read Paul, they do not have Matthew's Gospel before them, in which we find numerous passages urging forgiveness of sins within the church (Matt. 6:14–15; 9:12–13; 18:10–14, 21–22, 23–35; 26:28). According to Paul, God forgave our sins when we crossed from death to life, and from slavery to evil to service of God (Rom. 3:24–25). But Paul is almost mute about forgiveness of sins committed after becoming God's children (perhaps 1 Cor. 6:7–8; 2 Cor. 2:9–11). Whereas Hebrews 6:4–8 states that forgiveness of postbaptismal sins is precluded, Paul has no explicit comment. Yet we find his perceptions implied elsewhere.

As noted above, the "leaven" of illicit sexual unions and circumcision is not to be tolerated. It must be driven from the midst of the holy church. The same would apply to the presence of heretical doctrine in 2 Corinthians 11 and Galatians 1. The perception of boundaries threatened (e.g., 1 Cor. 5:9–10; 2 Cor. 6:14–7:1) does not leave much space for a conciliatory doctrine of forgiveness.

Furthermore, earlier in this book we noted Paul's broad semantic word field for the term *purity*. From that we learned how Paul exhorts the church to be "innocent" (*akeraios*; Rom. 16:19), "blameless" (*amōmos*; Phil. 2:15), "irreproachable" (*anegklētos*; 1 Cor. 1:8). He demands of the church perfect purity "so that he may establish your hearts unblamable (*amemptous*) before our God and Father, at the coming of our Lord Jesus with all his saints" (1 Thess. 3:13). Paul's Pharisaic socialization asserts itself in his perception of sin. Speaking of God's demand for total purity (*katharismos*) in marriage (1 Thess. 4:3), Paul describes God as "an avenger in all these things" (1 Thess. 4:6). "For God has not called us for uncleanness, but in holiness" (4:7). Perceiving sin as corruption, Paul correspondingly urges a strategy of intolerance in the presence of uncleanness.

In several places in this book, we examine Paul's use of anathemas and excommunication. We will study this in particular in the final two chapters in regard to Galatians and 2 Corinthians 10–13. But such a strategy makes sense only when one perceives the cause for such radical actions to be life threatening. Heresy for Paul was the worst sin, a corruption of the gospel. Confronted with it, his strategy was one of intolerance.

One final observation is in order here. Paul several times reminds us that he "persecuted the church" (1 Cor. 15:9; Gal. 1:13, 23; Phil. 3:6). As we noted earlier, his actions stem from his perception of Jesus and his teaching as a corruption of the Judaism into which Paul was socialized. Paul expresses this perception clearly in terms of purity and pollution: "As to the law a Pharisee, . . . as to righteousness under the law blameless" (Phil. 3:5–6). Hence Paul saw his Pharisaic thinking and behavior as fully in accord with God's holiness. This led him to consider Jesus and his gospel as a pollution, a perception that explains his reaction to Jesus and the Christian gospel: "As to zeal a persecutor of the church" (Phil. 3:6). Zealous for God, he must be the enemy of God's enemies. His strategy in this context was intolerance toward "the Way" (Donaldson 1989:668–680).

## 5.0 Summary

Paul, therefore, perceives sin and deviance in two different ways. At times, the formal breaking of God's commandments constitutes sin, but at other times, Paul understands sin as corruption and disease. God deals with sin-as-broken-rules in a variety of ways, which liberally include patience, slowness to judge, and time for repentance. But the perception of sin-as-corruption allows for no such time because it demands immediate and intolerant action. God may forgive the breaking of commandments, but God cannot tolerate corruption. Both perceptions are found in Paul's letters. Upon examination, moreover, this latter perception and its implied strategy prove to be the more typical perception in Paul's letters.

# 7

# Paul's Cosmology:
# War in a Dualistic World

We wanted to come to you . . . but Satan hindered us.
1 Thessalonians 2:18

## 1.0 Introduction: Cosmology

In one sense we have already examined certain aspects of the way Paul views his world. In Chapters 2 and 3 we noted the many maps whereby Paul's world is ordered and structured. As creation indicates, God has made a *kosmos* where there is a place for everything and everything is in its place. But in Chapter 4 we discovered that Paul also focuses much attention on boundaries, either making them or defending them. In fact, Paul and most people in his world perceive intense threats to the boundaries of their world, the boundaries both of country and city as well as those of the physical body. A world that should be orderly is under attack (Schweizer 1988:455–468). The perception of the cosmos under attack was confirmed by the recent examination of sin as corruption. Evil is perceived to have insinuated itself within the boundaries of the holy body of the church. Thus, when we formally take up the question of how Paul and others perceive their cosmos, we are already alerted to elements of dualism, boundaries attacked, and warring powers in the cosmos.

## 2.0 Paul's Dualistic World

It is surely an understatement to assert here that Paul perceives his world in terms of dualisms. Already in this book we have noted how many of the maps that structure his world are based on dualistic perspectives.

In the chapter on order and purity, we noted that Paul perceives both maps of time and maps of persons that dualistically divide reality into opposing polarities.

*2.1 Dualistic Map of Time*    Time for Paul was divided into periods of then and now. According to this pattern, the long period when humanity in the image of the old Adam lived in sin and subjection to death was contrasted with the new period when humanity in the image of the new Adam enjoys God's righteousness and "reigns in life" (see Rom. 5:12–21).

*2.2 Dualistic Map of Persons*    Paul perceives the world radically divided into dualistic camps of good and bad persons: saints/unrighteous (1 Cor. 6:1, 9), those within/those without (1 Cor. 5:12–13; 1 Thess. 4:12), enlightened/not enlightened (Rom. 10:2), Jacob who was loved/Esau who was hated (Rom. 9:12–13), and children of light/children of darkness (1 Thess. 5:4–11). This mode of description echoes similar dualistic expressions in the Gospels that compare and contrast the followers of Jesus with all others in terms of wheat/chaff, sheep/wolves, few/many who travel the narrow/wide path, good/bad fish, wise/foolish maidens, and sheep/goats.

*2.3 Dualistic Map of Masters*    The map of time only clarifies how with the coming of Christ we have changed masters. We leave slavery to sin and evil and become the slaves of God. Once we were "slaves of sin," when "sin reigned" in our mortal bodies to make us obey their passions (Rom. 6:12). But now we have been "set free from sin and have become slaves of God" (6:22).

***2.4 Dualism and Fences*** Paul's major form of ritual was the making and maintenance of boundaries. Boundaries necessarily separate and divide, thus reinforcing a sense of dualism. Clean must be separated from unclean and pure from polluted. Moreover, God's dealings with Israel can and should be divided into two covenants, which Paul presents in dualistic perspective.

***2.5 Dualistic Covenants*** In Galatians 3–4, Paul contrasts God's promise given to Abraham with the law given to Moses in dualistic terms: faith/works, blessing/curse, spirit/flesh and freedom/slavery. The basic dualistic perception implies that one cannot and should not belong to both. Because the covenants are contrasted as good and evil, good is always to be chosen and evil to be avoided.

**Spirit/Flesh:** When Paul compares and contrasts God's two covenants in Galatians, he begins in Galatians 3:1–5 with the dualism of spirit and flesh. He appeals to the Galatians' experience of receiving God's free gift of Spirit as their eyewitness basis for his argument: "Did you receive the Spirit by works of the law, or by hearing with faith?" (3:2). Stressing God's gift, he asks: "Does he who supplies the Spirit to you and works miracles among you do so by works of the law, or by hearing with faith?" (3:5). God elected these Gentile followers of Jesus and gave them the Spirit of adoption whereby they became God's own family (4:6–7). Gift of "Spirit," then, characterizes God's covenantal relationship with the followers of Jesus.

Yet "spirit" here stands in contrast to the covenant of Moses, which Paul labels "flesh." After all, Judaizing practices concentrated on the flesh, at least circumcision and diet. "Flesh" is how Paul describes Hagar's son, Ishmael (Gal. 4:23, 29), who is a symbol for Paul of the alternative covenant. Having begun in the "spirit," then, the Galatians would be foolish to "end with the flesh" (3:3).

**Blessing/Curse:** When contrasting the two covenants, Paul labels the arrangement with Abraham a "blessing" for him and for all the nations who share the saving faith of Abraham (Gal.

3:8–9). In contrast, those who belong to the covenant of Moses are they who "rely on works of the law," and they are "under a curse": "*Cursed* be every one who does not abide by all things written in the book of the law, and do them" (3:10). Except for foolish, deceived people, who would prefer curse to blessing?

**Freedom/Slavery:** Paul's distinguishing of the two covenants continues in Galatians 4:21–31, where he contrasts them by means of an "allegory," which is the story of Sarah and Hagar and their respective sons, Isaac and Ishmael. Hagar, the slave woman, "bears children for slavery" (i.e., Ishmael), whereas Sarah, "the free woman," bears free children, namely, Isaac. Hagar must be cast out, "For the son of the slave shall not inherit with the son of the free woman" (4:30). Free children remain, but slaves are cast out (see John 8:31–36).

If the comparison of the two covenants in Galatians 3:6–12 stressed blessing/curse and faith/works, the allegory in 4:21–31 emphasizes freedom/slavery, inheritance/dispossession, re-maining/being cast out, and spirit/flesh.

Paul draws these dualistic distinctions with emphatic sharp-ness, so that the contrasts might be as crisp as possible. His dualistic distinctions articulate patterns of values or worthless-ness and hence imply a moral stance: one covenant is to be highly valued and the other foresworn. Paul leaves no room for ambiguity, because the purpose of his dualistic description is to preclude the possibility of belonging to both covenants and to avoid any attempt at blending the two. They are mutually ex-clusive.

*2.6 Baptismal Contrasts* Following our examination of the dualisms used in the self-definition of the church, we recall the sharp contrasts used in regard to the ritual transition of bap-tism.

| "before" | vs. | "after" |
|---|---|---|
| darkness | vs. | light |
| ignorance | vs. | knowledge |
| passion/flesh | vs. | spirit |
| deceit | vs. | truth |
| death | vs. | life |
| drunken/asleep | vs. | sober/awake |
| lust | vs. | holiness |
| blindness | vs. | sight |

These dualisms affect not only perception, but also behavior.

As we noted in regard to 2 Corinthians 6:14–7:1, there can be no fellowship between light and darkness, no partnership between righteousness and iniquity. Just as Christ has nothing whatever in common with Belial, so also believers with unbelievers. Therefore, the appropriate strategy in this dualistic perspective is "Come out from them, and be separate from them" (6:17). From these examples and from the detailed presentation of maps and boundaries made earlier, we are safe in concluding that Paul tends to perceive the world and all in it in radically dualistic terms.

### 3.0 All Powers Personified: Anthropomorphism

Our study of Paul's dualistic perspective has focused on the distinctions in the earthly realm between Christians and Gentiles and Christians and Jews. But we must examine another set of dichotomous perceptions, namely, the dualisms in the heavenly realm both between God and Satan and between the good spirit and bad spirits. We note here that, like others in his world, Paul too perceives the malevolent heavenly powers as personified.

**3.1 Night, Death, and the Evil One** Twentieth-century Westerners describe night as the absence of light, death as the absence of life, and evil as the absence of good. Not so Paul and his world. They perceive Night as a somebody, not an absence of something. Matthew twice speaks of the Moon having an evil influence on people on earth (see *selēniazesthai*, "to be moonstruck," Matt. 4:24; 17:15), indicating that it is an active agent. Evil too is real, and in the Gospels we pray to "escape the Evil One" (Matt. 6:13) and to be "protected from the evil one" (John 17:15). It is in this vein that we note how Paul speaks of Sin and Death as personified phenomena.

Paul describes the period before Christ as a kingdom ruled over by Death: "Death reigned" (Rom. 5:14, 17, 21). And he says the same thing about Sin: "Sin reigned" (Rom. 5:21; 6:12). Paul does not consider these personifications of Sin and Death as mere figures of speech. Elsewhere he speaks of Death, the last enemy of Christ, who has not yet been put under the feet of this new Adam (1 Cor. 15:26). And, citing Hosea 13:14, he addresses it: "O Death, where is thy victory? O Death, where is thy sting?" (1 Cor. 15:55).

**3.2 The Army of God's Enemies** In the Pauline letters we find comparable examples of this typical personification of malevolent forces. The labels of these figures in Paul differ from those found in the Gospels (Wink 1984), for he never speaks of "the Devil" (*diabolos*) nor of an "unclean spirit" (*pneuma akatharon*). Only once does he mention "demon" *(daimonion,* 1 Cor. 10:20–21) and "spirit of the world" (*pneuma,* 1 Cor. 2:12). Yet his cosmos is crowded with other personified malevolent figures, as the following list indicates.

1. Death (1 Cor. 15:26; Rom. 5:14, 17)
2. Sin (Rom. 5:21; 6:12; 7:11–23)
3. Satan (Rom. 16:20; 1 Cor. 5:5; 7:5; 2 Cor. 2:11; 11:14; 12:7; 1 Thess. 2:18)
4. Rule/*archē* (1 Cor. 15:24; Rom. 8:38)
5. Rulers/*archontes* (1 Cor. 2:6, 8)
6. Power/*exousia* (1 Cor. 15:24)
7. Power/*dynamis* (1 Cor. 15:24; Rom. 8:38)
8. Tempter (1 Thess. 3:5)
9. Elements/*stoicheia* (Gal. 4:3, 9)
10. Beings that by nature are no gods (Gal. 4:8)
11. Spirit of the world (1 Cor. 2:12)
12. Demons (1 Cor. 10:20–21)
13. Angels (1 Cor. 6:3; 2 Cor. 11:14; 12:7; Gal. 1:8; Rom. 8:38)
14. God of this age (2 Cor. 4:4) (Hall 1973:132–160)

This impressive list suggests a well-populated heavenly realm. When we examine the activities of these personified figures, we learn that they constitute a formidable army waging deadly combat against God's holy ones. Certain of the figures are clearly perceived as personal: Death, Sin, Satan, Rulers, Tempters, Demons, Angels, Spirits and gods (Schlier 1961:18–19). The same perception should be extended to Rule, Power, and Elements, both because of the company they keep and the similarity of their common malevolent actions against God's creatures. The full force of this list of personified figures conveys its power when we examine the way they wage war on God's creatures.

## 4.0 Worlds at War

The dualistic, personified forces in Paul's world wage war against each other. Second-temple Jewish writings and early Christian documents often describe a cosmic war between Good and Evil. Of course, this is not thematic in every document, and in some it is not evident at all. But this apocalyptic viewpoint represents a typical perspective found in the Jewish world of Jesus and Paul. At its starkest, it reflects an experience of crisis, disaster, and injustice in the lives of people who claim faithfulness to God, but who experience war, not peace. It is not our task to describe this cosmic war in detail, but rather to suggest the form and emphasis it has in Paul's writings.

The war takes place both in the heavens and on earth. We read of instances of single combat, such as the angel Michael contending with Satan (Jude 9). More commonly, we find descriptions of war between God's angels and a host of demons (Rev. 16–18). Yet frequently we read of the war waged by the malevolent heavenly powers against God's creatures on earth, which seems more accurately to reflect the perception of the Gospels and Paul's letters. The following passage from a Qumran document adequately illustrates this second aspect of the war: "And all the blows that smite them [and] all the times of their distress are because of the dominion of his malevolence. And all the spirits of his lot cause the sons of light to stumble" (1QS 3:23–25).

**4.1 Jesus at War Against Satan**   Because it is important to insist that early Christian writings operate out of this perception, let us pause to examine how one evangelist understood the role of Jesus as warrior fighting Satan and his demons. This should give us some basis of comparison with Paul's point of view. Mark's earliest chapters describe Jesus confronting and defeating a host of Spirits that have warred on people and captured them as slaves (Robinson 1957:33–42).

In this regard, we can identify four points. First, we note that Mark labels these foes of Jesus as "unclean spirits" (Mark 1:23; 3:11; 5:8; 6:7, etc.), perhaps to distinguish them clearly from Jesus' "Holy Spirit" (Mark 1:8, 10, 12; 3:29–30). Second, "holy" and "unclean" are at war, as is acknowledged in the inaugural, and so programmatic, confrontation between Jesus and the Evil Spirits: "Have you come to destroy us? I know who you are, the Holy One of God" (Mark 1:24). In response to the charge that Jesus himself has a demon, he replies that allies do not war on each other, only enemies (Mark 3:23–26). Describing himself as a "stronger man," Jesus implies that it is his business "to enter a strong man's house and plunder his goods." The stronger man (Jesus) can do this to the strong man (Satan) only after he "first binds the strong man; then indeed he may plunder his house" (3:27). Jesus clearly is that stronger man (see *ischyroteros*, 1:7) who battles and defeats Satan (1:12–13). Third, illness is perceived as harm worked by "deaf and dumb spirits" (Mark 9:25) or as enslavement by Satan (e.g.,

Luke 13:16). We already noted that Matthew twice describes people suffering from the evil influence of the Moon (Matt. 4:24; 17:15). Finally, Mark perceives storms of wind as the work of Evil Spirits. He describes Jesus' dealing with the storm in 4:35–41 in terms identical with his victory over the "unclean spirits": he "rebuked it," commanded it "Be silent!" and it obeyed him (see Mark 1:21–28). Jesus, then, acts as God's champion in the war against Evil Spirits (see Mark 3:27).

**4.2 Paul and the War Against Satan**   Paul also describes Jesus continuing that same war, not so much in warring against Spirits on earth, but battling and conquering them in the heavenly realm. In a passage where an exact map of time plays an important role, Paul describes a future time, "the end," when Christ will present God a kingdom totally pacified and rid of Evil Spirits: "He delivers the kingdom to God . . . *after* destroying every Rule and every Authority and Power" (1 Cor. 15:24). Even then Paul indicates a protracted battle "until he has put all his enemies under his feet"; and "the last enemy" is Death (15:25–26). But this victory is not yet achieved; the war is not over; people on earth still suffer from the attacks of Evil Spirits. And they are still subject to Death (1 Thess. 4:13–18; 1 Cor. 11:30; 15:6).

Speaking more directly of the war of Spirits as this affects the church on earth, Paul has much to say about Satan and the harm he works on God's children. He reminds the Corinthians that despite baptism and their sharing in Christ's resurrection, they are nevertheless still subject to attacks from Satan: " . . . lest Satan tempt you through lack of self-control" (1 Cor. 7:5; see 2 Cor. 2:11). Although Paul prays at the end of Romans that "the God of peace will soon crush Satan under your feet" (16:20), he implies that Satan is still active. Satan still has a kingdom and power, to which Paul would assign an intolerable sinner: "You are to deliver this man to Satan" (1 Cor. 5:5).

As we see, in Paul's view Satan is still belligerently active. In 2 Corinthians he fears that as Satan disguised himself to seduce Eve, so "his servants" are even now working the same harm on this church (2 Cor. 11:14–15). Even Paul experienced harm from Satan. He planned several times to come to Thessalonika, yet Evil prevented him: "We wanted to come to you . . . but Satan hindered us" (1 Thess. 2:18; see Rom. 15:22 and perhaps 1:13). Thus, despite the proclamation of Jesus as the victorious warrior under whose feet God has put all enemies, Paul continues to remark about the continued war Satan wages against him and the church. Indeed, "The God of peace will soon crush Satan under your feet" (Rom. 16:20); but the war is still going on! And Satan remains a deadly foe.

Likewise, in regard to Jews who do not and cannot believe in the Gospel, Paul remarks: "In their case the god of this world has blinded the minds of the unbelievers, to keep them from seeing the light of the gospel of the glory of Christ" (2 Cor. 4:4). Such a remark resembles those found in Mark 4:10–12, where failure to see and hear is attributed to malevolent Evil Spirits (Marcus 1984:558–563). In an analogous way, Paul reminds the Galatians that before their adoption as God's offspring they were enslaved to malevolent Powers: "When we were children, we were slaves to the elemental spirits" (Gal. 4:3) and "How can you turn back again to the weak and beggarly elemental spirits" (4:9).

**4.3 Paul's Own War** Apart from the list of cosmic powers who act malevolently against God's people on earth, we can appreciate Paul's sense of a world at war in his exhortations to be armed against the foe. In two places Paul urges his readers to put on the armor of virtue: "Put on the breastplate of faith and love, and for a helmet the hope of salvation" (1 Thess. 5:8) and "Let us then cast off the works of darkness and put on the armor of light" (Rom. 13:12; see Eph. 6:11–17). This metaphorical language goes hand in hand with his perception that both he and his followers are truly engaged in a war. Of himself he says, "For though we live in the world we are not carrying on a worldly war, for the weapons of our warfare are not worldly but have divine power to destroy strongholds" (2 Cor. 10:3–4; see 6:7). Whether he is responding to the attack of false teachers upon the church or speaking more generally, Paul describes the task of the followers of Jesus as co-warriors in a cosmic battle against Evil, Satan, and heavenly Powers.

## 5.0 Unfinished Business

How goes the war? We find two different responses in Paul's letters. His repeated confession that "Jesus is Lord" (1 Cor. 12:3; Phil. 2:11; Rom. 10:9) implies some acknowledgment of his power and triumph. Alone of all his sisters and brothers, Jesus has broken the chains of slavery to Death: "Death no longer has dominion over him" (Rom. 6:9; see Rom. 5:12–21). And in time he will complete his triumph over Death, which still enslaves us (1 Cor. 15:25–26).

Yet in other letters, especially those that reflect situations where Paul fears for the integrity of the church or senses attacks on his authority, the perception of war remains acute, even a war that the church might well lose. Although he begins his letter to the Galatians with a greeting from Jesus, who "gave himself for our sins to deliver us from the present evil age" (1:4), the rest of the letter does not square with so positive a remark. The Galatians are indeed bewitched by powers still active; and they have not in fact escaped "the present evil age." Furthermore, we noted above the many references to Satan's attacks on Paul and the church. In a subsequent chapter we will take up the accusations of witchcraft found in 2 Corinthians 10–13 and Galatians. The perception behind these accusations indicates a world hardly pacified and certainly not safe from mortal assault.

The two perceptions of Paul, optimistic of eventual success and pessimistic in certain situations, do not cancel each other out; both are true, but are of different churches at different times. Nevertheless, in regard to dualistic, personal powers at war in his world, Paul is not a chronicler of times past; the war is personally real to him and his churches. The conflict still continues.

# 8

# Suffering and Misfortune
# in a World at War

We have become, and are now, as the refuse of the world, the offscouring of all things.

1 Corinthians 4:13

1.0 Suffering and Misfortune
2.0 Who Did This to Me?
3.0 Two Ways/Two Spirits
    3.1 Two Masters
    3.2 Two Spirits
    3.3 Two Sovereigns
        3.3.1 Sin, Death, and Satan
        3.3.2 God's Holy Spirit
4.0 Evil Attacks Good
5.0 Paul's Unjust Sufferings
    5.1 Misfortune Caused by Satan
    5.2 Imprisonment
    5.3 Bodily Illness
    5.4 Weakness and Opponents
    5.5 Catalogs of Hardships
    5.6 Sufferings of Others
6.0 Summary and Conclusions

## 1.0 Suffering and Misfortune

The question we ask here regards theodicy: How do Paul and others explain suffering and misfortune in their world? It should come as no surprise that there might be several explanations in Paul (Gager 1970:325–337).

Related to the perception of sin as the transgression of a formal law, suffering and misfortune might be described as God's just judgment, which requites evil according to a *lex talionis* (see Rom. 1:24–28; 2:6–10). Such a perspective presupposes a world of clear norms, fair treatment by a just God, and predictable, orderly arrangements: "For we must all appear before the judgment seat of Christ, so that each one may receive good or evil, according to what he has done in the body" (2 Cor. 5:10; see Rom. 2:6; 14:10–12). And the *lex talionis* accounts for suffering and misfortune here on earth as well. As we sow, so shall we reap (Gal. 6:7). Paul, then, perceives suffering and misfortune in terms of a strongly ordered view of the universe. This, however, is not the only perception in Paul's letters.

In a world of warring dualistic forces, suffering and misfortune also result from the undeserved assaults by Evil Powers. It seems not to matter whether one is faithful to God and observant of the laws of the covenant, for it is the painful experience that good people suffer from the envy and hostility of the Evil One (Wis. 2:24) and its attacks on them. We noted in the previous chapter how Paul experiences the assaults of Satan and Evil Powers on himself and his churches.

Both points of view are found in Paul's letters, not because he was confused in his thinking, but because he shared so deeply the typical cosmological perspectives of the people in his world. It is the latter understanding of suffering and misfortune as caused by the attacks of Evil Spirits that we continue to investigate. The operative question becomes: When and in what circumstances does Paul perceive suffering and misfortune as God's just judgment or as the attacks of God's enemies? And which perspective is found most frequently in Paul's letters? It is our hypothesis that suffering is most often understood by Paul as the attack of Satan and Evil Powers on God's holy people. This correlates with his experience of challenges to his own authority and the presence of "another gospel" in his churches.

## 2.0 Who Did This to Me?

In keeping with Paul's anthropomorphic cosmos, we take careful note of the way he and others in his world interpret all good or harm done to them in terms of some personal causality. "Who did this to me?" is the appropriate question to ask in case of illness, famine, shipwreck, death, and the like, as well as in regard to a good harvest, the birth of children, and success in business. In the case of good fortune, success is directly attributable to God, either the birth of a child to aged parents (Luke 1:13, 24–25), or a superabundant catch of fish (Luke 5:6), or an unusually bountiful harvest of grain (Luke 12:16). But a personal force is credited with the blessing, either God or God's messenger, such as the angel who aided Tobias.

The same is true for misfortune: a personal force is responsible. For example, when in John 9 Jesus' disciples see a blind man, the questions they ask illustrate this sense that "someone" has caused the blindness of the afflicted man. The disciples ask: "Who sinned, this man or his parents, that he was born blind?" (9:2). In this instance, Jesus rejects this popular perception to argue for God's involvement: " . . . but that the works of God might be made manifest in him" (9:3; see Luke 13:16). In the same vein, we noted above how illness and storms were attributed to the workings of Evil Spirits against men and women. In regard to evil, John Pilch has developed insightful anthropological perspectives about illness and healing in the New Testament. He argues that a major way of speaking about the misfortune of ill health among Jesus, Paul, and their contemporaries was the attribution of this to the agency of personified Evil Spirits.

We can extend this by recalling how the misfortune of death is understood. As we noted above, Paul perceives Death as a hostile power, an "enemy" who still "reigns" (1 Cor. 15:25–26). Or Death might be the ultimate power that Satan exercises over us; such seems to be the perspective in the Gospels, which did not hesitate to describe Satan as an agent working Jesus' death through Judas, his servant. At the beginning of the Passion Narrative, for example, Luke remarks that "Satan entered into Judas" (Luke 22:3), who then worked with Jesus' enemies to bring him to death (22:4–6; see also John 6:70 and 13:2, 27). The same Satan desired to "sift you [Peter] like wheat" (Luke 22:31–32), thus harming Jesus by isolating him from his closest followers and thereby making his ruin that much easier. It is argued by some that Luke 22:43–44 describes a conflict between Jesus and Satan similar to the battle described in 4:1–13, thus indicating a fight to the death. Finally, Jesus' arrest is ascribed to "the power of darkness" (22:53), who will work Jesus' death. However one tries to argue that such malevolent powers are still under God's ultimate control, the fact remains that in the Gospels and Paul's letters, suffering, misfortune, and even death are caused by Evil Powers. Paul is no exception to this, for he too credits Jesus' death to the malevolence of Evil Powers (1 Cor. 2:8).

## 3.0 Two Ways/Two Spirits

Paul was not the first or only Jew in his world to interpret
suffering and misfortune in terms of the activity of Evil Spirits.
Much earlier, the author of the *Testaments of the Twelve Patriarchs* gave expression to this belief. In the farewell speeches
of Jacob's sons, each patriarch speaks of the harm done to him
by an Evil Spirit. Reuben, for example, speaks of "seven spirits
appointed against man" (*T. Reub.* 2:2); Levi, in a vision of a
heavenly being, learns that this Spirit is appointed as his de-
fender against the Evil Spirits: "I am the angel who intercedes
for the nation of Israel, that they may not be smitten utterly,
for every Evil Spirit attacks it" (*T. Levi* 5:6). The activity of
these Spirits is threefold: they battle in the heavens, on the
earth, and within the individual person.

The fullest expression of this perspective can be found in the
Rule of the Community at Qumran. We cite the text at length
so that the reader may appreciate the depth and power of this
understanding of suffering and misfortune by the priests at
Qumran.

> And He allotted unto man two Spirits that he should walk in
> them until the time of His Visitation; they are the Spirits of
> truth and perversity. The origin of Truth is in a fountain of light,
> and the origin of Perversity is from a fountain of darkness. Do-
> minion over all the sons of righteousness is in the hand of the
> Prince of light; they walk in the ways of light. All dominion over
> the sons of perversity is in the hand of the Angel of darkness;
> they walk in the ways of darkness. And because of the Angel of
> darkness, all the sons of righteousness go astray; and all their sin
> and iniquities and faults, and all the rebellion of their deeds, are
> because of his dominion, according to the Mysteries of God un-
> til the end appointed by Him. And all the blows that smite them,
> and all the times of their distress, are because of the dominion of
> his malevolence. And all the spirits of his lot cause the sons of
> light to stumble. (1QS 3:18–24, Dupont-Sommer 1973:78–79)

Radical dualism is evident: light/darkness and truth/perversity.
From this and other Qumran documents, we know that these
two Angels and their armies are at war. And from this passage,
one infers that all people experience "dominion" over themselves by one or another Spirit: "Dominion over all the sons of
righteousness is in the hand of the Prince of light. . . . All dominion over the sons of perversity is in the hand of the Angel
of darkness." Yet according to this passage, the sons of light
and righteousness likewise experience attacks by the Evil

Spirit: "And all the blows that smite them, and all the times of their distress, are because of the dominion of his malevolence. And all the spirits of his lot cause the sons of light to stumble." In the case of suffering and misfortune, then, both the author of the *Testaments of the Twelve Patriarchs* and the Qumran Rule of the Community would ask, "*Who* did this to me?" And the answer would invariably be Satan, an Evil Spirit, or the Angel of darkness.

Recent studies have shown that this perspective common in Jewish literature was part of the symbolic universe of Mark and James (Marcus 1982, 1984), as well as Barnabas and Hermas (Seitz 1959). And, I would argue, it stands behind many passages in Paul's letters as well.

**3.1 Two Masters** In Paul's symbolic universe, all peoples always have some "lord" over them. They are servants of some sovereign, either God or God's opposite. The question, then, is, Which master? Which sovereign? "Do not yield your members to Sin as instruments of wickedness, but yield yourselves to God as [people] who have been brought from death to life. . . . For Sin will have no dominion over you, since you are not under law but under grace" (Rom. 6:13–14). For Paul, the issue of freedom lies in being "free *from*" Sin and Death, so as to become "free *for*" service of God: "Now that you have been set free from Sin and have become slaves of God, the return you get is sanctification and its end, eternal life" (Rom. 6:22). The same contrast between being servants of Evil and servants of Good can be found in Galatians 4:8–9 and 4:4–7. Yet one is not free to vote for one or another master; they exercise power over people and demand allegiance.

**3.2 Two Spirits** In Paul's correspondence, we find many references to the heavenly Spirits that lead, guide, and direct people's lives, both for good and for ill.

Paul's description of the "Two Ways" in Galatians 5:16–25 reflects a dualistic perception of Spirits warring for dominion over people's lives. Although the "Two Ways" motif is common to Greeks and Jews (Malherbe 1986b:135), as with the priests at Qumran, Paul reflects the Jewish perception that Two Spirits control our behavior for good or for evil. He contrasts lists of virtues and vices, ascribing virtue to the agency of "the Spirit" and vice to "Flesh." These two powers war with each other: "The desires of the flesh are against the Spirit, and the desires of the Spirit are against the flesh; for these are opposed to each other" (Gal. 5:17). If the Spirit dominates, then the individual is "led by the Spirit" (5:18) and does what is right; conversely, the Flesh strives "to prevent you from doing what you would" (5:17) and leads to evil.

Clearly, in the world of Spirits, not all are of God. Because of the danger of a deceiving and malevolent Spirit, all Spirits must be tested. We find such a test at the beginning of Paul's discussion of "spiritual gifts" (or "spiritual persons") in 1 Corinthians 12. Paul first reminds the Corinthians that prior to Christ, they had experience of Spirits, but not of good ones: "You know that when you were heathens, you were led astray to dumb idols, however you may have been moved" (12:2). This refers to an Evil Spirit that "leads astray," not to the true God, but to "dumb idols." Yet even for Christians led by Spirits, some discernment is needed, for not every Spirit is of God. Hence, Paul establishes criteria to judge Good from Evil Spirits.

Evil Spirits lead people to make false or blasphemous confessions. Such a Spirit inspires people to say "Jesus be cursed!" (12:3a; see 1 John 4:3). But God's Spirit inspires them to say "Jesus is Lord!" (12:3b). Paul's tempering of speaking in tongues and prophecy occasions his remarks about which Spirit inspires the church to speak. Even the content of the respective confessions is group specific, for elite, pneumatic people who focus on Christ's resurrection would probably devalue the cross (see 1:18–25). Therefore, orthodox people will affirm, not lawlessness or absolute freedom, but authority; hence, truly inspired speech is confession of Jesus' abiding authority: "Jesus is Lord!" Nevertheless, Paul characteristically perceives that two Spirits vie for leadership over people, the Good Spirit of God and the Evil Spirit of Satan. Readers can find an exact parallel to 1 Corinthians 12:1–3 in the discernment of the Spirits in 1 John 4:1–3, 6.

**3.3 Two Sovereigns**   In this perspective, we turn back to a difficult passage in Romans where Paul describes himself at the mercy of a power not of God. Modern readers have tended to give Romans 7:7–25 an existentialist, psychological interpretation (Stendahl 1976:78–96). But, with more accurate cultural lenses, readers sensitive to the shape of Paul's symbolic universe will perceive the story in terms of personified and warring powers.

**3.3.1 Sin, Death, and Satan**   The key to Romans 7:7–12 lies in hearing the echoes of Genesis 1–3 in Paul's remarks there, just as they inform the background to Romans 1:20–23 (Hyldahl

1956:285–288; Hooker 1959:297–306). In chapter 7 Paul describes how he is subject to "two laws" that war for dominion over him, the "law of God" and the "law of sin" (7:22–23). He would be free from the "law of sin," by which he does not mean the law(s) of the covenant found in the Scriptures. That law is "holy and just and good" (7:12). Indeed, the law of God alluded to here is not the Mosaic covenant at all, but the law given Adam and Eve in Genesis 2–3, which Satan subverted.

With Genesis 1–3 in mind, let us read Romans 7:7–12 with attention to Paul's perception of the world as a battleground of warring Sovereigns. Paul begins by declaring: "If it had not been for *the law*, I should not have known sin" (7:7). "The law" can adequately be understood here in terms of the law that God gave Adam and Eve: "Of the tree of the knowledge of good and evil you shall not eat, for in the day that you eat of it you shall die" (Gen. 2:17). It is about this law that Satan lied to Eve: "God knows that when you eat of it your eyes will be opened, and you will be like God, knowing good and evil" (Gen. 3:5). Yet when God gave this law, he intended to keep Adam and Eve sinless and deathless; they were not destined to know sin or death. What went wrong?

Paul then says: "I should not have known what it is to *desire* if the law had not said, 'You shall not *desire*' " (7:7b). Only when Satan had deceived Eve did humankind begin to desire what should not be desired: "So when the woman saw that the tree was good for food, and that it was a delight to the eyes, and that the tree was to be *desired* to make one wise, she took of its fruit and ate" (Gen. 3:6). God gave a good law to make Adam and Eve deathless, but Satan tricked them to desire evil instead.

Paul introduces a new figure into the scene, Sin. He remarks that "*Sin*, finding opportunity in the commandment, wrought in me all kinds of desire" (7:8). He says "Sin," meaning a personified agent of Satan, the twin of "Death" (i.e., "Death reigned," Rom. 5:14, 17). Although "in the world" (Rom. 5:13), Sin was absent from the scene until God gave Adam the law to prevent his death: "Apart from the law sin lies dead" (7:8c). If Adam was to live forever, then Death was dead.

But with an object of God now in view, Sin came alive to attack Adam and Eve: "But when the commandment came, sin revived and I *died*" (7:9). Once Adam was alive and Sin was dead; but then Sin revived and Adam died. But Adam's death was the work of Satan, Sin, and Death, all enemies of God (e.g., Rom. 5:12–14). In Scripture (Wis. 2:23–24) and legend, Adam was created "in the image and likeness of God," that is, deathless (Murphy-O'Connor 1976:32–36). And indeed God's law was intended to prevent his death: "You shall not eat of the fruit . . . lest you *die*" (Gen. 3:3).

It was precisely to subvert this that Satan lied to Eve: "You will not *die*" (Gen. 3:4). In Paul's paraphrase of this we read: "Sin, finding opportunity in the commandment, *deceived* me and by it killed me" (Rom. 7:11). This echoes Genesis 3:13: "The serpent *deceived* me, and I ate" (Gen. 3:13). And because of Sin's work, Death could then reign over them ("And he *died*," Gen. 5:5; see Rom. 5:17, 21).

Paul's remarks in Romans 7:7–12, then, tell a story of two Sovereigns, God and Satan. Satan is not formally mentioned, but his two chief agents, Sin and Death, do his work.

**3.3.2 God's Holy Spirit**   Romans 7:7–12, which tells the story of the attack by Evil Spirits, is balanced by 8:1–17, which describes the workings of God's Spirit unto salvation. Prefacing his remarks about God's Spirit, Paul describes a battle between Evil and God for the possession of his heart:

> I find it to be a law that when I want to do right, evil lies close at hand. For I delight in the law of God, in my inmost self, but I see in my members another law at war with the law of my mind and making me captive to the law of sin which dwells in my members.
>
> Romans 7:21–23

Paul's salvation lies in being set free from Sin and Death to be the servant of Christ: "The law of the Spirit of life in Christ Jesus has set me free from the law of Sin and Death" (Rom. 8:2). Paul labels these two powers "Spirit" and "Flesh" for several reasons. "Spirit" denotes freedom and suggests something heavenly; it is the Power whereby Jesus' mortal body was raised from death to holiness and life (Rom. 1:4; 8:10). "Flesh" here means slavery and suggests something earthly (or, outside of God's realm); flesh is associated with Death: "To set the mind on the flesh is death" (Rom. 8:6). And: "Flesh and blood cannot inherit the kingdom of God" (1 Cor. 15:50). The mind that is set on the flesh is hostile to God (Rom. 8:7). But Spirit and Flesh are at war over the minds of God's creatures, a war to the death.

Whence comes suffering and misfortune? One answer typically found in Paul and his world replies that human beings are constantly affected by the power of Spirits who exercise over them dominion and who attack them as enemies.

## 4.0 Evil Attacks Good

Some New Testament texts try to argue for an orderly world in which all suffering and misfortune are eventually credited to God according to some *lex talionis*. Yet experience suggests that such a perspective does not explain all suffering. Hence, further explanations are given: some suffering is said to be God's will (*dei*: Acts 9:16; 14:22; *thelēma*: Luke 22:42); it happened according to God's foreknowledge and plan (Acts 2:23; 4:28). Certain documents speak of it positively as God's purification of us, as gold tested in fire (1 Peter 1:7; see James 1:3). Suffering and misfortune on earth, then, need not imply God's displeasure at all; in fact, they may be strange marks of blessing (Luke 6:20–23).

Yet in other places we read of suffering and misfortune whose source may or may not be clearly stated but whose remedy lies in God's hand. One recalls first of all the example of the righteous man in The Wisdom of Solomon 2:12–20; his sufferings result from the envy and hatred of his enemies, but his vindication rests with God. Another example might be the four original beatitudes: "Blessed are the poor . . . the hungry . . . the mourning . . . the persecuted" (Luke 6:20–23//Matt. 5:3, 4, 6, 10–12). These misfortunes probably result from domestic hostility, from dispossession and excommunication from the family circle because of loyalty to Christ. As such they spring not from God, although God is their remedy. He pronounces them "Blessed!" and heralds their return to favor. A third phenomenon is the inevitable rejection and persecution of the prophets: "Jerusalem, Jerusalem, killing the prophets and stoning those who are sent to you!" (Matt. 23:37). Stephen asked: "Which of the prophets did not your fathers persecute?" (Acts 7:52). Their suffering and misfortune were caused, not by God, but by evil men; such suffering and misfortune represent a pattern followed by some of Jesus' followers: "Blessed are you when men hate you, and when they exclude you and revile you, and cast out your name as evil . . . for so their fathers did to the prophets" (Luke 6:22–23). One common denominator running through this material is the explanation of suffering and misfortune as the attack of evil upon good, either the righteous man of Wisdom, the loyal followers of Jesus, or God's prophets. As we saw in the case of Jesus, Satan and the Power of Darkness worked harm against him, even his death. Either God or God's enemies, then, are the source of suffering and misfortune. In both cases the good suffer.

All that we have said above about personified malevolent figures who war on God's creatures is surely relevant here. People regularly perceive themselves as the objects of the attacks of Satan and other Evil Spirits. In a world at war, those on earth often sense themselves as the target of hostility, not just from envious neighbors but from Evil Powers as well. Evil attacks Good; so has it been since the creation of the world. This implies also a perception that such suffering and misfortune are undeserved and unjust.

## 5.0 Paul's Unjust Sufferings

With this scenario in mind, let us examine Paul's sufferings. What are these misfortunes and whence do they come?

***5.1 Misfortune Caused by Satan*** From the preceding exposition, we expect to hear that Satan or an Evil Spirit caused suffering and misfortune to Paul and others, and such is the case. For example, we noted above that Satan often "hindered" Paul in his work (1 Thess. 2:18; Rom. 15:22) and attempted to seduce the bride he was honor bound to guard (2 Cor. 11:2, 14–15). We hear, moreover, of "an angel from Satan" who harassed him (2 Cor. 12:7); yet in this instance, the purpose seems to be to keep Paul from sin. Evil Spirits, then, cause part of Paul's misfortune, which is unjustly suffered.

***5.2 Imprisonment*** In three letters Paul speaks of imprisonment. Twice in 2 Corinthians he mentions frequent imprisonment as one of the great humiliations he suffered for the gospel (6:5; 11:23). Both Philemon (1, 9, 10, 13) and Philippians (1:7, 13–14) are written during imprisonment. Presumably, he was imprisoned by the civil authorities of the places where he spoke (see Acts 16:20–24; 22:24–26:32), but that should not preclude the perception of his imprisonment as the work of malevolent people or powers bent on stopping the spread of the gospel of Jesus Christ. There is no chaining of the word of God; Paul's imprisonment "has really served to advance the gospel" (Phil. 1:12).

***5.3 Bodily Illness*** Paul also mentions his physical condition. He describes it occasionally as "weakness . . . fear and trembling" (1 Cor. 2:3). But to others it suggests not just the absence of spiritual power, but even hypocrisy on Paul's part: "They say, 'His letters are weighty and strong, but his bodily presence is weak, and his speech of no account' " (2 Cor. 10:10). More significantly, Paul reminds the Galatians that when he first came to them he suffered from a "bodily ailment," which might rightly have caused them to scorn and despise him (4:13–14). About this two things need be said. In light of the scenario we have proposed, illness is thought to be caused by malevolent Spirits, and such evident absence of strength and power would probably be interpreted as the workings of an Evil Spirit. Either way, Paul suffers unjustly.

### 5.4 Weakness and Opponents

A recent scholar (Barré 1975, 1980) argued that "weakness" (*astheneia*) in 2 Corinthians 11:29 should be translated as "to cause to stumble, to be tripped up," suggesting that it is the result of the actions of evil persons, either human or demonic. Barré marshals his argument from parallel expressions in the Qumran literature and concludes that Paul's "weakness" results from persecution and from the attacks of his opponents. Such in fact is the meaning that is given by him and others to the "thorn in the flesh" in 2 Corinthians 12:7, namely, Paul's opponents. Such misfortunes, then, are unjustly suffered.

### 5.5 Catalogs of Hardships

In the Corinthian correspondence, Paul four times mentions his hardships (1 Cor. 4:8–13; 2 Cor. 4:7–12; 6:3–10; 11:23–30). An excellent study of these passages has recently appeared (Fitzgerald 1988), which quite rightly examines them in terms of the way wise men and sages in the Greco-Roman world describe their struggles toward wisdom and the conquering of passion. I am asking questions of these lists, however, which Fitzgerald did not ask, simply because they were outside the scope of his study. Whence come the sufferings, dishonors, humiliations, and misfortunes that Paul suffers so nobly? On occasion Fitzgerald indicates divine control over them (1 Cor. 4:9); in other places he indicates that they are the result of Fortune or God (pp. 70–87). But he is basically disinterested in their source, for his study concerns the overcoming of suffering and misfortune by *askēsis* and training in wisdom, which seems to be the case even in Paul's letters. But in light of the scenario we have developed, let us press the question, Whence come Paul's misfortunes and sufferings?

In the list of hardships in 1 Corinthians 4:8–13, we find not just Paul's comparison/contrast of himself with the elite of Corinth (4:9–10), but a description of an attack made on him and his success in overcoming it.

| Attack | Victory |
|--------|---------|
| When reviled, | we bless; |

when persecuted,   we endure;
when slandered,    we conciliate (4:12–13).

God's power may help Paul triumph over his misfortune and
suffering, but that should not obscure the fact that Paul is unjustly attacked and suffers undeservedly. The source of the attack is not clear, either evil men or Evil Powers.

Likewise, in 2 Corinthians 4:7–12 Paul narrates a series of
misfortunes that befell him and over which he wins the victory.
Our interest lies in the first part, the assaults and sufferings
inflicted on him.

| Attack | Victory |
|---|---|
| We are afflicted in every way, | but not crushed; |
| perplexed, | but not driven to despair; |
| persecuted, | but not forsaken; |
| struck down, | but not destroyed (4:8–9). |

Again, no source is specified here, either evil men or Evil Spirits; nevertheless, the sufferings are undeserved and therefore
unjust.

A third list (2 Cor. 6:3–10) catalogs many more unjust sufferings endured by Paul. Upon him are inflicted "beatings, imprisonments, tumults" (6:5). His fate is that of a victim of war, and
so he mentions the weapons needed to defend himself: "with the
weapons of righteousness for the right hand and for the left"
(6:7). Finally, he comments that he has endured two contrasting
fates, alternately caused by God and by evil people. He knows
"honor" and "dishonor," as well as "good repute" and "ill repute" (6:8). Finally, he lists four more misfortunes inflicted
upon him, over which he triumphs. God is the source of his
victory, but the misfortunes are unjustly inflicted by others.

| Attacks | Victory |
|---|---|
| We are treated as impostors, | and yet are true; |
| as unknown, | and yet well known; |
| as dying, | and behold we live; |
| as punished, | and yet not killed (6:8–9). |

In the fourth list, 2 Corinthians 11:23–32, Paul tells the full
extent of the hostility shown him and the sufferings inflicted on
him. He endured:

(1) many imprisonments
(2) countless beatings:
    five times by Jews
    three times by Romans
(3) shipwreck three times

(4) dangers:
    from my own people
    from Gentiles
    from city, wilderness, sea
    from King Aretas of Damascus (11:23–33)

From these lists we conclude that Paul perceived and indeed
experienced a hostile world that sought his harm and ruin. He
describes himself as Misfortune's number one target. He is a
man more acted upon than acting. God, of course, sustains
him and leads him to victory, but he suffers these misfortunes
nonetheless. His sufferings are undeserved and therefore unjust.

**5.6 Sufferings of Others**     Infrequently, Paul alludes to the misfortune and sufferings of others in ways that confirm the observations made above. He acknowledges the unjust suffering of
both the church in Judea and that in Thessalonika: "For you
. . . became imitators of the churches . . . in Judea; for you suffered the same things from your own countrymen as they did
from the Jews, who killed both the Lord Jesus and the
prophets, and drove us out, and displease God and oppose all
men by hindering us from speaking to the Gentiles" (1 Thess.
2:14–16). Yet others have pointed out how these remarks
should be read in light of another part of 1 Thessalonians:
"When we were with you, we told you beforehand that we were
to suffer affliction; just as it has come to pass, and as you
know" (3:4). It is argued that predictions of afflictions were
regularly made as part of the baptismal catechesis, thus indicating that good people would suffer evil and misfortune at the
hands of evil people or Evil Spirits (Meeks 1983b:691; Hill
1976:181–189). Not only Paul, but the church as well, experiences unjust suffering from the hands of evil people.

## 6.0 Summary and Conclusions

The discussion of these three topics, sin/deviance, cosmology, and suffering/misfortune brings us to the end of our exposition of the symbolic universe of Paul. It is perhaps in this
current chapter that a reader finally gets a sense of how different Paul's perceptions are from our own. Moreover, in the way
Paul understands sin/deviance, we find a complex point of
view that is not entirely consistent. If we have not done vio-
lence to Paul's letters, then a considerate reader will learn to

deal with both the unpleasantness of the point of view as well
as its lack of consistency.

What then do we know? On many occasions, Paul perceives
himself and his churches as the objects of attack. If sin is understood as corruption and disease, then someone has mortally
threatened the church by the introduction of sin within the
healthy and holy church. In the face of this life-threatening
danger, intolerance becomes a virtue. The good of the whole
demands the immediate, uncompromising attention of the
group to identify the evil and seek its removal from the organism. Given this perception, *not* to act intolerantly would be
suicide.

The world, moreover, is peopled with many evil powers who
are personified in Paul's perspective. They war on God's kingdom, attacking, seeking to ruin, and striving to kill. Jesus, the
Warrior of God, battled against them. Paul, his apostle, is besieged by them.

It follows, then, that when any misfortune or suffering is experienced, a personal cause is expected: Who did this to me?
God may lead God's saints through trials, but more often we
read that human suffering is caused by the attacks of Evil upon
Good. Hence, suffering tends to be understood in terms of injustice: the good suffer and the wicked prosper. And although
suffering can be ameliorated by promises of future vindication
and reward, it cannot be removed from the world, at least not
until the Evil Powers are finally conquered by the Lord Jesus.
The last enemy is Death, who will reign until "the end."

# 9

# Bewitched in Galatia: Paul's Accusations of Witchcraft

O foolish Galatians! Who has bewitched you?

Galatians 3:1

## 1.0 Introduction

People in the New Testament documents regularly accuse one another of sorcery or witchcraft. Certain people, it is argued, are slaves of Satan and his demons or are in league with them. By this power they work harm against their neighbors or gain false advantage. The accusations occur on the lips of outsiders speaking of Jesus and John the Baptizer. Jesus likewise speaks in the same way about others. The followers of Jesus also accuse other Christian disciples of the same charge. We find this widespread phenomenon in all the documents of the New Testament, in the Gospels (Mark, Q, and John) as well as Paul's and John's letters, as the following outline indicates.

### Accusations of Demon Possession in the New Testament

1. *Others accuse Jesus of demon possession*
   (a) Mark 3:23–30; Matt. 12:22–37//Luke 11:14–23
   (b) John 7:20; 8:48, 52; 10:20
2. *Jesus accuses others of demon possession*
   (a) Judas (John 6:70; see also Luke 22:3 and John 13:2, 27)
   (b) Peter (Mark 8:33)
   (c) Others (John 8:44; Matt. 12:43–44//Luke 11:24–26; Matt. 13:38–39)
3. *Paul accuses others of demon possession*
   (a) "Superlative Apostles" (2 Cor. 11:3, 13–15)
   (b) Judaizing Preachers (Gal. 3:1; 1:8)
   (c) Elymas the Magician (Acts 13:8–11)
4. *John the Baptizer is accused of demon possession*
   Matt. 11:18//Luke 7:33
5. *"Secessionists" who left the group are accused*
   1 John 2:18, 22; 3:8–10; 4:1–3; 2 John 7
6. *The Evil Eye* (Elliott 1988)
   (a) Mark 7:22 (*ophthalmos ponēros*)
   (b) Matt. 6:23 and esp. 20:15

Our interest lies primarily in Paul's accusations in Galatians and 2 Corinthians. In coming to understand its presence and function in the Pauline letters, what we learn about accusations of demon possession will equip us to study this phenomenon in the other documents.

In this chapter we argue that in 2 Corinthians 11:2–3, 13–15 and in Galatians 3:1 and 1:8 Paul formally accuses certain rival preachers of "witchcraft." He perceives a cosmos structured in such a way that it is quite plausible that someone is seducing the Corinthians and bewitching the Galatians. This means that

Paul argues that the false teachers who are spreading "another gospel" in Galatia and Corinth are either Satan himself or persons possessed and controlled by Satan. In this regard, Paul would be said to share with the rest of the authors of the New Testament a common view of the active presence of Satan and demons in the world. Like them, Paul would also engage in the common practice of accusing one's enemies and rivals of sorcery or demon possession, a phenomenon attributed to Jesus and his followers.

Modern Westerners find it difficult to take seriously not only belief in demon possession but also in witches who work evil. This indicates that we perceive our world in a way quite different from that of Paul, the four evangelists, Jesus, and other New Testament writers. Yet if we would see the world through Paul's eyes and appreciate the full force of these accusations of seduction and bewitchment, we must turn to the social sciences to find appropriate categories and scenarios to examine Paul's world and so to appreciate how his accusations functioned in the Mediterranean world, even in the New Testament.

In the social sciences, anthropologists discuss accusations of demon possession under the technical label of "witchcraft accusations," a term we will employ in this study. I propose, then, to examine 2 Corinthians 11:14–15 and Galatians 3:1 in the terms of the discussion of witchcraft accusations current among cultural anthropologists.

As regards a formal perspective, the works of Mary T. Douglas offer particularly useful insights in this endeavor for several reasons. First, in addition to her own fieldwork on witchcraft, she undertook to synthesize much of the work done by her colleagues, a task that makes available to us as much of a consensus on the topic as is likely to be found (Douglas 1970). Second, inasmuch as witchcraft accusations appear only in a certain type of social system and only under certain conditions, Douglas has attempted to describe both the symbolic cosmos of those who employ witchcraft accusations and the social function they play in that culture. Historians of ancient Mediterranean cultures are increasingly employing Douglas's basic anthropological work. Her modeling of witchcraft accusations has proved useful to students of religion as well (Brown 1970:17–45).

In Galatians 3:1 and 2 Corinthians 11:3, 13–15 Paul accuses his rivals of being Satan disguised as an angel of light, bewitching and seducing the church. These charges of demon association and/or possession are formal witchcraft accusations. This technical term indicates that, according to Paul's accusation, his rivals are either the Devil himself or persons controlled by him. The proper evaluation of these passages as formal accusations of sorcery will entail the use of two models from Douglas's works: first, a general sketch of the cosmology of Paul's world from an anthropological point of view, and second, a specific assessment of a witchcraft accusation that is a common feature of that type of cosmology. With these perspectives clearly detailed, we have an adequate scenario for understanding Paul's remarks.

## 2.0  Understanding Witchcraft Societies: Two Models

*2.1 General Symbolic Universe of Accusing Groups*  Here we draw heavily upon the first part of this book, where we used anthropological categories to describe the typical symbolic universe of Paul and others in his world. Douglas and other anthropologists would have us examine seven aspects of a group's cosmology to understand the basic symbolic structures and social dynamics of their world. We hope that by now readers are familiar with categories such as purity, ritual, personal identity, body, sin/deviance, cosmology, and suffering/misfortune. Although Douglas indicates the possibility of four ideal perspectives in the world at large, witchcraft accusations tend to occur in only one of these ideal types, namely, the particular worldview described in the earlier chapters of this book. As we noted above, Paul and other first-century Jews share a particular worldview in which witchcraft accusations frequently occur (see the summary on pp. 16–17 above). The three other descriptions of worldviews are conveniently found in Malina 1986b:14–15.

*2.2 Specific Characteristics of Witchcraft Societies*  In addition to understanding the general cosmos where witchcraft accusations flourish, we also must examine specific aspects of this phenomenon. Douglas has identified six characteristics of the social group that engages in such accusations. She has, moreover, defined in general terms applicable to many cultures who and what a witch is. Finally, she suggests the social function of accusations of witchcraft.

*2.2.1 Six Specific Characteristics*  Douglas identifies six specific characteristics of groups that she calls "witchcraft societies," that is, groups where accusations of witchcraft tend to occur. These are clearer definitions of the cosmology described earlier.

1. *External boundaries are clearly marked;* there is a clear sense of who belongs to the group and who does not.
2. *Internal relations are confused*; the internal lines of a map of persons that classifies, ranks, and locates people in some social hierarchy are confused.
3. *There is close, unavoidable interaction*; a witchcraft society is a small group living in close and unavoidable interaction. They draw water from the same well, forage in the same forest, bake bread at the same common ovens, shop in the same small marketplace, and sit in the same small house church.
4. *Tension-relieving techniques are underdeveloped*; there are no, or very weak, procedures for distancing, regulating, or reconciling conflicts.
5. *Weak authority characterizes this type of group.* Access to power or status is ambiguous because the routes of access are unclear, as are the factors that legitimate acquisition of power and authority.
6. *Intense and disorderly competition occurs constantly in this group.* This last item will be examined more intensely as a constant element in the challenge-riposte phenomenon that is typical of honor and shame societies.

**2.2.2 *Definition of a Witch*** Anthropologists define a witch in terms of the misfortune such a person is said to have caused and the context in which such misfortune appears. According to Douglas's model, witches appear in groups whose cosmos is perceived in dualistic terms as an arena of warring forces. Those who consider themselves to be in the correct place and to take the correct stand perceive themselves under attack, especially from hostile outsiders who would corrupt and poison them. This wickedness is experienced on a cosmic scale: those who immediately threaten them are from the Evil One. The witch, then, is a figure who sums up all of the above sense of dualism, cosmic evil, and hostility to the group.

In this milieu, there is a painful ambiguity between what is external and what is internal, between appearances and reality; the attacking Evil disguises itself as a wolf in sheep's clothing. In this context of ambiguity and deception, a witch may be defined as follows:

1. A witch is one whose *inside is corrupt.*
2. A witch has a *perverted nature*, a *reversal* of the ways

things ought to be; a witch is a *deceiver* whose external appearance does not betray its inner nature.
3. If a witch is seen as living within the group, it attacks the pure and innocent by *life-sucking* or by *poison*.

***2.2.3 Function of the Witchcraft Accusation***   According to Douglas's profile, the characteristic ritual of this kind of social group focuses on discernment and expulsion of the witch. The primary act in the process of grappling with the Evil that is perceived as attacking is the accusation of witchcraft or demon possession; for by the accusation, the threat to the group's boundaries is revealed, and its cause, the witch, is identified and can be expelled. This points up an important feature we discussed earlier, namely, that this is a highly competitive society marked with strong rivalry and strong ambition. In this context, the accusation functions to denigrate rivals and pull them down in the competition for leadership. Such accusations, in short, are idioms of social control.

An accusation might produce several results. If successful, the person accused of witchcraft would be expelled from the group. The competition for leadership would then moderate, but only temporarily, for the rules for ambitioning and gaining authority and status are ambiguous. A second possible result is that the accused might withdraw from the group (fission), claiming that it is an evil place that he or she can no longer abide. Third, the accusation may not succeed in expulsion or fission, so the accusing parties would continue to live in close and unavoidable contact in a state of intense competition and rivalry (Malina & Neyrey 1988:29–30). Yet the function of the accusation remains constant. It is a weapon used against a rival in a highly competitive situation; it aims to discredit and dislodge that rival.

## 3.0 Bewitched in Galatia

***3.1 Galatia and Paul's Symbolic Universe***   Earlier in this book we examined the symbolic universe of Paul, but in an eclectic way, picking and choosing illustrative passages from many of his letters. Now we focus on his letter to the Galatians in order to examine the symbolic universe contained there and so to learn the specific ways in which he expressed his worldview.

***3.1.1 Purity***   We know that temple and even synagogue Jews were strongly organized, a cultural impulse found also in the ex-Pharisee, Paul. On the one hand, prior to his faith in Jesus, Paul claims to have been a Pharisee's Pharisee (Gal. 1:14; Phil. 3:4–6); as such, this same Paul perceived the "purity" of Judaism polluted by Jesus and his followers, for which reason he persecuted them (Gal. 1:13; 1 Cor. 15:9). Even in Galatians Paul continued to be acutely sensitive to "dirt" that threatened his pure world, that is, to "another gospel," one that was other than the one he had preached. To appreciate the sense of "purity" and "dirt" that are reflected in Paul's worldview, let us sketch the orderly patterns of his perception of the cosmos in Galatians, with special attention to how Judaizers and "another gospel" are pollutions of the world he has established.

With his Pharisee's eye for clarity and precision, Paul describes in Galatians 3–4 the history of God's actions, indicating how God has successively related to the world in two systematic but different ways. For convenience sake, we call them the covenant with Abraham (3:6–9; 4:24) and the covenant with Moses (3:10–12). Each covenant systematically expresses God's will for humanity and indicates a way in which to walk, either by believing in God's promises or by the doing of God's halachic will. Covenant, then, symbolizes system or order in the Jewish cosmos.

God's Scriptures, moreover, contain these two divine orderings of the world. Not only are the general sketches of God's covenants found there, but particular details of the Scriptures are used by Paul to affirm aspects of the covenant system that Paul sees as currently valid in Christ. For example, when Paul talks about the "offspring" of Abraham (3:16–17), he narrows the correct line of descent to focus on offspring through Abraham's one legitimate son, Isaac. Certain details of these Scriptures become important for Paul's argument to establish the precedence of the covenant of Abraham over that of Moses. For example, the earlier character of God's dealing with Abraham (3:17) signals its priority in time and importance; the Hagar-Sarah story offers a host of details whereby the covenant with Abraham may be seen to come through Sarah and her free son, Isaac, not through Hagar and her slave son, Ishmael. Scripture, then, structures Paul's worldview.

Yet the world of Paul the Pharisee is structured as well by his faith in Jesus who died on the cross. Christ's death, moreover, marks the exact boundary line between the former covenant of law and the new covenant of faith and grace (3:13–14). Furthermore, Jesus sums up in himself the precise pattern of the covenant of faith, what it means and how it works. For example, Jesus is the unique "son" promised Abraham (3:16), the model of our "sonship" with God (4:5–7), a definition of our status. Just as Jesus prayed to God, so his followers are filled with the Spirit and pray "Abba! Father!" (4:6). The precision about one's relationship to God, which was formerly given Paul the Pharisee by Torah, now comes from Jesus. Paul's world, therefore, is strongly structured in terms of traditional belief in God and the Scriptures, at least as these are understood and configured in a certain way, that is, in Christ as the fulfillment of the covenant with Abraham, which ends the former covenant with Moses.

This basic pattern of ordering, moreover, attests to what Paul perceives as "holy" or "pure," a point that is clearly of considerable importance to him (Meeks 1983a:85–86; Newton 1985:52–78). For Jews, the unquestionable aim of all religious behavior was righteousness; but how does one arrive at that holy state? In characteristic dualistic fashion, Paul argues that holiness, which he typically calls "righteousness," does *not* come from the Law (2:16; 3:11). Rather, as God's Scriptures teach, holiness/righteousness comes only through faith. Abraham believed God, and "It was reckoned to him as righteousness" (3:6/Gen. 15:6), and those who are "righteous by faith" shall live (3:11/Hab. 2:4). The holy state of those who are righteous by faith is further expressed by the possession of the "holy" Spirit, which God pours into human hearts confirming and empowering them as "holy" (3:2, 5; 4:6).

Yet Paul's strong sense of an orderly, holy cosmos has come under fierce attack. Paul writes his letter to the Galatians precisely because some people, presumably Judaizers, have come to Galatia and attacked Paul's ordering of the world in the way described above. They urge a different system of ordering, not the covenant with Abraham but the covenant with Moses. Although it is important to know just what they said and why it should be persuasive to the Galatians, suffice it to say that Paul perceives their presence and preaching of "another gospel" as a pollution of God's holy church because it attacks the pure way of serving God that Paul enunciated. They are infecting the church like polluting leaven (5:9; see 1 Cor. 5:6–7) or gangrene (see 2 Tim. 2:17). Cast in this light, the conflict assumes cosmic proportions. Chaos threatens Paul's cosmos.

**3.1.2 Rituals**  Examining the structures of society, anthropologists like Mary Douglas pay special attention to the rites and ceremonies that either define the boundaries of a group (rituals) or celebrate and strengthen its values and structures (ceremonies). In Paul's cosmos, people focus attention primarily on rituals that establish and maintain boundaries. Because people here perceive their boundaries already breached by pollutants, they devote themselves to sounding the alarm and rallying to the perimeter under attack. That is, they aim at identifying the pollution and trying to expel it.

Galatians exhibits several kinds of rituals—those that create boundaries and those that would repel the invading pollutant who has crossed them. In understanding "boundaries," we need only look at Paul's enunciation of redundant dualistic patterns in Galatians. By the way he speaks of the two covenants, Paul clearly indicates where the primary boundary line lies between the two covenants, between synagogue Jews and Christians. First, he describes his own status, how he was originally an outsider to God's plan. Extremely zealous for the traditions of his fathers, Paul persecuted the church of God and tried to destroy it (Gal. 1:13–14). Yet God brought him across a boundary and made him an insider by an act of grace; that is, by freely setting him apart, calling him, and revealing his Son to him (1:15–16). Paul not only establishes his legitimacy by this rehearsal of his commission, thus indicating that he stands on the correct side of the boundary separating good from evil, but his experience serves as a paradigm of the correct boundary line, namely, the way God works to establish boundaries by grace and faith.

The Galatians, too, have crossed a significant boundary when God freely gave them the Spirit through faith (3:1–5). God thus changed their status from Gentile outsiders to covenant insiders (Sanders 1983a:4–9). Formerly outsiders who did not know God, they were shown grace and favor by God (4:9), proof of which is the gratuitous reception of the Spirit by hearing with faith (3:2–5).

Paul draws the main boundary lines most sharply in chapters 3 and 4, where he contrasts the covenant with Abraham, characterized by promise and faith, with the covenant with Moses, known by its emphasis on law and doing. Following the former, one finds blessing (3:8–9), but only curse in the latter (3:10, 13). Paul insists that the covenant with Moses is ended; Christ is the official boundary line, namely, the end of the Law. By being born under the Law and becoming a curse, Christ ended that covenant dispensation. Leaving aside for the moment the intricacies of Paul's argument, we are aware how this distinction functions as boundary language, firmly establishing where one thing ends and another begins. All of his arguments to buttress the validity of the covenant with Abraham only draw the boundary line that much clearer and distinguish insiders from outsiders that much more sharply. The allegory of Hagar and Sarah in 4:21–31 reinforces the basic boundary, contrasting free with slave, heaven with earth, and spirit with flesh, thus indicating the cosmic dimensions of the boundary drawn in Christ (Barrett 1982:154–170).

Paul expresses this boundary narratively in terms of historical covenants and traditional personages. But the dividing line becomes immediate when Paul affirms the effect and importance of Jesus' death in 2:15–21. The correct side of the boundary line is constituted by being "in Christ," that is, by having the "faith of Jesus" (Hays 1981; Johnson 1982). Here is found justification, which is "purity" in God's sight. The wrong side is that characterized by "the law" and works of the Law, where Paul implies sin is found (2:16–17; 6:13). In criticizing the wrong side, Paul describes himself as "tearing something down," emphasizing that Christ died for a purpose, to end the period of sin and curse. Of the right side, Paul claims that it is "the grace of God," which should not be nullified (2:21). Christ, then, is the boundary between Abraham and Moses, faith and works, and righteousness and sin. It matters on which side of the fence one stands.

The basic boundary, then, is expressed in terms of covenants, personages, and theoretical means of justification (grace, works). It is finally expressed in terms of spirit and flesh and the activity appropriate to each. Spirit and flesh are terms introduced in the Sarah-Hagar allegory, linking Isaac with birth through the Spirit (4:29) and Ishmael with birth according to the flesh (4:23). The terms are appropriate to Paul's argument, in that birth through spirit (4:6) and gift of spirit (3:2–5) characterize the correct side of the boundary, the covenant in Christ. Opposed to "spirit" is "flesh," not simply bodily descent through Ishmael, but works of the flesh; in particular, fleshly circumcision, which is the chief symbol of the Judaizers and the major ritual of the alternative covenant system.

Paul focuses on the boundary line that circumcision symbolizes. Those who cut in their flesh the mark of the Jewish synagogue system (of the Law of Moses, works) are themselves cut off: "You are severed [cut off] from Christ, you who would be justified by the law" (5:4). For a Gentile who began on the correct side of the boundary (faith/spirit) to submit now to circumcision would mean to cross back over the boundary to the wrong side (works/flesh).

Galatians, then, reflects Paul's incessant boundary making, a perception of two mutually exclusive systems or ways of serving God. The boundary is legitimated in history (3:6–13; 4:21–

31), exemplified in experience (1:15–17; 3:1–5) and illustrated by specific practices (2:16–17; 5:4). The boundary, moreover, is endlessly presented in a series of redundant dualisms that replicate and reinforce the basic distinction between Christians and Jews according to Paul (Martyn 1985:412–420).

### Redundant Dualisms in Galatians

| | | |
|---|---|---|
| Covenant with Abraham characterized by promise/faith | -1- | Covenant with Moses characterized by law/doing |
| Belonging through Sarah and Isaac | -2- | Belonging through Hagar and Ishmael |
| Blessing | -3- | Curse |
| Grace | -4- | Sin |
| Freedom | -5- | Slavery |
| Free gift of Spirit | -6- | Earned merit through deeds |
| Spirit | -7- | Flesh |
| Home: Jerusalem above | -8- | Home: Mount Sinai below |

Paul, then, is adept at erecting boundaries that become the major lines of his purity system. Yet according to Paul, the Judaizers have attacked that boundary by asking people who stand correctly to cross back into slavery, flesh, and curse—the covenant with Moses.

Besides the ritual of boundary making, Paul indicates a second kind of ritual that is appropriate for dealing with polluting invaders who are discovered to have breached the boundaries. They must be identified and expelled. In two clear places, Paul explicitly calls for the expulsion of the pollutants (and their ideas). Apropos of the Sarah-Hagar allegory, Paul formally cites from Genesis 21:10 Sarah's demand to Abraham that Hagar and her son be expelled from his household because of Ishmael's threats to Isaac's well-being: "Cast out the slave and her son" (4:30). In the context, Paul clearly intends this as a warrant for expelling those who are allegorically linked with Hagar, Ishmael, and the covenant of flesh, namely, those who preach "another gospel." Comparably, Paul also claims that the Judaizers are trying to build boundaries as well, boundaries that will "shut you out" of God's kingdom (4:17).

In a more symbolic statement, Paul prays that those who urge circumcision and so introduce polluting doctrine into the church would themselves be "cut off." In 5:4, Paul already indicated that those who "cut" themselves bodily in circumcision are automatically "cut off" from Christ. Then, in what is evidently a play on the term *cut*, Paul prays that "those who unsettle you would mutilate themselves" (5:12) by castration, which in a Jewish cultural system would mean being "cut off" from the temple of God and being rendered permanently unclean. Mutilation is a richly charged word here, suggesting ritual impurity, which comes from bodily mutilation. Leviticus 21:20 indicates that those with "crushed testicles" cannot approach to offer the bread of God (see Lev. 22:24; Deut. 23:1). Mutilation or castration meant that one's line of descendants is literally "cut off" from the covenant of Israel, a profound curse (see *b. Yeb.* 24a and 75a–75b; *Sabb.* 152a; *Sota* 26a; *Sanh.* 36b). Mutilation, moreover, would cancel "glory," which in 6:13 is a euphemism for the circumcised penis (see Phil. 3:19). Finally, mutilation symbolically suggests Paul's desire that these heretics be cut off from the church, made shameful, and rendered permanently unclean. Permanent removal from the holy body, then, is the ritual described by Paul in 5:12.

We should take passing notice of the anathema Paul directs at those who would introduce "another gospel" into his churches (1:8–9). The curse of anathema clearly labels those who bring deviant doctrines as pollutants, and demands their separation both now and forever from God's holy realm (Forkman 1972:171, 177). In Romans 9:3, Paul explains anathema as a form of expulsion or banning: "accursed and cut off from Christ."

### 3.1.3 Personal Identity

The identity of people in Paul's world is not individualistic, but is found in terms of some other person. For example, people are known in terms of the town of their birth (Paul of Tarsus), one's family (sons of Zebedee), trade (Paul, the worker in leather) or some other identifying stereotype (Malina 1981:51–60). Paul, for example, is always God's prophet or Jesus' apostle; he is always authorized by another. Peter, James, and John are not only Christians, but pillars of the Jerusalem church; they are, then, known in terms of role and place. The Galatians are the "true Israel"; and individual members of the church are known as "the household of faith" (6:10). They are, moreover, expected to learn their Christian identity by imitating Paul (4:12).

In this regard, Mary Douglas calls attention to a profound problem in learning the identity of people in this social script. Although this world would build exact boundaries to locate, classify, and identify people, this is also a world in which boundaries are breached and the system is under attack. But the precise problem here is the difficulty of identifying the invading pollutant, because in this world external appearances are not a sure guide to the interior. At best, ambiguity reigns here; but at worst, this world is full of deceit and masquerade which intends to deceive. Evil masquerades as good, and what is truly good may not be fully recognized as such because of some seemingly exterior defect. Paul in Galatians is intensely aware of both ambiguity and masquerade.

As regards Paul himself, ambiguity shrouds him on every side. Although he insists that he never preached circumcision or spoke in favor of Jewish practices, others at least perceive him as being two-faced, saying one thing and doing another. In several places he notes the criticism that he "pleases men" (1:10; see 1 Cor. 10:33 and 1 Thess. 2:4) or that he too has approved circumcision (5:11; see Acts 16:3). These are not implausible criticisms, inasmuch as Paul admits that he is extremely flexible in his preaching (1 Cor. 9:19–23; see Carson 1986:6–45).

Similarly, let us consider the ambiguity in Paul's explanations for his visit to Jerusalem in Galatians 2:1–10. First he insists on his seeming independence from Peter and the Jerusalem church (1:16–17) in terms of both authority and doctrine. Yet when he finally goes to Jerusalem, although he claims to go because of a "revelation" from God (2:2), he lays his gospel before the Jerusalem leaders expressly for the purpose of receiving their commendation (" . . . lest somehow I should be running or had run in vain," 2:2b).

Ambiguity extends as well to Paul's role and status; for although he claims to be an apostle, he is by his own admission the runt of the litter, one untimely born (1 Cor. 15:7) who does not deserve to be called an apostle because he persecuted the church (1:13; see 1 Cor. 15:9). Even on a bodily level, the one who preaches power, holiness, and life is ambiguous. He alludes to a "bodily ailment," which could in the eyes of some belie that he has a gospel of power or the words of life (4:13–14). In this regard, he noted how the Galatians originally saw through the ambiguity of his bodily ailment and "received me as an angel of God" (4:14). Yet his appearance, role, and status, and even his doctrine are ambiguous. He may take oaths to clear up ambiguity (1:20; see Sampley 1977:477–482), but that only indicates it already exists (see 2 Cor. 1:16–20).

Besides warning his churches about the ambiguity that exists between the way people present themselves and what they really are, Paul indicates that this discrepancy is probably a matter of deceit and masquerade. For example, in 6:3 he issues a general warning: "If any one thinks he is something, when he is nothing, he deceives himself" (see 1 Cor. 3:18; 8:2). In Galatians, the "pillars of Jerusalem" are clearly ambiguous to Paul, if not actually deceitful hypocrites. To begin with, Paul regularly characterizes them as those who *seem* to be truthful or holy. They are sarcastically called "those of repute" (2:2) and those who are "reputed to be something" (2:6–7, 9), ostensibly because they are bearers of the truth of the gospel of God. Their repute, however, rests on externals, which in this cosmos are ambiguous at best and potentially deceitful—their eyewitness experience of Jesus and their direct access to his words and teaching. Externally, then, they are impeccable and far more qualified to be leaders than Paul, who presumably never knew the earthly Jesus and even persecuted his followers. But Paul accuses Peter of hypocrisy for his behavior at table in Antioch (2:11–14).

In this vein, Paul himself is trying to make a counter argument to that of the Judaizers. They ostensibly preached a doctrine of "perfection" that comes with the full keeping of the law (Baasland 1984:139). But Paul accuses them of masquerading as good, whereas they are evil. For, he charges, when they demand an external action such as circumcision, which they claim will result in "glory," they would in reality destroy faith. Urging the observance of "days, months, seasons, years" (4:10), they effectively deny the importance of Jesus' faith and God's grace. Arguing the perfection that comes with the Law, they would cheat the Galatians of freedom and put them back in bondage (4:8–9).

We will return to these texts when we examine them under the rubric of witchcraft accusations, but 3:1 and 1:8 deserve to be considered here as examples of this masquerade. Paul, of course, does not consider his Judaizing opponents to have the truth that they claim when he exclaims, "Who has *bewitched* you?" (3:1). They have passed off as coin of the realm "another gospel" that is not just worthless but costly. And in his remark about "an angel from heaven [preaching] to you a gospel contrary to that which we preached" (1:8), Paul would seem to be alluding to the popular myth that Satan disguised himself as an angel of light to seduce Eve, a midrash that stands behind his accusations about the "Superapostles" in 2 Cor. 11:3, 13–15. It is correct for them to take Paul "as an angel of God" (4:14), but not other preachers, who are only demons in disguise.

***3.1.4 Body***  We saw in an earlier chapter the way anthropologists understand the physical body. The individual physical body is a microcosm of the social body, the macrocosm. Where people perceive a highly ordered cosmos, we have learned to expect this to be replicated in strong bodily control. We argued above that Paul sees the world strongly organized and structured, which suggests that he should also urge strong bodily control and discipline. This is verified in Galatians 5–6, where Paul emphatically indicates that freedom from the Law of Moses does not mean lawlessness: "Do not use your freedom as an opportunity for the flesh" (5:13). Lest the Galatians misunderstand him, he delivers a conventional moral exhortation in 5:16–25, which proscribes certain vices and prescribes specific virtues. Paul understands this catalog in terms of walking in the Spirit (5:16), that is, as a way of life based on clear, strong rules of conduct. Inasmuch as his aim is strict control of the "flesh," the dominant virtue is "self-control" (*egkrateia*, 5:23).

Mary Douglas suggests that when there is concern for social boundaries, entrances, and exits, there will be corresponding concern for control of the entrances and exits of the physical body. By this she means the sexual, oral, ocular, and aural orifices, which are entrances into the body's interior (Douglas 1966:123–124 and 1982a:70–71). In the list of vices of "the flesh" to be avoided (5:19–20), Paul typically identifies those that involve the body's orifices, for they should be controlled and guarded to prevent evil and pollution:

| | |
|---|---|
| *genitals:* | fornication, impurity, licentiousness |
| *mouth:* | drunkenness, carousing, anger |
| *eye:* | sorcery, envy, jealousy |

Furthermore, Paul focuses on two bodily orifices, the mouth and the genitals. In regard to the mouth, he typically expresses the Semitic preoccupation with mouth vis-à-vis speech, that is, concern with false witness, foolish speech, and wrong doctrine. He would regulate the mouth so that only certain things would be spoken (the gospel), whereas other things should never be spoken (Judaizing heresy). He proscribes "another gospel" (1:8–9) that would advocate circumcision or observance of the Law of Moses. And he prescribes other speech: (a) his correct gospel (1:11; 5:2), (b) public reproach of those who in any way advocate the other gospel, either reproach of Peter (2:11, 14) or sarcastic rebuke of the Galatians themselves (3:1–5; 4:20), and (c) speech in the Spirit (4:6).

The crisis over circumcision, moreover, focuses on the regulation of the genital orifice. Ironically, Paul might seem to stand for *no* control over this orifice because he abandons the practice of circumcision, but that would be misleading. He rigorously demands control of the genital orifice represented by circumcision, only he demands that it *not* be circumcised. Just as Jesus' insistence that hands need *not* be washed did not mean that he had no purity concerns, only concerns quite different from those of the Pharisees, so Paul's insistence that the male genital orifice *not* be circumcised is also a purity concern and a demand for strict control of that orifice.

In general, Paul urges self-control, which implies bodily discipline. The reader should not mistake Paul's emphasis on spirit vs. flesh and freedom vs. slavery to imply that he does not urge bodily control. Abandoning circumcision and other Jewish bodily practices, he nevertheless enjoins a bodily control corresponding to the social structures he claims characterize the true covenant of God (see Rom. 6:15–22).

**3.1.5 Sin and Deviance**   Given the strong sense of purity and social organization, one would expect to find sin defined in terms of the violation of society's (and God's) basic laws. This is indeed the case in 5:18–21, where the condemned "works of the flesh" echo the prohibitions basically covered in the Ten Commandments. Transgression of them will cause the loss of eternal salvation: "I warn you, as I warned you before, that those who do such things shall not inherit the kingdom of God" (5:21; see 1 Cor. 6:9–10).

Yet in this ambiguous world, Evil attacks the boundaries of society and physical bodies alike. Comparably, Paul perceives sin as pollution that totally corrupts the body. In this regard, Paul labels the doctrine and practice of the Judaizers as "leaven" that corrupts the purity of God's people (5:9). Although we tend to view leaven positively, the ancients regularly described it as the stuff that causes fermentation, and so corruption. Paul exhorted the Corinthians to be "unleavened bread," freed from "the old leaven of malice and evil" (1 Cor. 5:8). Therefore, when he labels the evil of the Judaizers as "leaven," he perceives it as a pollution that is corrupting the Galatians. It must be expelled.

**3.1.6 Cosmology**   Paul perceives this cosmos in anthropomorphic terms. He no doubt understands Israel's God as a person who is Father (4:4–6) and as Patron who is benevolent (3:2–5), merciful (1:13–16), and just (6:7–8). But Paul's cosmos is also disturbingly full of other personal agents of power who work harm against us, as the following list indicates (Hall 1973:132–160):

1. Satan (1 Cor. 7:5; 2 Cor. 2:11; 11:14; 12:7; 1 Thess. 2:18)
2. Principality (1 Cor. 15:24; Rom. 8:38)
3. Rulers (1 Cor. 2:6, 8)

4. Powers/*exousia* (1 Cor. 15:24)
5. Power/*dynamis* (1 Cor. 15:24; Rom. 8:38)
6. Tempter (1 Thess. 3:5)
7. Elements (Gal. 4:3, 9)
8. Beings that by nature are no gods (Gal. 4:8)
9. Spirit of the world (1 Cor. 2:12)
10. Demons (1 Cor. 10:20–21)
11. God of this age (2 Cor. 4:4)

But in this world there also exists a dominant evil force who is perceived anthropomorphically. Paul identifies this personal Evil in his accusation that some*one* is bewitching the Galatians (3:1) or some*one* is disguising himself as an angel of God (1:8). Although individuals are personally responsible for their own behavior and will be judged accordingly (6:8), yet personal Evil exists in this world; it attacks and seduces people, thus causing their ruin as surely as if they had broken all of God's commandments.

In an earlier chapter, we cited the numerous times that Paul speaks of himself (1 Thess. 2:18; 2 Cor. 12:7) and his churches as being attacked by Satan (2 Cor. 11:13–15). He readily concedes that all of them must regularly strive "to keep Satan from gaining the advantage over us" (2 Cor. 2:11). For an evil figure still tempts them (1 Cor. 7:5) and works to keep people from believing the gospel (2 Cor. 4:4). In Galatians, moreover, Paul speaks of an Evil that enslaves humans (4:9) and bewitches them (3:1). Through its earthly agents, it "persecutes him who is born according to the spirit" (4:29), not just Isaac but those of his lineage (see 1 Thess. 2:14–15). In short, Paul tends to ascribe to the agency of this evil figure all the evils of this world—sickness, death, and especially heresy.

This world, moreover, is dualistically perceived. Just as everything in the cosmos is dualistically divided into two kingdoms, so the two kingdoms are themselves ruled respectively by two figures at war with each other, God and Satan. Apropos of the warring cosmic powers, some scholars would invite us to consider the doctrine of the "two spirits," the *yetzer ha-tob* and the *yetzer ha-ra'* (May 1963:1-7; Marcus 1982:606–621). These terms describe the two spirits at war in human hearts, a suggestion that I find plausible in light of the current discussion. This cosmos, then, is a battlefield of warring spirits, many of whom are disguised as angels of light.

### 3.1.7 Suffering and Misfortune
In a dualistic world where Evil attacks the boundaries of the holy cosmos, the world seems

unjust at times. Paul himself serves as an excellent example of cosmic injustice whereby the good suffer, despite their being God's chosen ones who are blessed with grace and Spirit. A prophet called by God (1:13–16), an apostle legitimated by Jerusalem (2:7–9), Paul is nevertheless held in low regard and even viciously attacked (Baasland 1984:140–143). But then, such has always been the lot of God's true prophets, as it was of Isaac at the hands of Ishmael (4:29). Beyond the fact that Paul interprets the cross of Jesus as the official boundary line between the covenants of Moses and Abraham, Paul glories in this cross and the symbolic suffering attached to it as indication of where he stands. For identification with Christ crucified would indicate that he not only knows the truth about Jesus, but bodily imitates him (6:17). Thus, he accepts suffering as proof that he is being attacked unjustly by Evil, God's enemy.

In summary, in the earlier part of this book we examined in a general way the basic elements of Paul's cosmology and worldview. Here we have studied the particular shape of Paul's symbolic world as this is reflected in his letter to the Galatians. As a result of this we now appreciate several important facts: (1) Paul perceives himself under constant attack, even as he engages in interminable conflict with others. (2) He perceives his world in radically dualistic terms (God vs. Satan; good vs. evil; spirit vs. flesh; Abraham vs. Moses, etc.). As a result, he contrasts his theological position point for point with that of the Judaizers. (3) At best Paul perceives the cosmos as ambiguous, but actually as a dangerous world of deceit and masquerade. (4) He perceives Evil attacking and polluting his churches. This model allows us to examine texts that might not at first seem important; but, of more importance, it allows us to see a coherence in Paul's perceptions. As the anthropologists suggest, this is the type of world in which we are likely to find witchcraft accusations. This first part of our inquiry, then, has given us a basic framework in which to consider more formally the accusation made in 3:1 and implied in 1:8.

**3.2 Specific Characteristics of Witchcraft Society**  From the beginning, it must be clear that when we speak of "witchcraft accusations" we are not envisioning black cats, broomsticks, or Halloween decorations. We are discussing the social phenomenon where people accuse their enemy or rival of being either the Devil himself or acting under the Devil's power. We focus, then, on the *accusation* of demon possession (witchcraft accusation) and how this *functions* in the social relations within a group.

Besides teaching us how to discover the symbolic universe where witchcraft accusations occur, Mary Douglas offers a second and more specific model for studying this phenomenon. This second model contains three elements needed to understand witches and witchcraft accusations: (1) specific characteristics of witchcraft societies, (2) the anthropological definition of a witch, and (3) the function of accusations of witchcraft or bewitchment (Douglas 1963:123–141; 1970:xiii–xxxviii; 1982b: 99–124).

### 3.2.1 Six Specific Characteristics

*3.2.1 Six Specific Characteristics* Douglas identifies six specific characteristics of what she calls "witchcraft societies," that is, societies where accusations of witchcraft possession tend to occur. These are clearer definitions of the cosmology described earlier.

**Clearly Marked External Boundaries:** As we noted above, in Galatians there is no ambiguity in Paul's mind about who is "in" and who is "out", for the primary ritual in which Paul engages is boundary building and maintenance.

**Confused Internal Relations:** In the churches of Galatia there appears to be a vacuum of leadership. It seems to have been Paul's custom to found his churches and move on. The letter mentions no one by name, no Stephanas whom he might appoint as regent in his absence (1 Cor. 16:15–16), no Euodia and Syntyche, who might be the owners of the house churches where Christians met (Phil. 4:2–3). Although absent, Paul tries to maintain leadership of the group; no one is allowed to take his place. Yet in this vacuum, we learn of "teachers" whose credentials are never mentioned, much less refuted. Even Paul's own claims to leadership are contested here. Although claims and legitimacy might be tested and validated in Jerusalem (2:6–9), there is apparently no mechanism in Galatia to sort out the competing claims of Paul or his opponents. We find instead an absence of leadership and competing claims to authority, a very confusing situation.

The letter, moreover, indicates considerable confusion on Paul's part about roles and statuses in the church. Paul knows of leaders at Jerusalem, "pillars" (2:9), but he slurs their authority by describing them as those who only seem to have legitimate status. Paul himself would like to be considered "an apostle," a term that many in Galatia deny him (1:10). When Paul tells the story that functions as the legitimation of his role and authority (1:15–16), he presents himself using language from the prophetic tradition. This suggests that he perceives himself in some way as a prophet, a category that should command respect but is very difficult to test or define. There are apparently "teachers" in Galatia, but we know nothing about their status or legitimation (see 1:6–9; 3:1–2, 5; 4:17; 5:7–12; 6:12–14). Paul, then, disputes the authority and status of all others, even as his own is contested. The internal relations in these churches, then, are extremely confused.

**Close and Unavoidable Interaction:** Although Paul was absent from the Galatian churches, he remained in close contact with them, just as he did with the churches at Corinth and Philippi. Because of his claim to be their founder and father, he cannot and will not abandon them; he chooses to remain in close interaction with them, even if this means unavoidable and constant friction.

Although it is not clear how Paul comes to know about the crisis in Galatia, from his other letters we get the sense of a person in very close contact with his churches, especially when absent. As he himself says, although absent he is present (1 Cor. 5:3) in a variety of ways:

1. Through his messengers to them (1 Cor. 4:17; 16:10; 1 Thess. 3:2), who return to him with news (1 Thess. 3:6; 2 Cor. 7:6, 13–14)
2. By oral reports from members of the churches (1 Cor. 1:11)
3. By letters from them (1 Cor. 7:1)
4. By his own letters to them

The contact, then, is intense and unrelenting.

**Underdeveloped Tension-Relieving Techniques:** Techniques for distancing, regulating, and reconciling these conflicts are little developed here. Whereas in Jerusalem issues may be decided, at Antioch Paul resorts to name calling. Paul accuses Cephas of hypocrisy, although by his own admission he himself is a "Greek with Greeks and a Jew with Jews" (1 Cor. 9:19–21); and according to his critics at Galatia, he seems to be less than consistent about circumcision (1:10; 5:11). It is especially in regard to the conflicting claims of Paul and the Judaizers that we recognize how underdeveloped are the techniques for settling leadership and doctrinal disputes in Galatia. There is no formal procedure for regulating this intense competition, adjudicating rival claims, or even separating the parties.

**Weak Authority:** Paul is simply unable to control effectively the behavior of people in Galatia. It is presumed that Paul's rivals cite to their own purposes the only authority, the Scriptures, just as Paul construes the Scriptures in his own idiosyncratic way. But who is right, and how can the Galatians know? Paul's authority, moreover, is being fiercely attacked by those who denigrate his "apostleship," point out his inconsistencies, and highlight his distance from Jerusalem and its traditions. It is not incidental that whereas Paul previously laid before Cephas and the Jerusalem "pillars" his doctrine, "lest somehow I should be running . . . in vain" (2:2), he does not appeal to Jerusalem to adjudicate the present crisis. Implicit in this stance is Paul's sense of his own weak authority in Jerusalem as well as his attack on its alleged authority (2:6, 8).

It is noteworthy that when Paul's apostleship comes under attack (1:1), he redefines the legitimacy of his position by describing his role as that of a prophet. Like Jeremiah and Isaiah, he claims to be set apart even from his mother's womb (1:15). God, not Jesus, "called him" and gave him a revelation to proclaim (1:16). Nowhere else in his letters does he pass himself off as a prophet like the prophets of Israel. But here, where he is denied one role (apostle), he searches for another label to explain his status and authority (prophet). If he were able to establish this, he would be superior to any apostle commissioned by mere men or confirmed by them, for he would be a prophet to whom God has directly revealed the truth. The very confusion of roles Paul assumes (apostle, prophet) indicates the weakness of his authority in the conflict.

**Intense, Disorderly Competition:** Accusations of demonic possession tend to occur in groups characterized by intense, disorderly competition for leadership. Galatians records numerous examples of intense competition:

1. Paul vs. the pillars at Jerusalem (2:1–10)
2. Paul vs. Cephas at Antioch (2:11–14)
3. Paul vs. the teachers in Galatia

At every level we find competition and rivalry. Although scholars tend to focus primarily on the doctrinal issues in Galatians, the fact is that Paul here, as elsewhere, remained in an intense state of competition with rival preachers, a competition that was disorderly. We should not ignore this when trying to understand his theology in its historical context.

**3.2.2 Definition of the Galatian Witch**   Earlier in this chapter we cited three aspects of how anthropologists define a witch.

1. A witch's *inside is corrupt.*
2. A witch has a *perverted nature,* a *reversal* of the ways things ought to be; a witch is a *deceiver* whose external appearance hides its inner nature.
3. A witch attacks by *life-sucking* or by *poison.*

Although Paul does not formally name or describe his Judaizing opponents, there are bits of evidence in the letter that indicate that he perceives them as "witches."

**Corrupt Insides**   Paul understands the covenant with Moses (Law/works) as producing a "curse" (3:10–11). It was, after all, given "because of transgressions" (3:19), and according to the Scriptures "all were consigned to sin" (3:22) who live in it. Conversely, no one can be justified before God by the Law (3:11; 2:16). It follows, then, that the Judaizers who urge a return to this covenant must themselves be sinners still, under God's curse, and definitely *not* justified before God. Paul infers, then, that they are still in sin; in anthropological terms, their insides are corrupt.

**Perversion/Deception:**   In some way, Paul links the Judaizers in Galatia with "false brethren" in the Jerusalem church (2:4), in that both of them urge slavery. They are false because they deliberately claim to be zealous for God and to belong to the disciples of Jesus, but in Paul's view they are enemies of God's plan in Christ and are only masquerading as brothers of God's family. They urge, moreover, a doctrine and a practice that they claim leads to perfection or glory. They indeed seem to argue their case from God's holy Word, but from a part that Paul describes as a temporary covenant given because of sin to sinners, a part of the Scriptures that Paul calls "curse." They, however, exalt that part of the Scriptures as necessary and desirable, disguising the curse and slavery of their covenant under the lie of perfection and glory. They are deceivers, only pretending to be Christians. In fact, they are enemies of the cross of Christ, for whom the cross is a stumbling block (5:11) that achieved nothing. They are really disciples of Moses, but only pretend to be disciples of Jesus. They disguise their errors and pretend to teach truth.

**Poison/Life-Sucking:**   In one telltale remark, Paul describes the false doctrine of the Judaizers as "leaven," even a pinch of which necessarily corrupts the whole batch of pure flour (5:9). Paul understands "leaven" here as a metaphor for wickedness and pollution, just as he did in 1 Corinthians 5:8. This doctrinal "leaven" corresponds to the witch's poison, which corrupts and kills when ingested (see Matt. 16:11–12).

As regards "life-sucking," we should attend to two phenomena in Galatians. Paul himself is concerned that he be "full" and not "empty" (*kenos*), and so he goes to Jerusalem to lay his own doctrine before the church, lest he have created "emptiness" in others (2:2; see 1 Cor. 15:10, 14, 58). He, then, is not empty, nor does he cause others to become empty, sucked of life.

Yet his portrayal of the rival teachers implies that they cause emptiness, the loss of previous life in the soul. As Paul argues in 3:3, when they urge circumcision and the Law, these Judaizers cause people who "began in the Spirit" (an inside full of God's life) to "end in the flesh" (a shell of a person). They are causing the loss of Spirit, leaving their disciples empty, sucked of life. As Paul says, if they observe "days, months, seasons, and years," then he has labored "emptily"; for the Galatians shall have lost all that Paul would have put in them (4:10–11) through the life-sucking of the preachers of "another gospel."

### 3.2.3 Function of Witchcraft Accusations in Galatia

There are two "witchcraft accusations" in Galatians 3:1 and 1:8. When Paul asks, "Who has *bewitched* you?" the word used there ("bewitched" = *baskanein*) is the technical term in the classical Mediterranean world for "the evil eye" that harms and kills (Elliott 1988:42, 54–57). The anthropological model we are using suggests that we understand this term as a genuine accusation by Paul that the churches in Galatia have been attacked by an evil figure, Satan or one of his minions. Paul, then, is not using a metaphor here, but speaks literally about someone harming the church both by soul-sucking and by poison. Given his perception of a dualistic cosmos of warring figures, he labels the Judaizing preachers as agents of Satan who are corrupting God's people.

The proper labeling of 1:8 depends on our appreciation of a clearer use of this language in 2 Corinthians 11. Paul accused the "Superapostles" who preach at Corinth of being demon possessed. He drew an analogy between Satan's seduction of Eve and the seduction of the holy Corinthian church by these rival preachers (11:3). Noting that Satan is wont to disguise himself as an angel of light (11:14), he argues that the same tactic is used by Satan's servants, the Superapostles: "So it is not strange if his servants also disguise themselves as servants of righteousness" (11:15).

An angel of light, then, is a fundamentally ambiguous figure who might be God's messenger (e.g., Paul, Gal. 4:14), but who might just as well be Satan in disguise. I suggest that Paul's remark in Galatians 1:8 about an "angel from heaven" who preaches "a gospel contrary to that which we preached to you" should be unmasked as a deceiving angel of light, that is, as Satan in disguise. The unfortunate fact for Paul is that such a gospel has already been taught at Galatia by teachers whom he considers to be capable of bewitchment. Galatians 1:8, then, contains no positive reference to angelic revelations, but a warning of a potential and even actual deception by a disguised angel of light. Galatians 3:1 and 1:8, then, should be formally labeled "witchcraft accusations." But what is their function?

It would be an understatement to say that Paul is fiercely jealous of his turf. In letter after letter, he either states his policy of "making it my ambition to preach the gospel, not where Christ has already been named, lest I build on another['s] foundation" (Rom. 15:20) or he complains bitterly about those who have crossed the line and come on to his turf to poach: "We will not boast beyond limit, but will keep to the limits God has apportioned us, . . . for we are not overextending ourselves; . . . we do not boast beyond limit, in other['s] labors, . . . boasting of work already done in another's field" (2 Cor. 10:13–16; see Barrett 1973:262–268). On this occasion Paul accused the Superapostles at Corinth of being Satan in disguise (2 Cor. 11:3, 13–15). For the sake of peace, Paul may say that he welcomes Apollos' labors at Corinth and considers him his equal in the ministry (1 Cor. 3:5), but there is no doubt that Paul planted the seed (3:6) and laid the foundation (3:10). And anyone who would build on that foundation had better look out (3:12–14)! Paul's distress with others' coming into his churches springs from his sense of competition from them. Whereas theologians focus on these conflicts in terms of conflicting theologies, a social science model urges us to see them as evidence of an intense sense of rivalry, competition, and even jealousy.

Galatians fairly bristles with a sense of rivalry and competition. We recall Paul's competition with the Jerusalem "pillars," at whose "repute" he sneers (2:6). We do not know the particulars of the division of the apostolate between Cephas/Jewish mission and Paul/Gentile mission in 2:6–8, but there are hints that Paul came to understand it as a territorial division, which implies a certain exclusivity. He appears reluctant to go on

Peter's turf, to Jerusalem (1:16–24); ánd the text suggests Paul's discomfort at anyone coming on to his turf, either the advent of certain men from Jerusalem (2:12) or the coming of rival teachers into his churches in Galatia.

Paul's church at Antioch became the scene of conflict with the arrival of "outsiders" (2:11–12). The apparent harmony that Cephas and Paul shared was shattered when "men from James," presumably "the circumcision party," occasioned a division between them. On one level the conflict is over eating rituals, which symbolizes theological issues. The use of social science modeling draws attention to Paul's sense that his turf is violated by these men from James, whose theology he considered evil. Cephas' presence at Antioch then becomes a scandal. Although stopping short of calling Cephas a witch, Paul accuses him of "insincerity" or hypocrisy (*tē hypokrisei*, 2:13).

But the most intense rivalry occurs between Paul and his opponents for leadership over the churches of Galatia that are his turf. I do not doubt that Paul reacted to their very coming on to his territory in the same way he took offense at "certain men [who] came from James" (2:12). Their coming, of course, was linked with their preaching "another gospel." Yet to judge from the intense apology for his own role and status, Paul seems to have perceived and experienced their coming as an explicit attack on his leadership in a church from which he is absent. The issue is not just theology but rivalry as well.

A mirror reading of his statements about himself suggests the shape of the polemic, either real or perceived. He is no genuine apostle (1:1); he hides the truth from these churches and so is a false teacher (5:11; 1:10); his ties with the mother church are tenuous at best, implying that he is a maverick figure (2:1–10) with perhaps a defective doctrine. The fact that Paul hastens to find alternate legitimation of his authority and role (1:13–16) suggests a strategy of one-upmanship in the rivalry with the Judaizers (see Phil. 3:3–6 and 2 Cor. 11:21–23).

If apology serves to deflect their criticism of Paul, his own witchcraft accusations against these rival preachers function offensively to reduce their status. The Judaizers are those who not only "pervert the gospel" (1:7), but they act as disguised agents of the devil by "bewitching" the poor Galatians (3:1). Yet it is not enough to identify the Judaizers as demons in disguise. Such evil persons should then be expelled from the church. Paul explicitly calls for this when he cites Genesis 21:10: "Cast out the slave and her son" (4:30).

Witchcraft accusations serve two purposes, either expulsion or fission (Douglas 1970:xviii; 1982b:114). It does not appear that Paul quit the fight, abandoned the churches in Galatia, and moved on—not fission! From the document, his strategy was clearly to expel the witches and so to purify the holy group. His anathemas and his demand that they be "cast out of the house" like Hagar and Ishmael (4:30) indicate that Paul's purpose in labeling the Judaizing preachers as "witches" is to expel them. The accusations are intended to discredit his rivals. History does not tell us the outcome of the struggle, but presumably Paul succeeded.

The models from cultural anthropology have sharpened our perception of both the general symbolic universe of Paul and the particular social dynamics in the Galatian churches. Labels function as social weapons, whether presidential candidates label each other as "wimp" or "liberal," whether politicians label each other as "strong on law and order" or "weak on communism" (Malina and Neyrey 1988:35–67). We have examined Paul's use of a powerful label, his accusation that those who promote Judaizing doctrines are Satan's agents. This chapter has been able to explain how such an accusation of witchcraft is part and parcel of Paul's symbolic universe. We have gained a fresh insight into how such a label functions in the contest for leadership of the Galatian churches. In the next chapter, we will examine another example of Pauline witchcraft accusations. He accuses his rivals in Corinth of being disguised angels of light who are seducing the virgin bride of Christ.

# 10

## Seduced in Corinth:
## More Witchcraft Accusations

Satan disguises himself as an angel of light.
                              2 Corinthians 11:14

### 1.0  Disguised in Corinth

When we turn to 2 Corinthians 10–13, we find Paul employing witchcraft accusations against certain members of the Corinthian church. By employing the anthropological models once more, we test their appropriateness for understanding Paul, even as their successful application confirms their correctness and utility. Two examples are better than one. They confirm, moreover, the general patterns of Paul's perception that we have tried to examine in this book.

Paul accuses some people of being servants of Satan, even demons disguised as angels of light (11:13–15). Such labeling of prominent and respected members of his church is clearly an act of social aggression, which he does with utmost seriousness. Why does Paul use the accusation of sorcery here? Why does this function as his best weapon in the conflict? What does he hope to achieve by this labeling? Our model of witchcraft accusations can serve us well in explaining Paul's perceptions and his strategy in employing this language.

## 2.0 Corinth and Paul's Symbolic Universe

One might ask why we must examine once more Paul's symbolic universe. We studied its broad outlines in the early chapters of this book. But there we were attending to large and general patterns that seem common to all the Pauline letters. And in the preceding study of Galatians, we noted that those general patterns took quite specific shape according to the issues discussed and the crisis addressed in that particular document. Because each Pauline epistle is an "occasional" letter, we must attend not only to general patterns of Pauline perception but to their specific and concrete expression in an individual letter. The actual way Paul expresses himself in 2 Corinthians will be different from that done in Galatians, although the general point of view will be the same.

In this chapter we are focusing on 2 Corinthians 10–13. The second letter to Corinth is often described as a collection of different letters (Georgi 1986). Although that correspondence reflects general aspects of Paul's symbolic universe, we restrict our attention here to the specific materials contained in 2 Corinthians 10–13. Once more, we begin our investigation of witchcraft accusations in 2 Corinthians 11 by examining first the way 2 Corinthians 10–13 reflects the general shape of Paul's symbolic universe.

*2.1 Purity* Paul's universe is shaped into a strongly ordered purity system by virtue of the simple phrase "the gospel of Christ" (2 Cor. 10:14; see 10:16). This presupposes an extensive, articulated kerygma about Jesus. Moreover, by citing Jeremiah 9:24 in 2 Corinthians 10:17, Paul indicates that he continues to value the Scriptures as normative for him and his churches, as do the allusions to the Genesis story of Satan and Eve in 11:3 (see also Deut. 19:15 cited in 2 Cor. 13:1). Furthermore, traditional Christian customs are assumed in the typical reference to financial support of apostolic preachers (11:7–9; see 1 Cor. 9:3–

12). Therefore, the gospel about Jesus, the Scriptures, and early church traditions together determine the specific patterns of Paul's orderly, structured cosmos. It was a highly ordered cosmos with an exact classification system.

Yet despite his desire for an ordered world, Paul speaks of threats to it and of pollutants attacking it. He speaks, for example, of a state of warfare in which he is engaged, referring to his "weapons of warfare," his attempts to "destroy strongholds," and his "taking captive" opposing thoughts (10:4–5). The threat of polluting heresy disturbs him most, that is, the preaching of "another Jesus . . . a different gospel" (11:4). He claims that the false apostles preach this to seduce the pure bride of Christ (11:2, 13–15).

Pollution, moreover, threatens the physical as well as the social body. Just as the social body's unity is attacked by "quarreling, jealousy, slander" (12:20), so the individual's physical body is correspondingly polluted by "impurity, immorality, and licentiousness" (12:21). Paul's cosmos, then, is engaged in warfare and is subject to seduction. The order of truth is being subverted by the chaos of error, and the stakes are very high indeed.

**2.2 Ritual** Belief in Jesus as God's Son, Christ, and agent of the true covenant constitutes the main boundary line distinguishing Christian insiders from all others. Yet the crisis for Corinth resides not at these boundaries, because all parties to the dispute in 2 Corinthians 10–13 appear to be "Christians." Rather, Paul's attention focuses on the pollution that has already breached this boundary. The conflict resides in the ambiguous internal relationships among the members of the group, namely, the question of legitimate leadership in the Corinthian church—Paul versus Superapostles.

As founder of that church, Paul repeatedly claims special honor as the group's head and "father" (12:14; see 1 Cor. 4:14–15; 1 Thess. 2:11). In this capacity he speaks of himself as the elder male of the family whose role it is to betroth the virgin church to Christ (2 Cor. 11:2). The legitimacy of Paul's claims rests partly on his initial, but past, apostolic actions, his claims of pedigree (11:22), and his claims to have suffered like Jesus (11:23–33; 13:3–4). Covering other bases, Paul claims legitimation through achievements such as heavenly revelations (12:1–4; see 1 Cor. 2:6–16; Gal. 1:15–16). These achievements suggest that he claims the role of a prophet, because others at Corinth dispute his claim to be an "apostle" (1 Cor. 9:1; 15:9; see Gal. 1:1).

Yet Paul *has been*, *is*, and *will remain* absent from this group over which he claims absolute and enduring authority. Other leaders, however, have moved into this vacuum to preach to and preside over the Corinthian church. Paul denigrates these rivals in highly polemical terms, calling them Superapostles (11:5), "false apostles, deceitful workmen" (11:13), boastful persons (10:12–13; 11:16–19, 22), and seductive suitors (11:3, 12–15).

He speaks from a sense of Corinth as *his* turf. These rival preachers are trespassing on his turf: "We are not overextending ourselves. . . . We do not boast beyond limit, in another['s] labors; but our hope is that as your faith increases, our field among you may be greatly enlarged, so that we may preach the gospel in lands beyond you, without boasting of work already done in another's fields" (10:14–16; see Rom. 15:20 and 1 Cor. 3:10–15). Paul, moreover, interprets the presence of rivals on his turf as a pollution that has breached the boundaries of the social and individual bodies, and threatens a fatal corruption. Paul versus Superapostles—the critical issue rests in the confusing roles and ambiguous status of the rival preachers at Corinth, including Paul himself.

Paul's characteristic ritual actions have to do with boundary making and maintenance. The fences around his turf have been breached, which summons Paul's attention to the periphery. In his view, those who climbed the fences are not only trespassers but saboteurs. They have spread poison in the Corinthian church. Paul's rituals, then, focus both on identifying the pollution that has crossed the boundaries of the group and forcing its removal.

**2.3 Personal Identity**   We are reminded that persons in Paul's world appear ambiguous to others. People regularly make distinctions between a person's exterior and interior, between appearances and reality. Some see such ambiguity in Paul, and he sees it in them.

In 2 Corinthians, Paul repeats the invaders' own accusations that he is duplicitous: "I who am humble when face to face with you, but bold to you when I am away!" (10:1) and: "They say, 'His letters are weighty and strong, but his bodily presence is weak, and his speech of no account' " (10:10). According to them, Paul has many faces (see 1 Cor. 9:19–23). For his own part, he accuses his very accusers of duplicity, calling them "deceitful workmen, disguising themselves as apostles of Christ" (11:13). After comparing their tactics with Satan's deceit and seduction of Eve, Paul concludes: "It is not strange if his [Satan's] servants also disguise themselves as servants of righteousness" (11:15). Personal identity, then, remains painfully ambiguous on both sides.

The personal identity of Paul is still more ambiguous when we notice the debate over his "weakness." Paul occasionally claims achieved legitimate authority by virtue of his display of charismatic strength and power (Gal. 3:3–5; 1 Thess. 1:5; 1 Cor. 14:18). Yet on the whole, it would seem that his presentation of himself was, as 2 Corinthians indicates, "weak, and . . . of no account" (2 Cor. 10:10; see 1 Cor. 2:1–5; Gal. 4:13–14). Paul, however, boasts that appearances may be deceiving, for weakness is strength, just as foolishness is wisdom (13:3–4; see 1 Cor. 1:18–25). The boast of physical hardships for the sake of the gospel in 11:23–33 is a further example of the ambiguity of appearances (see 6:4–10 and 1 Cor. 4:8–13). Paul's sufferings, humiliations, and weakness become in his eyes signs of his legitimation, not of his disqualification, as seems to have been thought at Corinth (see 1 Cor. 1:17; 2:3–5; 2 Cor. 4:7–11).

The plausible explanation for the confusion of appearance and reality most likely stems from Paul's preaching of the Crucified Christ as God's power and wisdom against the celebration of pneumatic power as the source of legitimate authority (1 Cor. 1:18–25). Yet, as Paul proclaims of himself, *things are seldom what they seem.* Weakness is strength. Paul's own world, then, remains fundamentally ambiguous.

**2.4 Body** In 1 Corinthians 6 and 12, Paul compared the church to a physical body, a metaphor that yields in 2 Corinthians 11 to the image of the church as the spotless bride of Christ. Stringent bodily control is an appropriate defensive strategy for a holy body or a spotless bride (Malina 1981:42–46). This control takes the form of guarding the bodily orifices, especially the ears (against seductive flattery, 11:4, 13–15) and the genitals (where sexual pollution symbolizes doctrinal pollution). Yet Paul charges that this body is already being seduced and polluted (11:13–15).

**2.5 Sin and Deviance** Although in 1 Corinthians 6:9–10 Paul defines sin as the formal violation of the Ten Commandments, in 2 Corinthians he perceives sin primarily as pollution, seduction, and heresy (see "leaven" in 1 Cor. 5:8). His preoccupation with "another gospel . . . another Jesus" suggests that he perceives the sin of the trespassing Superapostles as a type of all-corrupting pollution.

**2.6 *Cosmology***  By his own account, Paul describes himself at war in the cosmos (10:1–6). We note his thoroughly dualistic view of the cosmos as completely polarized into opposing forces of good and evil. Not only is God involved in the lives of the Corinthians; God's rival, Satan, likewise operates in the world. Satan once seduced Eve, causing unspeakable harm to God's creatures (11:3), and Satan returns to work further harm on the followers of Jesus (11:13–15). Even Paul himself is harassed by "a messenger of Satan" (12:7).

Not only are God and Satan at war in Paul's world, their respective agents are likewise battling. Using Paul's own metaphors, we understand these agents as two opposing armies or two warring camps locked in mortal combat:

| | | |
|---|---|---|
| Paul the Apostle | vs. | Superapostles/False Apostles |
| The Gospel of Christ | vs. | Another Jesus/A Different Gospel |
| Authorized Preacher from God | vs. | Unauthorized Agents of Satan |

The Superapostles who propose "another gospel" are identified as Satan's servants. As Paul sees it, he enjoys authentic, legitimate authority, they do not; he is spiritual, but they are worldly; he is God's agent, they are Satan's henchmen. Heaven and earth, then, are thoroughly divided into opposing armies of good and evil.

**2.7 *Suffering and Misfortune***  Paul sees the world as an unjust cosmos. After all, Paul, who is God's authorized agent, suffers terribly as the legitimate preacher of the gospel, whereas the Superapostles are honored by worldly recommendations (10:17–18), boasts (11:18), and mighty works (12:11–12). Suffering is unfair. God's agent, Paul, even on the occasion of his great revelations, was given a thorn in the flesh, a painful experience that was not suffering merited by sin (12:7–10). Paul, then, does not deserve the dishonor or humiliation or pain that he experiences. In fact, he ascribes his suffering and misfortunes to the agency of God's enemy, Satan (e.g., 12:7; see 1 Thess. 2:18).

In summary, the various details provided by Paul in 2 Corinthians 10–13 correspond quite closely to the general profile of a witchcraft society as described by anthropological students of this phenomenon. The perceptions in 2 Corinthians basically resemble those of Galatians, allowing for the "occasional" quality of each of Paul's letters. The net impression is that of the following:

1. A system threatened and under seige
2. Pollution infiltrating boundaries
3. A cosmos stricken with ambiguity and deceit
4. A world of pervasive and cosmic evil

## 3.0 Specific Characteristics of Witchcraft Society

*3.1 Specific Characteristics* Applying Douglas's model once more, we note the following specific aspects of a witchcraft society in Paul's perception of the situation at Corinth.

**External Boundaries Clearly Marked:** Paul addresses a small group whose external boundaries are tightly drawn; they all belong to the church of Christ at Corinth.

**Confused Internal Relations:** Although all are Christians, the internal relations within the group are confused in terms of role, office, and authority. Legitimation has become the persistent and dominant problem for Paul and for the Superapostles. Paul seems always to be intensely self-conscious of this issue (see 1 Cor. 9:1–2; 15:8–11; Gal. 1:1). In fact, he seems to live in a state of rivalry with other preachers (see Phil. 1:15–18; 1 Cor. 1:12; 3:4; Gal. 1:6–9), indicating a persistent problem in the early church with legitimate role and status. The problem is compounded by his long absence from them and the inevitable emergence of other leaders, but the criteria for legitimate authority are unclear.

**Close and Unavoidable Interaction:** Paul is absent from the churches to which he writes, an absence quite permanent despite his protestations of an imminent return (see 1:16–17; 13:2, 10; 1 Cor. 4:18–19). Yet he stays in close, unavoidable conflict with them through letters and emissaries (1 Cor. 1:11; 11:18 and 16:10).

**Underdeveloped Tension-Relieving Techniques:** We have scant information about any tension-relieving techniques for the conflicts described in his letters. How is authority legitimated? Paul does not appeal to Jerusalem and its apostolic leadership to validate the legitimacy of his claims (see Gal. 2:2, 7–9). He occasionally claims Jesus' direct designation of him as an apostle (1 Cor. 9:1); but, when faced with pneumatic rivals, he claims legitimation through achievement (1 Cor. 2:6–16; 14:18; see 2 Cor. 12:1–4). At other times, he presents himself as a prophet (Gal. 1:15). Considerable evidence suggests that Paul was not readily accepted as a true apostle on a par with the pillars of the church (see 1 Cor. 9:2). In 1 Corinthians 15:8–9, he speaks of himself as "the runt of the litter," not worthy to be called an apostle. From all of this we learn that Paul's role and status as an apostle and the legitimation of his apostolic authority remained a continual problem. There seems to have been no definitive criterion at Corinth (or elsewhere) for determining the legitimacy either of the absent Paul or his rivals who are present.

**Weak Authority:** Paul speaks constantly about authority, either God's authority, Christ's authority, or that of husbands (1 Cor. 11:3; 15:22–28). Yet authority is weak in the Pauline churches. Paul himself is absent; apparently he did not name successors, except Stephanas (1 Cor. 16:15–18). Into this vacuum moved other leaders, people who appear to have been pneumatic, eloquent, powerful figures. Paul refuses to acknowledge their legitimacy, but seems impotent to unseat them. At best he may discredit them.

**Intense, Disorderly Competition:** Evidence of intense and disorderly competition surfaces as a palpable feature of Paul's correspondence. He battles constantly with other preachers: pneumatics, Judaizers, Superapostles, rival preachers, Apollos. Like the situation in Galatia, Paul's dealings with Corinth according to 2 Corinthians 10–13 may be described adequately as satisfying the conditions in which witchcraft accusations occur.

*3.2 Witches at Corinth*  Paul regularly describes his rivals according to what we have come to learn as the anthropological definition of a witch:

**Corrupt Insides:** In Paul's eyes, they are false apostles (11:13) who act out of perverse motives (11:20; see Phil. 1:15).

**Perversion/Deception:** They are perverted figures, deceivers who mask their corruption in a show of wisdom and power: "Such men are . . . deceitful workmen, disguising themselves as apostles of Christ" (11:13). Paul compares them with Satan, who "disguises himself as an angel of light" (11:14). They are, in effect, Satan's very agents.

**Poison/Life-Sucking:** As secret witches, Paul perceives his rival preachers as attacking their victims with the poison of heresy ("another Jesus . . . a different gospel," 11:4). They seduce their victims, offering tainted doctrine for the truth, thus corrupting the church's "sincere and pure devotion to Christ" (11:3). From an anthropological perspective, then, Paul perceives his rivals as "witches," and labels them as such with "witchcraft accusations."

**3.3 Social Function of Witchcraft Accusations**  The social function of typical witchcraft accusations applies to the charges made by Paul in 2 Corinthians 10–13. By calling public attention to the pollutions of his rivals, Paul expects them to be discredited in the eyes of the church and dismissed from the group. His accusations function as an idiom of social control in the competition for leadership in the Corinthian church. In the intense and disorderly competition, Paul's labeling of his rivals, if successful, would dishonor them and leave him alone in the field to face inevitable new challenges to his authority.

## 4.0 Summary and Conclusions

What have we learned in this investigation? We focused on passages in two of Paul's letters: Galatians 1:8 and 3:1 and 2 Corinthians 11:3, 13–15. These record Paul's accusation that some people are corrupting the churches and that they are in league with Satan and the demonic world. We learned that such accusations were quite common in the world of early Christianity, indeed throughout the Mediterranean world. To understand them correctly, however, we had to learn to perceive Paul's world more accurately, for contemporary biblical criticism simply is not capable of understanding these verses. We needed to hear Paul *in other words*. For this reason we employed the aid of a complex anthropological model about the nature and workings of social groups who typically use such accusations. We have added, then, a valuable reading tool to our toolbox; we can understand things that previously were impervious to us.

The anthropological model was not entirely new to us. It has two parts: one familiar to readers of this book (i.e., general symbolic universe) and a second part new to us (i.e., specific characteristics of witchcraft societies). Earlier in this book, we examined the general cosmos of Paul in terms of the component perspectives that make up a symbolic universe. We were able to take that general material and examine in detail two specific documents of Paul, Galatians and 2 Corinthians 10–13. In this we came to see the applicability and utility of using that model. It genuinely equipped us to begin seeing the world as Paul saw it, albeit in other words. Whereas traditional New Testament criticism focuses on the theological controversies between Paul and his opponents, we looked further and deeper to perceive the world as Paul did. Therefore, we were able to see why and how he acted the way he did. In the process, we gained a strong, coherent sense of how his world worked. Furthermore, with the practice gained in using this model, we have acquired skill in using it to read other New Testament documents with more accuracy and sympathy.

That basic model was expanded with specific considerations about witchcraft societies. We learned the specific characteristics of such groups, as well as a generic definition of "witch" applicable to many other situations. And we discovered the function of such accusations. This part of the model forced us to focus on new aspects of the Pauline letters, namely, the issues of authority and status, of weak community structures, and of rivalry and competition. These are not the typical topics discussed in Paul's letters, because over the years we have been socialized to ask theological questions of Paul, not social questions. And the agenda for reading Paul has been largely shaped by reformation polemics. But we are learning to ask new questions of the documents we study, questions that require us to learn new ways of perceiving and understanding.

Indeed, the materials in this chapter might leave a reader with a feeling of embarrassment, if not revulsion. Our Western world has scant place for demons and cosmic wars, and it is uncomfortable with any talk about Satan. Moreover, it is hardly inspirational to look into the foundational documents of Christian faith and find "witchcraft accusations." It may not disquiet us much when we read that Pharisees call Jesus a witch, but we would rather not notice that Jesus or Paul or John accuse others of witchcraft, even other community members. Furthermore, in studying this material, Paul begins to look less like *Saint* Paul because of his use of these social weapons. Yet an honest reader must strive to pay attention to what writers say, and understand them as sympathetically as possible. If Paul indeed speaks the language of witchcraft accusations, it would be naive to ignore this. Our error would be compounded if we tried to bowdlerize the text for the sake of piety. Ignoring unpleasantness does not make it go away. Understanding is needed.

What we have learned, then, is a way of perceiving the world and a social strategy quite different from those to which we

are socialized. This should not surprise us, given the distance
in time, place, and social location between modern, Western,
postindustrial people, and ancient, Mediterranean, peasant societies. We need special tools to allow us to hear Paul on
his own terms, for he speaks in words other than those familiar
to us.

The net benefit of this chapter, then, lies in the perceptions
learned and the skills mastered. Not only have we read two
documents in greater depth and breadth, but we have ready
scenarios that can aid us in understanding other places in the
New Testament where accusations of Satanic or demonic possession occur.

As a result of our reading, we can define the shape of Paul's
world more clearly. In terms of his symbolic universe, Paul
perceives a world divided into warring cosmic forces. Suffering
and misfortune unjustly come upon us as a result of the attacks
of Evil against Good. This world is profoundly ambiguous; disguise and deception are everywhere. Hostility is presumed until otherwise proven. Mirroring this heavenly macrocosm is the
earthly microcosm, which Paul perceives as a highly conflic-
tual, competitive society. This should not surprise us, for our
Gospels record endless confrontations between Jesus and Pharisees, scribes, lawyers, Sadducees, and others. Paul too belonged to that world of endless challenge and riposte.

The test of any model lies in its ability to account plausibly
for the most data and to suggest fresh insights and new lines of
inquiry. In this regard, Douglas's models for understanding
witchcraft accusations seem particularly successful. Not only
do they give us a valid procedure for understanding the accusations of demon possession in Paul's writings and other writings
in the New Testament; they suggest a fresh way of investigating
Paul's basic cultural viewpoint and social dynamic.

Whereas typical scholarly readings of Galatians and 2 Corinthians tend to focus on the theological issues argued, the nitty-
gritty social world of Paul rarely gets addressed. The current
use of anthropological models fills that void and offers important insights into the social problems and dynamics of Paul
and the early church. The issue is not the reduction of the New
Testament from theology to sociology, but a fuller reading of
the theology embedded in a lively social context. One might
say that by reading Paul this way, we pay closer attention to the
way grace is incarnated in genuinely human beings. Indeed, it
has been worth our while to listen to Paul, in other words.

# Conclusion

1.0 How Paul Perceived the Cosmos
2.0 Consonance
3.0 Unfinished Agenda
4.0 Anthropology and History
5.0 On Using This Book

## 1.0 How Paul Perceived the Cosmos

This book has aimed at describing the shape of the cosmos as Paul perceived it. Because the focus is that of cultural anthropology, we learned to speak about Paul *in other words*. We are in a position now to summarize the main aspects of his perception of the cosmos, both his socialization as a Pharisee and his shared worldview with first-century, eastern Mediterranean non-elites.

Paul views the world as a highly organized cosmos, where every person, thing, place, and time has its proper place. He classifies all persons and things in terms of "in" or "out" and "pure" or "unclean." His strong sense of classification leads him to make lists of persons and things, always with a sense of some order or ranking. He is no stranger to social hierarchy. Paul, moreover, expresses this acute sense of proper order in the customary terminology of "purity" and its contravention as "pollution." He is ever seeking to classify all the objects in his world as accurately as possible.

He is best identified as a type of reformer, for he maintains his loyalty to the essentials of Jewish faith: belief in the one, true God and acceptance of God's Sacred Writings. Yet he is no longer Paul the Pharisee; nor does he worship any more in synagogue or temple. Hence, although his instincts to classify all persons and things remain, as a follower of Jesus he develops new systems of classification, different boundary lines and structures to express the order of the cosmos-in-Christ.

Paul's attention is focused on the boundaries of his social group and on the lines that define and classify. He is highly sensitive to persons or things that cross the boundary lines. For those who cross legitimately, there are formal rites of passage and clear behavioral expectations of the new status. Yet he often perceives others as illegitimately trespassing. Whether they be Superapostles or "another gospel," he labels them "unclean" and sounds the alarm at their intrusion into his holy church.

Paul views the physical human body the same way he views the social body. It is an orderly organism that is subject to the same control and discipline that governs the social body. He pays acute attention to its orifices (sexual, oral, aural), as boundaries that must be guarded against unwarranted and illegitimate trespass.

He views sin and deviance as the violation of community rules, but more frequently as a pollution, even a pinch of which will corrupt the whole organism. This helps to explain his intolerance of certain evils in the community and his need to instigate procedures of excommunication. If sin is truly perceived as leaven or gangrene, failure to act means total corruption and death.

Paul perceives the cosmos and everything in it in dualistic terms. Moreover, he understands it as a battleground where God and God's allies wage mortal combat with Satan and his minions. To judge from his many references to Satan and cosmic hostile powers, Paul's world was peopled with personified forces such as Sin and Death.

Consonant with his perception of dualistic, personified powers at war in the world, Paul interprets the suffering and misfortune that befall him and others as unjustly deserved. But in a world where Evil attacks all that is good and godly, such is the inevitable fate of God's followers.

These are generalized summary statements of Paul's perceptions. I would argue that they are shared by Jews and Greeks alike in Paul's world, although different nations and places would incarnate them in terms specific to their geography, ancestral traditions, mythic histories, and the like. In the course of the book, we labored to show the specific Jewish and Pharisaic character they took in light of Paul's socialization as a

Pharisee's Pharisee. After all, he was socialized into Jewish cultural and religious patterns, especially those of a person zealous for the Law.

Admittedly, the questions asked here are not typical of current Pauline scholarship. Although we may study the Greek or Jewish background of Paul, scholars have been more interested in describing Paul's "theology" than his worldview. Hence, Paul may sound a bit strange when described *in other words*. Yet this study of his symbolic universe should contribute significantly to any sketch of his "dogmatic universe."

## 2.0 Consonance

This way of reading Paul's letters indicates a strong sense of coherence in his symbolic perceptions. As a person who classifies every person and thing, Paul necessarily drew lines to define and identify. He was a superb maker and maintainer of boundary lines, both around and within the church. His perceptions were cast in the language of "pure" and "polluted" or "clean" and "unclean." Thus, he viewed the cosmos in dualistic terms. Dualistic classification systems, moreover, make for intolerance. For, if some person or thing is labeled evil and perceived as corrupting, that person or thing is seen as life threatening. Furthermore, the world is perceived as filled with warring Powers and Persons; mortals in the earthly microcosm experience their full share of the battle raging in the macrocosm.

There is strong coherence, then, in Paul's perceptions. He pursues order and values exact classification. Yet this leads to an acute sense of pervasive dualism. His own experience of hostility and conflict confirms the cultural view of the cosmos as a battlefield. Paul worries about the attacks of Satan or Evil upon Christ's church; he sees these persistent assaults as a corruption threatening to destroy all that is good and godly. Whatever else we might say of this worldview, it enjoys considerable internal consonance. The various perceptions reinforce each other.

Is it any wonder, then, that Paul engages in "witchcraft accusations"? The two chapters in which we examined his accusations of bewitchment in Galatia and seduction in Corinth indicate how perceptions lead to action. For if Paul truly perceives the new gospel in Galatia as a harm worked by Satan's disguised agents, he would be crazy not to call for its expulsion. If he genuinely understood the Superapostles at Corinth as disguised angels of light, his clamorous behavior is plausible.

These two chapters in particular illustrate the consonance of Paul's perceptions.

## 3.0 Unfinished Agenda

Much remains to be done if we would truly understand Paul in terms of his specific Mediterranean, first-century, non-elite culture. We would want to know more about the kinship patterns that make up the basic social institution in Paul's world, the family (Todd 1985). In line with this, we could legitimately inquire about the economics of such kinship groups, their forms of reciprocity, and their basic patron-client relations (Elliott 1987; Malina 1988). We would want to know more about the anthropology of a preindustrial city (Sjoberg 1960) and the social relations that took place in such an environment. This would have a considerable impact on Paul's communities, which are comprised of elites and non-elites, aristocrats and workers.

Apart from investigation of these basic institutions and structures in Paul's social world, we should inquire further into the way first-century persons are perceived. How difficult it is for modern Westerners, who are characterized by *Habits of the Heart* and individualism, to perceive, much less appreciate, people who are anti-individualistic! Whereas we eschew social pressures for conformity, such was the dominant force that shaped Paul's personality and others in his world (Malina 1989:127–141).

Unlike our world, ancient Mediterranean culture was strongly structured around the pivotal values of honor and shame. Their world was divided into male and female spheres, with specific places, objects, and actions appropriate to males and corresponding ones for females. This must be taken into account if Paul's remarks about women are to be understood in terms of his culture. Honor and shame, moreover, explain the highly agonistic nature of Paul's culture. Honor, name, and reputation were the primary values of an individual, but ones that could be lost when challenged. Even a cursory reading of Paul indicates that in every letter he was either challenging others or being challenged himself. His honor formed a crucial issue in all of his dealings with his churches.

Examining the symbolic universe of Paul is but the opening gambit in attempting to understand the apostle in terms of his true and complete *Sitz im Leben*, but it is a welcome and fruitful beginning.

## 4.0 Anthropology and History

Readers trained in traditional exegetical methods will surely note that this small volume has not done what is currently recognized as historical studies. It presumes the standard discussion of the historical setting of each letter, which can be conveniently found in introductions to the New Testament. There is no need to repeat that material here. Nor has it set out in detail the specific influences of Hellenistic culture upon Paul. That too is presumed.

This book has stressed the Jewish background of Paul, in particular his socialization as a Pharisee's Pharisee. Yet the interest in this was not strictly historical, but cultural. How orderly did Pharisees perceive the universe? How did they classify persons, places, times, and objects? How did they label things "pure" or "polluted"? In short, the symbolic universe of Pharisaic Judaism was more accurately our historical interest because, as I have argued, in his most basic understanding of the cosmos Paul never ceased viewing the world as a Pharisee, even though he was a follower of Jesus.

History and historical background should not be ignored. Nor does this book treat them lightly, because many of the judgments and perceptions here are informed by such studies. Nevertheless, this book is about Paul's symbolic universe; it employs concepts and models from cultural anthropology.

## 5.0 On Using This Book

All Pauline scholars either knowingly or unknowingly favor certain letters as most representative of Paul's perspective. Traditionally, reformation scholarship has promoted Galatians and Romans as the true Paul, the "canon within the canon." In this book we have favored the Corinthian correspondence as well as Galatians. But this emphasis arose from the utilitarian desire to find the clearest and most typical examples of his perceptions. First Corinthians best illustrates the basic cultural impulse in Paul to perceive all reality as part of an orderly cosmos. Moreover, it embodies Paul's clearest and most systematic treatment of the physical human body. Yet the patterns noted there are not exclusive to that letter. Similar perceptions of the body can be studied in Romans 12–15; comparable tendencies to order and classify can be found in 1 Thessalonians.

This book might well be used as a model for reading each of Paul's letters in cultural perspective. Each of the six aspects (purity, rites, body, sin, cosmology, and suffering) can profitably be employed as lenses for interpreting a specific document. They may not be evident in each letter as clearly as they appeared in the illustrations presented here, but that in itself may be a clue to the specific or "occasional" character of the document. A more thematic perspective might be developed from this book. One might survey all the letters to see how each of the six anthropological perspectives informs each of them.

Traditional readers of Paul have sought in his letters spiritual nourishment, theological grounding, and pastoral guidance. In a true sense, this book is about Paul's "thought" and his "theology." Only, using anthropological categories, we have covered much of that ground *in other words*. A reader might well take the theme of "God," "Christ," "church," and so forth, from the topical index and pull together the various perceptions from the six perspectives developed here.

Indubitably, contemporary readers of Paul will find that these anthropological perspectives can tend to make him sound less modern, less relevant, and even problematic for social and political life in the 1990s. If cultural perceptions in Paul's letters disturb modern readers, we should not dismiss them for this reason. Are they an accurate reading of Paul? Of his culture? This project is not advocating the Pauline cultural perspectives, nor claiming that they have the weight of inerrancy in forming our modern consciences. In fact, the success of this book lies in aiding readers to discover just how differently Paul viewed the cosmos from the way we do. This book surely invites a modern reader to a greater sense of ecumenism, that is, the appreciation of other Christians in their distinctive otherness. Cultural uniformity is neither possible nor desirable.

# Abbreviations

| | |
|---|---|
| *ANRW* | *Aufstieg und Niedergang der römischen Welt* |
| AOAT | Alter Orient und Altes Testament |
| *ATR* | *Anglican Theological Review* |
| *AusBR* | *Australian Biblical Review* |
| *AUSS* | *Andrews University Seminary Studies* |
| *BA* | *Biblical Archeologist* |
| *Bib* | *Biblica* |
| *BJRL* | *Bulletin of the John Rylands Library* |
| *BTB* | *Biblical Theology Bulletin* |
| *BZ* | *Biblische Zeitschrift* |
| *CBQ* | *Catholic Biblical Quarterly* |
| *ETL* | *Ephemerides theologicae lovanienses* |
| HNTC | Harper's New Testament Commentaries |
| *HR* | *History of Religions* |
| *HTR* | *Harvard Theological Review* |
| *IEJ* | *Israel Exploration Journal* |
| *Int* | *Interpretation* |
| *JAAR* | *Journal of the American Academy of Religion* |
| *JBL* | *Journal of Biblical Literature* |
| *JES* | *Journal of Ecumenical Studies* |
| *JJS* | *Journal of Jewish Studies* |
| *JQR* | *Jewish Quarterly Review* |
| *JR* | *Journal of Religion* |
| *JRelS* | *Journal of Religious Studies* |
| *JRH* | *Journal of Religious History* |
| *JRS* | *Journal of Roman Studies* |
| *JSNT* | *Journal for the Study of the New Testament* |
| *JTS* | *Journal of Theological Studies* |

| | |
|---|---|
| *Neot* | *Neotestamentica* |
| *NovT* | *Novum Testamentum* |
| *NRT* | *La nouvelle revue théologique* |
| *NTS* | *New Testament Studies* |
| *RAC* | *Reallexikon für Antike und Christentum* |
| *RB* | *Revue biblique* |
| *RelSRev* | *Religious Studies Review* |
| *ResQ* | *Restoration Quarterly* |
| *RevQ* | *Revue de Qumran* |
| *RSR* | *Recherches de science religieuse* |
| SBLASP | Society of Biblical Literature Abstracts and Seminaı Papers |
| SBLDS | Society of Biblical Literature Dissertation Series |
| SBLSBS | Society of Biblical Literature Sources for Biblical Study |
| *SCent* | *Second Century* |
| *SEA* | *Svensk exegetisk årsbok* |
| *SJTh* | *Scottish Journal of Theology* |
| SNTSMS | Society for New Testament Studies Monograph Series |
| *ST* | *Studia Theologica* |
| SBT | Studies in Biblical Theology |
| *StudR/SciRel* | *Studies in Religion/Sciences Religieuses* |
| *TDNT* | *Theological Dictionary of the New Testament* |
| *TynBul* | *Tyndale Bulletin* |
| *VC* | *Vigiliae Christianae* |
| *VT* | *Vetus Testamentum* |
| WUNT | Wissenschaftliche Untersuchungen zum Neuen Testament |
| *ZNW* | *Zeitschrift für die neutestamentliche Wissenschaft* |

# Bibliography

Aalders, G. J. D. 1979. "The Hellenistic Concept of the Enviousness of Fate." In *Studies in Hellenistic Religions,* edited by M. J. Vermaseren, 1–8. Leiden: E. J. Brill.

Abu-Hilal, Ahmad. 1982. "Arab and North-American Social Attitudes: Some Cross-Cultural Comparisons." *Mankind* 22:193–207.

Baasland, Ernst. 1984. "Persecution: A Neglected Factor in the Letter to the Galatians." *ST* 38:135–150.

Bailey, Kenneth E. 1983a. *Poet and Peasant.* Grand Rapids: Wm. B. Eerdmans Publishing Co.

———. 1983b. *Through Peasant Eyes: A Literary Cultural Approach to the Parables of Luke.* Grand Rapids: Wm. B. Eerdmans Publishing Co.

Balch, David L. 1983. "1 Cor. 7:32–35 and Stoic Debates About Marriage, Anxiety, and Distraction." *JBL* 102:429–439.

———. 1988. "Household Codes." In *Graeco-Roman Literature and the New Testament: Selected Forms and Genres,* edited by David Aune, 24–50. SBLSBS 21. Atlanta: Scholars Press.

Barkan, Leonard. 1975. *Nature's Work of Art: The Human Body as Image of the World.* New Haven: Yale University Press.

Barré, Michael. 1975. "Paul as an 'Eschatological Person': A New Look at 2 Cor. 11:29." *CBQ* 37:500–526.

———. 1980. "Qumran and the 'Weakness' of Paul." *CBQ* 42:216–227.

———. 1981. " 'Fear of God' and the World of Wisdom." *BTB* 11:41–43.

Barrett, C. K. 1962. *From First Adam to Last: A Study in Pauline Theology.* New York: Charles Scribner's Sons.

——. 1968. *A Commentary on the First Epistle to the Corinthians*. HNTC. New York: Harper & Row.

——. 1973. *A Commentary on the Second Epistle to the Corinthians*. HNTC. New York: Harper & Row.

——. 1982. "The Allegory of Abraham, Sarah, and Hagar in the Argument of Galatians." In *Essays on Paul*, by C. K. Barrett, 154–170. Philadelphia: Westminster Press.

Barton, Stephen. 1982. "Paul and the Cross: A Sociological Approach." *Theology* 85:16–19.

——. 1984. "Paul and the Resurrection: A Sociological Approach." *Religion* 14:67–75.

——. 1986. "Paul's Sense of Place: An Anthropological Approach to Community Formation in Corinth." *NTS* 32:225–246.

Bassler, Jouette M. 1982. *Divine Impartiality: Paul and a Theological Axiom*. Chico, Calif.: Scholars Press.

——. 1984. "Divine Impartiality in Paul's Letter to the Romans." *NovT* 26:43–58.

Baumgarten, J. M. 1980. "The Pharisaic-Sadducean Controversies About Purity and the Qumran Texts." *JJS* 31:157–170.

Behm, Johannes. 1964. *"Anathema." TDNT* 1:354–356.

Beker, Johan C. 1980. *Paul the Apostle: The Triumph of God in Life and Thought*. Philadelphia: Fortress Press.

Benthall, Jonathan, and Ted Polhemus, eds. 1975. *The Body as Medium of Expression*. New York: E. P. Dutton & Co.

Berger, Peter, and Thomas Luckmann. 1966. *The Social Construction of Reality: A Treatise in the Sociology of Knowledge*. Garden City, N.Y.: Doubleday & Co.

Best, Ernest. 1955. *One Body in Christ: A Study in the Relationship of the Church to Christ in the Epistles of the Apostle Paul*. London: SPCK.

Betz, Hans Dieter. 1970. "The Delphic Maxim '*GNŌTHI SAUTON*' in Hermetic Interpretation." *HTR* 63:465–484.

——. 1973. "2 Cor. 6:14–7:1: An Anti-Pauline Fragment?" *JBL* 92:88–108.

——. 1979. *Galatians: A Commentary on Paul's Letter to the Churches in Galatia*. Philadelphia: Fortress Press.

Blacking, John, ed. 1977. *The Anthropology of the Body*. Association of Social Anthropologists Monograph 15. New York: Academic Press.

Blasi, A. J. 1986. "Role Structures in the Early Hellenistic Church." *Sociological Analysis* 47:226–248.

Boissevain, J. 1974. *Friends of Friends: Networks, Manipulators, and Coalitions*. New York: St. Martin's Press.

Booth, Roger P. 1986. *Jesus and the Laws of Purity: Tradition History and Legal History in Mark 7*. Sheffield: JSOT Press.

Borg, Marcus J. 1984. *Conflict, Holiness, and Politics in the Teaching of Jesus*. Lewiston, N.Y.: Edwin Mellen Press.

Borgen, Peder. 1968. "Agency in the Fourth Gospel." In *Religions in Antiquity*, edited by Jacob Neusner, 137–148. Leiden: E. J. Brill.

Bossman, David. 1979. "Ezra's Marriage Reform: Israel Redefined." *BTB* 9:32–38.

———. 1988. "Images of God in the Letters of Paul." *BTB* 18:67–76.

Bradley, David G. 1953. "The *Topos* as a Form in the Pauline Paraenesis." *JBL* 72:238–246.

Brilliant, Richard. 1963. *Gesture and Rank in Roman Art: The Use of Gestures to Denote Status in Roman Sculpture and Coinage*. Memoirs of the Connecticut Academy of Arts and Sciences, 14. New Haven, Conn.

Broshi, Magen. 1986. "The Diet of Palestine in the Roman Period: Introductory Notes." *The Israel Museum Journal* 5:41–56.

Brown, John Pairman. 1976. "Techniques of Imperial Control: Background of Gospel Events." In *The Bible and Liberation: Political and Social Hermeneutics. A Radical Religion Reader*, edited by Norman Gottwald and Antoinette Wire, 73–83. Berkeley, Calif.: Community for Religious Research and Communication.

Brown, Peter. 1970. "Sorcery, Demons, and the Rise of Christianity from Late Antiquity Into the Middle Ages." In *Witchcraft Confessions and Accusations*, edited by Mary T. Douglas, 17–45. New York: Tavistock Publications.

———. 1971. "The Rise and Function of the Holy Man in Late Antiquity." *JRS* 61:80–101. Reprinted in *Society and the Holy in Late Antiquity*, 103–152. London: Faber & Faber, 1982.

———. 1988. *The Body and Society: Men, Women, and Sexual Renunciation in Early Christianity*. New York: Columbia University Press.

Bruce, F. F. 1980. *1 and 2 Corinthians*. Grand Rapids: Wm. B. Eerdmans Publishing Co.

Buchanan, George W. 1963. "The Role of Purity in the Structure of the Essene Sect." *ResQ* 4:397–406.

Burke, Peter. 1980. *Sociology and History*. London: George Allen & Unwin.

Callan, T. 1985. "Prophecy and Ecstasy in Greco-Roman Religion and in 1 Corinthians." *NovT* 27:125–140.

———. 1986. "Competition and Boasting: Toward a Psychological Portrait of Paul." *JRelS* 13:27–51.

Carney, Thomas F. 1975. *The Shape of the Past: Models and Antiquity*. Lawrence, Kans.: Coronado Press.

Carson, D. 1986. "Pauline Inconsistency: Reflections on 1 Corinthians 9:19–23 and Galatians 2:11–14." *Churchman* 100:6–45.

Cerfaux, Lucien. 1951. "L'antinomie paulinienne de la vie apostolique." *RSR* 39:221–235.

Chadwick, Henry. 1955. " 'All Things to All Men' (1 Cor. IX.22)." *NTS* 1:261–275.

———. 1962. "Enkrateia." *RAC* 5:343–365.

Charlesworth, James H., ed. 1972. "A Critical Comparison of the Dualism in 1QS 3:13–4:26 and the 'Dualism' Contained in the Gospel of John." In *John and Qumran*, 77–89. London: Geoffrey Chapman.

Church, F. Forrester. 1978. "Rhetorical Structure and Design in Paul's Letter to Philemon." *HTR* 71:17–33.

Clements, R. E. 1967. *Abraham and David: Genesis XV and Its Meaning for Israelite Tradition*. Naperville, Ill.: Alec R. Allenson.

Cohn, Robert L. 1980. *The Shape of Sacred Space: Four Biblical Studies*. Chico, Calif.: Scholars Press.

Collins, John J. 1975. "The Mythology of Holy War in Daniel and the Qumran War Scroll." *VT* 25:596–612.

Collins, John N. 1984. "Diakonia as an Authoritative Capacity in Sacred Affairs and as the Model of Ministry." *Compass Theology Review* 18:29–34.

Conzelmann, Hans. 1975. *1 Corinthians: A Commentary on the First Epistle to the Corinthians*. Philadelphia: Fortress Press.

Cook, Michael J. 1978. "Jesus and the Pharisees: The Problem as It Stands Today." *JES* 15:441–460.

Corrigan, G. M. 1986. "Paul's Shame for the Gospel." *BTB* 16:23–27.

Dahl, Nils A. 1964. "Der Erstgeborene Satans und der Vater des Teufels (Polyk 7:1 und John 8:44)." In *Apophoreta*, edited by Walter Eltester, 70–84. Berlin: Alfred Töpelmann.

———. 1976. *Jesus in the Memory of the Early Church: Essays*. Minneapolis: Augsburg Publishing House.

———. 1977. *Studies in Paul: Theology for the Early Christian Mission*. Minneapolis: Augsburg Publishing House.

Danker, Frederick W. 1982. *Benefactor: Epigraphic Study of a Graeco-Roman and New Testament Semantic Field*. St. Louis: Clayton Publishing House.

Daube, David. 1982. "Shame Culture in Luke." In *Paul and Paulinism: Essays in Honour of C. K. Barrett*, edited by M. D. Hooker and S. G. Wilson, 355–372. London: SPCK.

Davies, W. D. 1948. *Paul and Rabbinic Judaism*. London: SPCK.

———. 1957. "Paul and the Dead Sea Scrolls: Flesh and Spirit." In

*The Scrolls and the New Testament*, edited by Krister Stendahl, 169–172. New York: Harper & Brothers.

Davis, John. 1987. "Family and State in the Mediterranean." In *Honor and Shame and the Unity of the Mediterranean*, edited by David D. Gilmore, 22–34. American Anthropological Association Special Publication 22. Washington, D.C.: American Anthropological Association.

de Boer, Martinus. 1980. "Images of Paul in the Post-Apostolic Period." *CBQ* 42:359–380.

————. 1988. *The Defeat of Death: Apocalyptic Eschatology in 1 Corinthians 15 and Romans 5*. JSNT Supp. Series, 22. Sheffield: JSOT Press.

De Geradon, Bernard. 1958. "L'homme à l'image de Dieu." *NRT* 80:683–695.

Delaney, Carol. 1986. "The Meaning of Paternity and the Virgin Birth Debate." *Man* 21:494–513.

————. 1987. "Seeds of Honor, Fields of Shame." In *Honor and Shame and the Unity of the Mediterranean*, edited by David D. Gilmore, 35–48. American Anthropological Association Special Publication 22. Washington, D.C.: American Anthropological Association.

Derrett, J. D. M. 1973. *Jesus' Audience: The Social and Psychological Environment in Which He Worked*. New York: Seabury Press.

————. 1977. "Religious Hair." In *Studies in the New Testament*, vol. 1, 170–175. Leiden: E. J. Brill.

Dewey, A. J. 1985. "A Matter of Honor: A Social-Historical Analysis of 2 Corinthians 10." *HTR* 78:209–217.

Doeve, J. W. 1963. "Paulus der Pharisäer und Galater 1.13–15." *NovT* 6:170–181.

Donaldson, Terence L. 1989. "Zealot and Convert: The Origin of Paul's Christ-Torah Antithesis." *CBQ* 51:655–682.

Douglas, Mary. 1963. "Techniques of Sorcery Control." In *Witchcraft and Sorcery in East Africa*, edited by J. F. M. Middleton and E. H. Winter, 123–141. London: Routledge & Kegan Paul.

————. 1966. *Purity and Danger*. London: Routledge & Kegan Paul.

————. 1967. "Witch Beliefs in Central Africa." *Africa* 37:72–80.

————. 1968. "Pollution." In *International Encyclopedia of the Social Sciences*, edited by David Sills, vol. 12, 336–342. New York: Macmillan Co. and Free Press.

————. 1969. "Social Preconditions of Enthusiasm and Heterodoxy." In *Forms of Symbolic Action*, edited by Robert F. Spenser, 69–80. Proceedings of the 1969 Annual Spring Meeting of the American Ethnological Society. Seattle: University of Washington Press.

————. 1970. "Thirty Years After *Witchcraft, Oracles and Magic*." In

*Witchcraft Confessions and Accusations*, edited by Mary Douglas, xiii–xxxviii. New York: Tavistock Publications.

———. 1975. "Deciphering a Meal." In *Implicit Meanings*, 249–275. London: Routledge & Kegan Paul.

———. 1982a. *Natural Symbols: Explorations in Cosmology*. New York: Pantheon Books.

———. 1982b. "Food as a System of Communication." In *In the Active Voice*, 82–124. London: Routledge & Kegan Paul.

Douglas, Mary, and Baron Isherwood. 1979. *The World of Goods*. New York: Basic Books.

Douglas, Mary, and Aaron Wildavsky. 1983. *Risk and Culture: An Essay on the Selection of Technical and Environmental Dangers*. Berkeley, Calif.: University of California Press.

Driver, Godfrey R. 1957. "Problems of Interpretation in the Heptateuch." In *Mélanges bibliques redigés en l'honneur de André Robert*, 66–76. Paris: Institute Catholique.

Dunn, James D. G. 1982. "The Relationship Between Paul and Jerusalem According to Galatians 1 and 2." *NTS* 28:461–478.

———. 1983. "The Incident at Antioch (Gal. 2:11–18)." *JSNT* 18:3–57.

———. 1985. "Works of the Law and the Curse of the Law (Gal. 3.10–14)." *NTS* 31:523–542.

Dupont-Sommer, A. 1973. *The Essene Writings from Qumran*. Translated by Geza Vermes. Gloucester, Mass.: Peter Smith.

Dyson, Stephen L. 1985. *The Creation of the Roman Frontier*. Princeton, N.J.: Princeton University Press.

Eilberg-Schwartz, Howard. 1987. "Creation and Classification in Judaism: From Priestly to Rabbinic Concepts." *HR* 26:357–381.

Eisenstadt, S. N., and L. Roniger. 1980. "Patron-Client Relations as a Model of Structuring Social Exchange." *Comparative Studies in Society and History* 22:42–77.

———. 1984. *Patrons, Clients, and Friends: Interpersonal Relations and the Structure of Trust in Society*. Cambridge: Cambridge University Press.

Elliot, John H. 1981. *A Home for the Homeless: A Sociological Exegesis of 1 Peter, Its Situation and Strategy*. Philadelphia: Fortress Press.

———. 1986. *Social-Scientific Criticism of the New Testament and Its Social World*. Semeia 35.

———. 1987. "Patronage and Clientism in Early Christian Society." *Forum* 3/4:39–48.

———. 1988. "The Fear of the Leer: The Evil Eye from the Bible to Li'l Abner." *Forum* 4/4:42–71.

Ellis, E. Earle. 1961. *Paul and His Recent Interpreters.* Grand Rapids: Wm. B. Eerdmans Publishing Co.

Erickson, Kai T. 1966. *Wayward Puritans.* New York: John Wiley & Sons.

Esler, Philip F. 1987. *Community and Gospel in Luke-Acts: The Social and Political Motivations of Lucan Theology.* Cambridge: Cambridge University Press.

Evans-Pritchard, E. E. 1937. *Witchcraft, Oracles, and Magic Among the Azande.* Oxford: Clarendon Press.

Farwell, Lyndon James. 1976. "Betwixt and Between: The Anthropological Contributions of Mary Douglas and Victor Turner Toward a Renewal of Roman Catholic Ritual." Dissertation, Claremont University.

Fennelly, James M. 1983. "The Jerusalem Community and Kashrut Shatnes." SBLASP, 273–288.

Fensham, F. C. 1967. "The Good and Evil Eye in the Sermon on the Mount." *Neot* 1:51–58.

Ferguson, Everett. 1984. *Demonology of the Early Christian World.* Lewiston, N.Y.: Edwin Mellen Press.

Festugiere, André-Jean. 1954. *Personal Religion Among the Greeks.* Berkeley, Calif.: University of California Press.

Finley, M. I. 1962. *The World of Odysseus.* London: Penguin Books.

Firth, Raymond W. 1973. *Symbols: Public and Private.* Ithaca, N.Y.: Cornell University Press.

Fisher, Seymour, and Sidney Cleveland. 1958. *Body Image and Personality.* Princeton, N.J.: Princeton University Press.

Fitzgerald, John T. 1988. *Cracks in an Earthen Vessel: An Examination of the Catalogues of Hardships in the Corinthian Correspondence.* SBLDS 99. Atlanta: Scholars Press.

Fitzmyer, Joseph A. 1957. "A Feature of Qumran Angelology and the Angels of 1 Cor. XI.10." *NTS* 4:48–58. Reprinted in *Paul and Qumran,* edited by Jerome Murphy-O'Connor, 31–47. London: Geoffrey Chapman.

———. 1961. "Qumran and the Interpolated Paragraph in 2 Cor. 6:14–7:1." *CBQ* 23:271–280.

———. 1989. *Paul and His Theology: A Brief Sketch.* 2nd edition. Englewood Cliffs, N.J.: Prentice-Hall.

Forbes, Christopher. 1986a. "Comparison, Self-Praise, and Irony: Paul's Boasting and the Conventions of Hellenistic Rhetoric." *NTS* 32:1–30.

———. 1986b. "Early Christian Inspired Speech and Hellenistic Popular Religion." *NovT* 28:257–270.

Ford, Josephine M. 1974. "You are God's 'Sukkah' (1 Cor. 3:10–17)." *NTS* 21:139–142.

Forkman, Göran. 1972. *The Limits of Religious Community: Expulsion from the Religious Community Within the Qumran Sect, Within Rabbinic Judaism, and Within Primitive Christianity.* Lund: G. W. K. Gleerup.

Foster, George. 1965. "Peasant Society and the Image of Limited Good." *American Anthropologist* 67:293–315.

———. 1967. "The Image of Limited Good." In *Peasant Society: A Reader*, edited by J. Potter, M. Diaz, and G. Foster, 300–323. Boston: Little, Brown & Co.

Furnish, Victor P. 1984. *II Corinthians.* Anchor Bible, vol. 32A. Garden City, N.Y.: Doubleday & Co.

Gager, John G. 1970. "Functional Diversity in Paul's Use of End Time Language." *JBL* 89:325–337.

———. 1981. "Some Notes on Paul's Conversion." *NTS* 27:697–704.

———. 1982a. "Shall We Marry Our Enemies? Sociology and the New Testament." *Int* 36:256–265.

———. 1982b. "Body-Symbols and Social Reality: Resurrection, Incarnation, and Asceticism in Early Christianity." *Religion* 12:345–364.

Gärtner, Bertil. 1965. *The Temple and the Community in Qumran and the New Testament.* Cambridge: Cambridge University Press.

Gaston, Lloyd. 1984. "Paul and Jerusalem." In *From Paul to Jesus*, edited by Peter Richardson and John Hurd, 61–72. Waterloo, Ont.: Wilfrid Laurier University Press.

Gaventa, B. R. 1980. "Comparing Paul and Judaism: Rethinking Our Methods." *BTB* 10:37–44.

———. 1986. *From Darkness to Light: Aspects of Conversion in the New Testament.* Philadelphia: Fortress Press.

Geertz, Clifford. 1973. *The Interpretation of Cultures: Selected Essays.* New York: Basic Books.

———. 1976. " 'From the Native's Point of View': On the Nature of Anthropological Understanding." In *Meaning and Anthropology*, edited by Keith H. Basso and Henry A. Selby, 221–237. Albuquerque, N.M.: University of New Mexico Press.

Gellner, E., and J. Waterbury. 1977. *Patrons and Clients in Mediterranean Societies.* London: Gerald Duckworth & Co.

Georgi, Dieter. 1986. *The Opponents of Paul in Second Corinthians: A Study of Religious Propaganda in Late Antiquity.* Philadelphia: Fortress Press.

Ghosh, Amitav. 1983. "The Relations of Envy in an Egyptian Village." *Ethnology* 32:211–223.

Gilmore, David D. 1982. "Anthropology of the Mediterranean Area." *Annual Review of Anthropology* 11:175–205.

———, ed. 1987. *Honor and Shame and the Unity of the Mediterra-*

*nean.* American Anthropological Association Special Publication 22. Washington, D.C.: American Anthropological Association.

Giovannini, Maureen J. 1987. "Female Chastity Codes in the Circum-Mediterranean: Comparative Perspectives." In *Honor and Shame and the Unity of the Mediterranean,* edited by David D. Gilmore, 61–74. American Anthropological Association Special Publication 22. Washington, D.C.: American Anthropological Association.

Gnilka, Joachim. 1968. "2 Cor. 6:14–7:1 in the Light of the Qumran Texts and the Testaments of the Twelve Patriarchs." In *Paul and Qumran,* edited by Jerome Murphy-O'Connor, 46–68. London: Geoffrey Chapman.

Goffman, Erving. 1959. *Presentation of Self in Everyday Life.* Garden City, N.Y.: Doubleday & Co.

Gordon, B. L. 1971. "Sacred Directions, Orientation, and the Top of the Map." *HR* 10:211–227.

Gottwald, Norman K. 1985. *The Hebrew Bible: A Socio-Literary Introduction.* Philadelphia: Fortress Press.

Grant, Robert M. 1947. "The Decalogue in Early Christianity." *HTR* 40:1–17.

———. 1969. "Chain of Being in Early Christianity." In *Myths and Symbols,* edited by Joseph Kitagawa, 279–289. Chicago: University of Chicago Press.

———. 1982. "The Problem of Miraculous Feedings in the Graeco-Roman World." Protocol of the 42nd Colloquy. Berkeley, Calif.: Center for Hermeneutical Studies.

Grollig, F. X., and Harold B. Haley, eds. 1976. *Medical Anthropology.* The Hague: Mouton Publishers.

Grundmann, Walter. 1964. "*Egkrateia.*" *TDNT* 2:339–342.

Gundry, Robert H. 1974. *Soma in Biblical Theology with Emphasis on Pauline Anthropology.* SNTSMS 29. Cambridge: Cambridge University Press.

Hall, Barbara. 1973. "Battle Imagery in Paul's Letters: An Exegetical Study." Dissertation, Union Theological Seminary.

Hall, Edward. 1959. *The Silent Language.* Garden City, N.Y.: Doubleday & Co.

———. 1983. *The Dance of Life: The Other Dimension of Time.* Garden City, N.Y.: Doubleday & Co.

Harrington, Daniel J. 1988. "Second Testament Exegesis and the Social Sciences: A Bibliography." *BTB* 18:77–85.

Harris, Marvin. 1976. "History and Significance of the Emic/Etic Distinction." *Annual Review of Anthropology* 5:329–350.

Hay, David M. 1973. *Glory at the Right Hand: Psalm 110 in Early Christianity.* Nashville: Abingdon Press.

Hays, Richard. 1981. *The Faith of Jesus Christ.* SBLDS 56. Chico, Calif.: Scholars Press.

Helgeland, John. 1980. "Time and Space: Christian and Roman." *ANRW* II.23.2:1285–1305.

Hemer, Colin J. 1986. "Medicine in the New Testament World." In *Medicine and the Bible*, edited by Bernard Palmer, 43–83. Exeter: Paternoster Press.

Hill, David. 1976. "On Suffering and Baptism in 1 Peter." *NovT* 18:181–189.

Hock, Ronald F. 1980. *The Social Context of Paul's Ministry: Tentmaking and Apostleship.* Philadelphia: Fortress Press.

Hoffner, H. A. 1966. "Symbols for Masculinity and Femininity: Their Use in Ancient Near Eastern Sympathetic Magic Rituals." *JBL* 85:326–334.

———. 1973. "Incest, Sodomy, and Bestiality in the Ancient Near East." In *Orient and Occident: Essays Presented to Cyrus H. Gordon*, edited by H. Hoffner, 81–90. AOAT 22. Neukirchen: Butzon & Bercker.

Hollenbach, B. 1979. "Col. ii.23: Which Things Lead to the Fulfillment of the Flesh." *NTS* 25:254–261.

Hollenbach, Paul W. 1982. "Jesus, Demoniacs, and Public Authorities: A Socio-historical Study." *JAAR* 49:567–588.

———. 1987. "Defining Rich and Poor Using the Social Sciences." SBLASP, 50–63.

Holmberg, Bengt. 1980. *Paul and Power: The Structure of Authority in the Primitive Church as Reflected in the Pauline Epistles.* Philadelphia: Fortress Press.

Hooker, Morna D. 1959. "Adam in Romans 1." *NTS* 6:297–306.

Hooker, Morna D., and S. G. Wilson, eds. 1982. *Paul and Paulinism: Essays in Honour of C. K. Barrett.* London: SPCK.

Horsley, Richard A. 1976. "Pneumatikos vs. Psychikos: Distinctions of Spiritual Status Among the Corinthians." *HTR* 69:269–288.

———. 1978a. "Consciousness and Freedom Among the Corinthians: 1 Corinthians 8–10." *CBQ* 40:574–589.

———. 1978b. " 'How Can Some of You Say That There Is No Resurrection of the Dead?' Spiritual Elitism in Corinth." *NovT* 20:203–231.

Horsley, Richard A., and J. S. Hanson. 1985. *Bandits, Prophets, and Messiahs: Popular Movements at the Time of Jesus.* San Francisco: Harper & Row.

House, Colin. 1983. "Defilement by Association: Some Insights from the Usage of *Koinos/Koinoō* in Acts 10 and 11." *AUSS* 21:143–153.

Hunzinger, C. H. 1954. *Die jüdische Bannpraxis im neutestamentlicher Zeitalter.* Göttingen: Vandenhoeck & Ruprecht.

Hurd, John C. 1983. *The Origin of 1 Corinthians.* Macon, Ga.: Mercer University Press.

Hyldahl, N. 1956. "A Reminiscence of the Old Testament at Romans i.23." *NTS* 2:285–288.

Isenberg, Sheldon K. 1975. "Mary Douglas and Hellenistic Religions: The Case of Qumran." SBLASP, 179–185.

Isenberg, Sheldon K., and Dennis E. Owens. 1977. "Bodies Natural and Contrived: The Work of Mary Douglas." *RelSRev* 3:1–16.

Jackson, Ralph. 1988. *Doctors and Diseases in the Roman Empire.* London: British Museum Publications.

Jäger, Bernd. 1985. "Body, House, and City: The Intertwinings of Embodiment, Inhabitation, and Civilization." In *Dwelling, Place, and Environment: Towards a Phenomenology of Person and World,* edited by David Seamon and R. Mugerauer, 215–225. Dordrecht: Martinus Nijhoff.

Jeremias, Joachim. 1955. "Flesh and Blood Cannot Inherit the Kingdom of God (1 Cor. XV.50)." *NTS* 2:151–159.

———. 1969. *Jerusalem in the Time of Jesus.* Philadelphia: Fortress Press.

Jewett, Robert. 1971. *Paul's Anthropological Terms: A Study of Their Use in Conflict Settings.* Leiden: E. J. Brill.

———. 1986. *The Thessalonian Correspondence: Pauline Rhetoric and Millenarian Piety.* Philadelphia: Fortress Press.

Johnson, Luke T. 1977. *The Literary Function of Possessions in Luke-Acts.* SBLDS 39. Missoula, Mont.: Scholars Press.

———. 1982. "Romans 3:21–26 and the Faith of Jesus." *CBQ* 44:77–90.

———. 1983. "James 3:13—4:10 and the *topos PERI PHTHONOU.*" *NovT* 25:327–347.

Judge, E. A. 1968. "Paul's Boasting in Relation to Contemporary Professional Practice." *AusBR* 16:37–50.

———. 1980. "The Social Identity of the First Christians: A Question of Method in Religious History." *JRH* 11:201–217.

———. 1982. *Rank and Status in the World of the Caesars and St. Paul.* Christchurch, New Zealand: University of Canterbury.

———. 1984. "Cultural Conformity and Innovation in Paul: Some Clues from Contemporary Documents." *TynBul* 35:3–24.

Kampen, N. 1981. *Image and Status: Roman Working Women in Ostia.* Berlin: Mann.

Käsemann, Ernst. 1969. *New Testament Questions of Today.* London: SCM Press.

———. 1971. *Perspectives on Paul.* Philadelphia: Fortress Press.

———. 1980. *Commentary on Romans.* Grand Rapids: Wm B. Eerdmans Publishing Co.

Kaufman, Gershen. 1974. "The Meaning of Shame: Toward a Self-Affirming Identity." *Journal of Counseling Psychology* 21:568–574.

———. 1980. *Shame: The Power of Caring.* Cambridge, Mass.: Schenkman Publishing Co.

Kautsky, John. 1982. *The Politics of Aristocratic Empires.* Chapel Hill, N.C.: University of North Carolina Press.

Kee, Doyle. 1980. "Who Were the 'Super-Apostles' of 2 Corinthians?" *ResQ* 23:65–76.

Keightley, G. M. 1987. "The Church's Memory of Jesus: A Social Science Analysis of 1 Thessalonians." *BTB* 17:149–156.

Kennedy, Charles A. 1987. "The Cult of the Dead in Corinth." In *Love and Death in the Ancient Near East,* edited by John Marks and Robert Good, 227–236. Guilford, Conn.: Four Quarters Publishing Co.

Klimkeit, H. J. 1975. "Spatial Orientation in Mythical Thinking as Exemplified in Ancient Egypt: Considerations Toward a Geography of Religions." *HR* 14:269–281.

Koenig, John. 1985. *New Testament Hospitality: Partnership with Strangers as Promise and Mission.* Philadelphia: Fortress Press.

Kraemer, R. S. 1979. "Ecstasy and Possession: The Attraction of Women to the Cult of Dionysius." *HTR* 71:55–80.

Kuhn, Karl Georg. 1957. "New Light on Temptation, Sin, and Flesh in the New Testament." In *The Scrolls and the New Testament,* edited by Krister Stendahl, 94–113. New York: Harper & Brothers.

Kurtz, Ernest. 1981. *Shame and Guilt: Characteristics of the Dependency Cycle: A Historical Perspective for Professionals.* Center City, Minn.: Hazelden Foundation.

Kurzinger, J. 1978. "Frau and Mann nach 1 Kor 11,11f." *BZ* 22:270–275.

Leach, E. R. 1958. "Magical Hair." *Journal of the Royal Anthropological Institute* 88:147–164.

Lenski, Gerhard. 1966. *Power and Privilege: A Theory of Social Stratification.* New York: McGraw-Hill Book Co.

Lenski, Gerhard, and Jean Lenski. 1974. *Human Societies: An Introduction to Macrosociology.* 2nd ed. New York: McGraw-Hill Book Co.

Lincoln, A. T. 1979. " 'Paul the Visionary': The Setting and Significance of the Rapture to Paradise in II Corinthians XII.1–10." *NTS* 25:204–220.

Long, William R. 1983. "The *Paulusbild* in the Trial of Paul in Acts." SBLASP, 87–105.

Lührmann, Dieter. 1989. "Paul and the Pharisaic Tradition." *JSNT* 36:75–94.

Lull, D. J. 1986a. "The Servant-Benefactor as a Model of Greatness (Luke 22:24–30)." *NovT* 28:289–305.

———. 1986b. " 'The Law Was Our Pedagogue': A Study of Galatians 3:19–25." *JBL* 105:481–498.

MacDonald, Dennis R. 1983. *The Legend and the Apostle: The Battle for Paul in Story and Canon.* Philadelphia: Westminster Press.

MacDowell, D. M. 1976. "*Hybris* in Athens." *Greece and Rome* 23:14–31.

MacMullen, Ramsay. 1966. *Enemies of the Roman Order: Treason, Unrest, and Alienation in the Empire.* Cambridge, Mass.: Harvard University Press.

———. 1974. *Roman Social Relations: 50 B.C. to A.D. 284.* New Haven: Yale University Press.

———. 1980. "Women in Public in the Roman Empire." *Historia* 29:208–218.

———. 1983. "Two Types of Conversion to Early Christianity." *VC* 37:174–192.

———. 1985. "Conversion: A Historian's View." *SCent* 5:67–81.

MacRae, Donald G. 1975. "The Body and Social Metaphor." In *The Body as a Medium of Expression*, edited by J. Benthall and T. Polhemus, 55–73. London: Allen Lane.

Mair, Lucy. 1969. *Witchcraft.* New York: McGraw-Hill Book Co.

Malherbe, Abraham. 1968. "The Beasts at Ephesus." *JBL* 87:71–80.

———. 1970. " 'Gentle as a Nurse': The Cynic Background to I Thess ii." *NovT* 12:203–217.

———. 1982. "Self-Definition Among Epicureans and Cynics." In *Self-Definition in the Greco-Roman World*, edited by B. F. Meyer and E. P. Sanders, vol. 3, 46–59. Philadelphia: Fortress Press.

———. 1983a. *Social Aspects of Early Christianity.* 2d ed. Philadelphia: Fortress Press.

———. 1983b. "Antisthenes and Odysseus, and Paul at War." *HTR* 76:143–173.

———. 1986a. "A Physical Description of Paul." *HTR* 79:170–175.

———. 1986b. *Moral Exhortation: A Greco-Roman Sourcebook.* Philadelphia: Westminster Press.

———. 1987. *Paul and the Thessalonians: The Philosophic Tradition of Pastoral Care.* Philadelphia: Fortress Press.

Malina, Bruce J. 1978a. "The Social World Implied in the Letters of the Christian Bishop (Named Ignatius of Antioch)." SBLASP, 71–119.

———. 1978b. "Limited Good and the Social World of Early Christianity." *BTB* 8:162–176.

———. 1978c. "Freedom: A Theological Inquiry Into the Dimensions of a Symbol." *BTB* 8:62–75.

———. 1979. "The Individual and the Community—Personality in the Social World of Early Christianity." *BTB* 9:126–138.

———. 1980. "What Is Prayer?" *The Bible Today* 18:214–222.

———. 1981. *The New Testament World: Insights from Cultural Anthropology*. Atlanta: John Knox Press.

———. 1982. "The Social Sciences and Biblical Interpretation." *Int* 36:229–242.

———. 1984. "Jesus as a Charismatic Leader." *BTB* 14:55–62.

———. 1986a. " 'Religion' in the World of Paul: A Preliminary Sketch." *BTB* 16:92–101.

———. 1986b. *Christian Origins and Cultural Anthropology: Practical Models for Biblical Interpretation*. Atlanta: John Knox Press.

———. 1986c. "Interpreting the Bible with Anthropology: The Case of the Poor and the Rich." *Listening* 21:148–159.

———. 1988. "Patron and Client: The Analogy Behind Synoptic Theology." *Forum* 4/1:2–32.

———. 1989. "Dealing with Biblical (Mediterranean) Characters: A Guide for U.S. Consumers." *BTB* 19:127–141.

Malina, Bruce J., and Jerome H. Neyrey. 1988. *Calling Jesus Names: The Social Value of Labels in Matthew*. Sonoma, Calif.: Polebridge Press.

Malul, M. 1985. "More on *Pahad Yishaq* (Genesis xxxi 42,53) and the Oath by the Thigh." *VT* 35:192–200.

———. 1987. "Touching the Sexual Organs as an Oath Ceremony in an Akkadian Letter." *VT* 37: 491–492.

Marcus, Joel. 1982. "The Evil Inclination in the Epistle of James." *CBQ* 44:606–621.

———. 1984. "Mark 4:10–12 and Marcan Epistemology." *JBL* 103:557–574.

Marshall, Peter. 1983. "A Metaphor of Social Shame: *Thriambeuein* in 2 Cor. 2:14." *NovT* 25:303–317.

———. 1987. *Enmity in Corinth: Social Conventions in Paul's Relations with the Corinthians*. WUNT 23. Tübingen: J. C. B. Mohr (Paul Siebeck).

Martyn, J. Louis. 1985a. "Apocalyptic Antinomies in Paul's Letter to the Galatians." *NTS* 31:412–420.

———. 1985b. "A Law-Observant Mission to Gentiles: The Background of Galatians." *SJTh* 38:307–324.

Mauss, Marcel. 1973. "Techniques of the Body." *Economy and Society* 2:70–88.

May, Herbert. 1963. "Cosmological Reference in the Qumran Doctrine of the Two Spirits and in Old Testament Imagery." *JBL* 82:1–7.

Meeks, Wayne. 1972. *The Writings of St. Paul.* New York: W. W. Norton & Co.

———. 1974. "The Image of the Androgyne: Some Uses of a Symbol in Earliest Christianity." *HR* 13:165–208.

———. 1977. "In One Body: The Unity of Humankind in Colossians and Ephesians." In *God's Christ and His People*, edited by Wayne Meeks and Jacob Jervell, 209–221. Oslo: Universitetsforlaget.

———. 1979. " 'Since Then You Would Need to Go Out of the World': Group Boundaries in Pauline Christianity." In *Critical History and Biblical Faith*, edited by T. J. Ryan, 4–29. Villanova, Pa.: Villanova University, College Theology Society/Horizons.

———. 1982a. "The Social Context of Pauline Theology." *Int* 36:266–277.

———. 1982b. " 'And Rose Up to Play': Midrash and Paraenesis in 1 Corinthians 10:1–22." *JSNT* 16:64–78.

———. 1983a. *The First Urban Christians: The Social World of the Apostle Paul.* New Haven: Yale University Press.

———. 1983b. "Social Functions of Apocalyptic Language in Pauline Christianity." In *Apocalypticism in the Mediterranean World and the Near East*, edited by D. Hellholm, 687–706. Tübingen: J. C. B. Mohr (Paul Siebeck).

———. 1986. "A Hermeneutic of Social Embodiment." *HTR* 79:176–186.

Menoud, Philippe H. 1978. "The Thorn in the Flesh and Satan's Angel." In *Jesus Christ and Faith: A Collection of Studies by Philippe H. Menoud*, 19–27. Pittsburgh: Pickwick Press.

Miguens, M. 1975. "1 Cor. 13:8–13 Reconsidered." *CBQ* 37:86–97.

Morrison, Clinton. 1960. *The Powers That Be: Earthly Rulers and Demonic Powers in Romans 13:1–7.* London: SCM Press.

Moxnes, Halvor. 1980. *Theology in Conflict: Studies in Paul's Understanding of God in Romans.* Leiden: E. J. Brill.

———. 1986. "Meals and the New Community in Luke." *SEA* 51:158–167.

———. 1988a. *The Economy of the Kingdom: Social Conflict and Economic Interaction in Luke's Gospel.* Philadelphia: Fortress Press.

———. 1988b. "Honour and Righteousness in Romans." *JSNT* 32:61–77.

———. 1988c. "Honor, Shame, and the Outside World in Paul's Letter to the Romans." In *The Social World of Formative Christianity and Judaism*, edited by Jacob Neusner, 207–218. Philadelphia: Fortress Press.

Murdock, George Peter. 1980. *Theories of Illness: A World Survey.* Pittsburgh: University of Pittsburgh Press.

Murphy-O'Connor, Jerome. 1968. "Truth: Paul and Qumran." In

*Paul and Qumran*, edited by J. Murphy-O'Connor, 179–230. London: Geoffrey Chapman.

———. 1976. "Christological Anthropology in Phil., II, 6–11." *RB* 83:25–50.

———. 1978a. "Corinthian Slogans in 1 Cor. 6:12–20." *CBQ* 40:391–396.

———. 1978b. "Freedom of the Ghetto (1 Cor., viii,1–13; x,23–xi,1)." *RB* 85:543–574.

———. 1979. "Food and Spiritual Gifts in 1 Cor. 8:8." *CBQ* 41:292–298.

———. 1980. "Sex and Logic in 1 Cor. 11:2–16." *CBQ* 42:482–500.

———. 1982. *Becoming Human Together: The Pastoral Anthropology of St. Paul.* Wilmington, Del.: Michael Glazier.

Myers, Jacob, and Edwin Freed. 1966. "Is Paul Also Among the Prophets?" *Int* 20:44–49.

Needham, Rodney, ed. 1973. *Right and Left: Essays on Dual Symbolic Classification.* Chicago: University of Chicago Press.

Nestle, W. 1927. "Die Fabel des Menenius Agrippa." *Klio* 21:350–360.

Neusner, Jacob. 1973a. *The Idea of Purity in Ancient Judaism.* Leiden: E. J. Brill.

———. 1973b. *From Politics to Piety: The Emergence of Pharisaic Judaism.* Englewood Cliffs, N. J.: Prentice-Hall.

———. 1975. "The Idea of Purity in Ancient Judaism." *JAAR* 43:15–26.

———. 1976. " 'First Cleanse the Inside': The 'Halakhic' Background of a Controversy Saying." *NTS* 22:486–495.

———. 1978. "History and Purity in First-Century Judaism." *HR* 18:1–17.

———. 1979. "Map Without Territory: Mishnah's System of Sacrifices and Sanctuary." *HR* 19:103–127.

———. 1980. "The Talmud as Anthropology." *Religious Traditions* 3:12–35.

———. 1982. "Two Pictures of the Pharisees: Philosophical Circle or Eating Club." *ATR* 64:525–538.

Newton, Michael. 1985. *The Concept of Purity at Qumran and in the Letters of Paul.* SNTSMS 53. Cambridge: Cambridge University Press.

Neyrey, Jerome H. 1984. "The Forensic Defense Speech and Paul's Trial Speeches in Acts 22–26: Form and Function." In *Luke-Acts: New Perspectives from the Society of Biblical Literature Seminar,* edited by Charles Talbert, 210–224. New York: Crossroad.

———. 1985. *Christ Is Community: The Christologies of the New Testament.* Wilmington, Del.: Michael Glazier.

———. 1986a. "The Idea of Purity in Mark's Gospel." In *Social-Scientific Criticism of the New Testament and Its Social World*, edited by John H. Elliott, 91–128. *Semeia* 35.

———. 1986b. "Body Language in 1 Corinthians: The Use of Anthropological Models for Understanding Paul and His Opponents." In *Social-Scientific Criticism of the New Testament and Its Social World*, edited by John H. Elliott, 129–170. *Semeia* 35.

———. 1986c. "Witchcraft Accusations in 2 Cor. 10–13: Paul in Social-Science Perspective." *Listening* 21:160–171.

———. 1987a. "Jesus the Judge: Forensic Process in John 8:21–59." *Bib* 68:509–541.

———. 1987b. "Hope Against Hope." *The Way* 27:264–273.

———. 1988a. "Bewitched in Galatia: Paul and Cultural Anthropology." *CBQ* 50:72–100.

———. 1988b. "A Symbolic Approach to Mark 7." *Forum* 4/3:63–92.

———. 1988c. "Unclean, Common, Polluted, and Taboo." *Forum* 4/4:72–82.

———. 1988d. *An Ideology of Revolt: John's Christology in Social-Science Perspective*. Philadelphia: Fortress Press.

Niebuhr, H. Richard. 1951. *Christ and Culture*. New York: Harper & Brothers.

Nineham, D. 1982. "The Strangeness of the New Testament World." *Theology* 85:171–172, 247–255.

Nock, A. D. 1925. "Eunuchs in Ancient Religion." *Archiv für Religionswissenschaft* 23:25–33.

North, Helen. 1966. *Sophrosyne: Self-Knowledge and Self-Restraint in Greek Literature*. Cornell Studies in Classical Philology, 34. Ithaca, N.Y.: Cornell University Press.

Oakman, Douglas E. 1986. *Jesus and the Economic Questions of His Day*. Lewiston, N.Y.: Edwin Mellen Press.

Osiek, Carolyn. 1984. *What Are They Saying About the Social Setting of the New Testament?* New York: Paulist Press.

Osten-Sacken, P. von. 1969. *Gott und Belial*. Göttingen: Vandenhoeck & Ruprecht.

Pamment, Margaret. 1981. "Witch-Hunt." *Theology* 84:98–106.

Parker, Robert. 1983. *Miasma: Pollution and Purification in Early Greek Religion*. Oxford: Clarendon Press.

Parsons, Talcott, and Neil Smelser. 1956. *Society and Economy*. London: Routledge & Kegan Paul.

Patai, Raphael. 1983. *The Arab Mind*. Rev. ed. New York: Charles Scribner's Sons.

Pearson, Birger. 1973. *The Pneumatikos-Psychikos Terminology in 1 Corinthians: A Study in the Theology of the Corinthian Opponents of Paul in Relation to Gnosticism.* Cambridge: Cambridge University Press.

Perdue, Leo. 1981. "Paraenesis and the Epistle of James." *ZNW* 72:241–256.

Péristiany, J. G., ed. 1966. *Honour and Shame: The Values of Mediterranean Society.* Chicago: University of Chicago Press.

Petersen, Norman. 1985. *Rediscovering Paul: Philemon and the Sociology of Paul's Narrative World.* Philadelphia: Fortress Press.

Pilch, John J. 1981. "Biblical Leprosy and Body Symbolism." *BTB* 11:119–133.

———. 1985. "Healing in Mark: A Social Science Analysis." *BTB* 15:142–150.

———. 1986. "The Health Care System in Matthew: A Social Science Analysis." *BTB* 16:102–106.

———. 1989. "Your Abba Is Not Your Daddy." *Modern Liturgy* 16/1:26.

Pitt-Rivers, Julian. 1961. *The People of the Sierra.* Chicago: University of Chicago Press.

———. 1968. "Honor." In *International Encyclopedia of the Social Sciences*, 503–511. New York: Macmillan Co.

———. 1977. *The Fate of Shechem; or, the Politics of Sex: Essays in the Anthropology of the Mediterranean.* Cambridge: Cambridge University Press.

Polhemus, Ted. 1975. "Social Bodies." In *The Body as a Medium of Expression*, edited by J. Benthall and T. Polhemus, 13–35. London: Allen Lane.

———, ed. 1978. *The Body Reader: Social Aspects of the Human Body.* New York: Pantheon Books.

Postal, Susan Koessler. 1965. "Body-Image and Identity: A Comparison of Kwatiutl and Hopi." *American Anthropologist* 67:455–460.

Purvo, Richard I. 1985. "Wisdom and Power: Petronius' *Satyricon* and the Social World of Early Christianity." *ATR* 67:307–328.

Räisänen, Heikki. 1986. *The Torah and Christ: Essays in German and English on the Problem of the Law in Early Christianity.* Helsinki: Finnish Exegetical Society.

———. 1987a. *Paul and the Law.* Tübingen: J. C. B. Mohr (Paul Siebeck).

———. 1987b. "Paul's Conversion and the Development of His View of the Law." *NTS* 33:404–419.

Rich, A. N. M. 1956. "The Cynic Conception of *AUTARKEIA.*" *Mnemosyne*, Series 4, 9:23–29.

Richardson, Peter. 1980a. "Pauline Inconsistency: 1 Corinthians 9:19–23 and Galatians 2:11–14." *NTS* 26:347–362.

———. 1980b. "Judgment, Immorality, and Sexual Ethics in 1 Corinthians 6." SBLASP, 337–357.

Robinson, J. A. T. 1952. *The Body: A Study in Pauline Theology* SBT 5. London: SCM Press.

Robinson, James M. 1957. *The Problem of History in Mark.* SBT 21. London: SPCK.

Rohrbaugh, Richard L. 1978. *The Biblical Interpreter: An Agrarian Bible in an Industrial Age.* Philadelphia: Fortress Press.

———. 1987a. " 'Social Location of Thought' as a Heuristic Construct in New Testament Study." *JAAR* 30:103–119.

———. 1987b. "Muddles and Models." *Forum* 3/2:23–34.

Rousselle, Aline. 1988. *Porneia: On Desire and the Body in Antiquity.* Oxford: Basil Blackwell.

Sack, Robert David. 1986. *Human Territoriality: Its Theory and History.* New York: Cambridge University Press.

Sahlins, Marshall D. 1965. "On the Sociology of Primitive Exchange." In *The Relevance of Models for Social Anthropology*, edited by Michael Banton, 139–236. Association of Social Anthropologists Monograph 1. London: Tavistock Publications.

———. 1976. *Culture and Practical Reason.* Chicago: University of Chicago Press.

Saller, R. P. 1982. *Personal Patronage Under the Early Empire.* Cambridge: Cambridge University Press.

Sampley, Paul. 1977. " 'Before God, I Do Not Lie' (Gal I.20): Paul's Self-Defense in the Light of Roman Legal Praxis." *NTS* 23:477–482.

Sanders, E. P. 1977. *Paul and Palestinian Judaism.* Philadelphia: Fortress Press.

———. 1980. *Jewish and Christian Self-Definition.* Vol. 1, *The Shaping of Christianity in the Second and Third Centuries.* Philadelphia: Fortress Press.

———. 1983a. *Paul, the Law, and the Jewish People.* Philadelphia: Fortress Press.

———. 1983b. "Jesus and the Sinners." *JSNT* 19:5–36.

———. 1985. *Jesus and Judaism.* London: SCM Press.

Schaberg, Jane. 1987. *The Illegitimacy of Jesus: A Feminist Theological Interpretation of the Infancy Narratives.* San Francisco: Harper & Row.

Scheflen, Albert, and Alice Scheflen. 1972. *Body Language and the Social Order: Communication as Behavioral Control.* Englewood Cliffs, N.J.: Prentice-Hall.

Schiffman, Lawrence H. 1979. "Communal Meals at Qumran." *RevQ* 10:45–56.

Schilder, Paul. 1950. *The Image and Appearance of the Human Body.* New York: International University Press.

Schlier, Heinrich. 1961. *Principalities and Powers in the New Testament.* New York: Herder & Herder.

Schmidt, S. W., ed. 1977. *Friends, Followers, and Factions: A Reader in Political Clientelism."* Berkeley, Calif.: University of California Press.

Schütz, John H. 1974. "Charisma and Social Reality in Primitive Christianity." *JR* 54:51–70.

———. 1975. *Paul and the Anatomy of Apostolic Authority.* New York: Cambridge University Press.

Schwartz, Barry. 1981. *Vertical Classification: A Study in Structuralism and the Sociology of Knowledge.* Chicago: University of Chicago Press.

Schwartz, Theodore, ed. 1976. *Socialization as Cultural Communication.* Berkeley, Calif.: University of California Press.

Schweizer, Eduard. 1988. "Slaves of the Elements and Worshippers of Angels: Gal. 4:3, 9 and Col. 2:8, 18, 20." *JBL* 107:455–468.

Scott, James C. 1977. *The Moral Economy of the Peasant: Rebellion and Subsistence in Southeast Asia.* New Haven: Yale University Press.

Scroggs, Robin. 1972. "Paul and the Eschatological Woman." *JAAR* 40:283–303.

———. 1974. "Paul and the Eschatological Woman: Revisited." *JAAR* 42:532–537.

———. 1983. *The New Testament and Homosexuality.* Philadelphia: Fortress Press.

———. 1986. "Sociology and the New Testament." *Listening* 21:138–147.

Segal, Alan F. 1986. "Romans 7 and Jewish Dietary Law." *StudR/SciRel* 15:361–374.

———. 1988. "The Costs of Proselytism and Conversion," SBLASP, 336–369.

Segal, Peretz. 1989. "The Penalty of the Warning Inscription from the Temple of Jerusalem." *IEJ* 39:79–84.

Segal, R. A. 1984. "The Application of Symbolic Anthropology to Religions in the Greco-Roman World." *RelSRev* 10:216–223.

Seitz, O. J. F. 1947. "Antecedents and Signification of the Term *Dipsychos.*" *JBL* 66:211–219.

———. 1959. "Two Spirits in Man: An Essay in Biblical Exegesis." *NTS* 6:82–94.

Sherwin-White, A. N. 1963. *Roman Society and Roman Law in the New Testament.* New York: Oxford University Press.

Sider, R. J. 1975. "The Pauline Conception of the Resurrection Body in 1 Corinthians XV.35–54." *NTS* 21:428–439.

———. 1977. "St. Paul's Understanding of the Nature and Significance of the Resurrection in 1 Corinthians XV.1–19." *NovT* 19:124–141.

Silverman, S. 1977. "Patronage as Myth." In *Patrons and Clients in Mediterranean Societies*, edited by E. Gellner and J. Waterbury, 7–20. London: Gerald Duckworth & Co.

Simon, Marcel. 1967. *Jewish Sects at the Time of Jesus*. Philadelphia: Fortress Press.

———. 1970. "The Apostolic Decree and Its Setting in the Ancient Church." *BJRL* 52:437–460.

Sjoberg, Gideon. 1960. *The Pre-Industrial City*. New York: Macmillan Co.

Sloyan, Gerald S. 1985. "Jewish Rituals of the First Century C.E. and Christian Sacramental Behavior." *BTB* 15:98–103.

Smith, Dennis. 1980. "Social Obligation in the Context of Communal Meals." Th.D. thesis, Harvard University.

———. 1985. "Jesus and the Pharisees in Socio-Anthropological Perspective." *Trinity Journal* 6:151–156.

———. 1987. "Table Fellowship as a Literary Motif in the Gospel of Luke." *JBL* 106:613–638.

Smith, Jonathan Z. 1978. *Map Is Not Territory*. Leiden: E. J. Brill.

Smith, M. 1980. "Pauline Worship as Seen by Pagans." *HTR* 73:241–249.

Soler, Jean. 1979. "The Dietary Prohibitions of the Hebrews." *New York Review of Books*, June 14: 24–30. Reprinted in *Food and Drink in History*, edited by Robert Forster and Orest Ranum, 126–138. Baltimore: Johns Hopkins University Press.

Spicq, C. 1937. "L'image sportive de II Corinthiens, IV.7–9." *ETL* 14:209–229.

Stark, Rodney. 1986. "Jewish Conversion and the Rise of Christianity: Rethinking Received Wisdom." SBLASP, 314–329.

Stein, S. 1957. "The Influence of Symposia Literature on the Literary Form of the Pesah Haggadah." *JJS* 8:13–44.

Stendahl, Krister. 1976. *Paul Among Jews and Gentiles*. Philadelphia: Fortress Press.

Stock, Augustine. 1984. "Chiastic Awareness and Education." *BTB* 14:23–27.

Stoops, R. F. 1986. "Patronage in the *Acts of Peter*." *Semeia* 38:91–100.

Stowers, Stanley K. 1981. *The Diatribe and Paul's Letter to the Romans*. SBLDS 57. Chico, Calif.: Scholars Press.

————. 1984. "Social Status, Public Speaking, and Private Teaching: The Circumstances of Paul's Preaching Activity." *NovT* 26:59–82.

————. 1985. "The Social Sciences and the Study of Early Christianity." In *Approaches to Ancient Judaism. Vol. 5, Studies in Judaism and Its Greco-Roman Context*, 373–374. Atlanta: Scholars Press.

Strugnell, John. 1960. "The Angelic Liturgy at Qumran." *VT* Supp. 7:318–345.

Theissen, Gerd. 1978. *Sociology of Early Palestinian Christianity*. Philadelphia: Fortress Press.

————. 1982. *The Social Setting of Pauline Christianity*. Philadelphia: Fortress Press.

————. 1983. *Psychological Aspects of Pauline Theology*. Philadelphia: Fortress Press.

Thiselton, A. C. 1973. "The Meaning of *Sarx* in 1 Corinthians 5:5: A Fresh Approach in the Light of Logical and Semantic Factors." *SJTh* 26:204–227.

————. 1978. "Realized Eschatology at Corinth." *NTS* 24:510–526.

————. 1979. "The 'Interpretation' of Tongues: A New Suggestion in Light of Greek Usage in Philo and Josephus." *JTS* 30:15–36.

Thompson, Cynthia L. 1988. "Hairstyles, Head-coverings, and St. Paul: Portraits from Roman Corinth." *BA* 51:99–115.

Thompson, L. 1986. "A Sociological Analysis of Tribulation in the Apocalypse of John." *Semeia* 36:147–174.

Thrall, M. E. 1967. "The Pauline Use of *Syneidēsis*." *NTS* 14:118–125.

————. 1977. "The Problem of II Cor VI.14–VII.1 in Some Recent Discussion." *NTS* 24:132–148.

Todd, Emmanuel. 1985. *The Explanation of Ideology: Family Structures and Social Systems*. Oxford: Basil Blackwell.

Turner, Victor. 1969. *The Ritual Process: Structure and Anti-Structure*. Chicago: Aldine Press.

Tyson, J. B. 1983. "Acts 6:1–7 and Dietary Regulations in Early Christianity." *Perspective in Religious Studies* 10:145–161.

Ullendorf, E. 1979. "The Bawdy Bible." *Bulletin of the School of Oriental and African Studies* 42:426–456.

Verner, David C. 1983. *The Household of God: The Social World of the Pastoral Epistles*. SBLDS 71. Chico, Calif.: Scholars Press.

Walcot, Peter. 1978. *Envy and the Greeks: A Study of Human Behaviour*. Warminster, Wiltshire: Aris & Phillips.

Waterbury, J. 1977. "An Attempt to Put Patrons and Clients in Their Place." In *Patrons and Clients in Mediterranean Societies*, edited by E. Gellner and J. Waterbury, 329–342. London: Gerald Duckworth & Co.

Watson, Francis. 1986. *Paul, Judaism, and the Gentiles: A Sociological Approach.* New York: Cambridge University Press.

Wedderburn, A. J. M. 1981. "The Problem of the Denial of the Resurrection in 1 Cor. XV." *NovT* 23:229–241.

White, Leland. 1985. "Grid and Group in Matthew's Community: The Righteousness/Honor Code in the Sermon on the Mount." In *Social-Scientific Criticism of the New Testament and Its Social World,* edited by John H. Elliott, 61–90. *Semeia* 35.

Wilcox, Max. 1977. " 'Upon the Tree': Deut. 21:22–23 in the New Testament." *JBL* 96:85–99.

Willis, Wendell Lee. 1985. *Idol Meat in Corinth: The Pauline Argument in 1 Corinthians 8 and 10.* SBLDS 68. Chico, Calif.: Scholars Press.

Wimbush, Vincent. 1987. *Paul: The Worldly Ascetic.* Macon, Ga.: Mercer University Press.

Wink, Walter. 1984. *Naming the Powers.* Philadelphia: Fortress Press.

———. 1986. *Unmasking the Powers.* Philadelphia: Fortress Press.

Winter, Bruce. 1988. "The Public Honouring of Christian Benefactors." *JSNT* 34:87–103.

Wire, A. 1974. "Pauline Theology as an Understanding of God." Dissertation, Claremont Graduate School.

Wolf, Eric. 1966. *Peasants.* Englewood Cliffs, N.J.: Prentice-Hall.

Wolfson, Elliot R. 1987. "Circumcision and the Divine Name: A Study in the Transmission of Esoteric Doctrine." *JQR* 78:77–111.

Worgul, G. S. 1979. "Anthropological Consciousness and Biblical Theology." *BTB* 9:3–12.

Wright, David P. 1987. *The Disposal of Impurity.* SBLDS 101. Atlanta: Scholars Press.

Wright, Lawrence. 1960. *Clean and Decent: The Fascinating History of the Bathroom and the Water Closet.* London: Routledge & Kegan Paul.

Yadin, Yigael. 1985. *The Temple Scroll: The Hidden Law of the Dead Sea Sect.* New York: Random House.

Yarbrough, O. Larry. 1985. *Not Like the Gentiles: Marriage Rules in the Churches of Paul.* SBLDS 80. Atlanta: Scholars Press.

# Index of
# Scripture Passages

# Index of
# Topics